REWRITING COMPOSITION

Rewriting Composition

Terms of Exchange

BRUCE HORNER

Southern Illinois University Press ▪ *Carbondale*

Printed in the United States of America

19 18 17 16 4 3 2 1

Library of Congress Cataloging-in-Publication Data
Horner, Bruce, [date]
Rewriting composition : terms of exchange / Bruce Horner.
pages cm
Summary: "Bruce Horner's *Rewriting Composition: Terms of Exchange* shows how dominant inflections of key terms in composition—language, labor, value/evaluation, discipline, and composition itself—reinforce composition's low institutional status and the poor working conditions of many of its instructors and tutors."— Provided by publisher.
Includes bibliographical references and index.
ISBN 978-0-8093-3450-6 (paperback)
ISBN 978-0-8093-3451-3 (e-book)
1. English language—Rhetoric—Study and teaching. 2. English language—Composition and exercises—Study and teaching. 3. Report writing—Study and teaching. I. Title.
PE1404.R469 2016
808'.0420711—dc23 2015022162

Printed on recycled paper. ♻

The paper used in this publication meets the minimum requirements of American National Standard for Information Sciences—Permanence of Paper for Printed Library Materials, ANSI Z39.48-1992. ∞

For Min

Contents

Acknowledgments ix

Introduction 1
1. Composition 8
2. Language 55
3. Labor 92
4. Value/Evaluation 121
5. Discipline 163

Epilogue 206

Notes 211
Works Cited 225
Index 253

Acknowledgments

I thank Karl Kageff of Southern Illinois University Press for his support and encouragement throughout the writing of this book, and Wayne Larsen, Linda Buhman, Bridget Brown, Amy J. Etcheson, Lynanne Page, and Ryan Masteller, also of Southern Illinois University Press, for their assiduous care in seeing this project through to completion. I am grateful to Kathryn Perry and Laura Tetreault for providing valuable research assistance and to Paula Durbin-Westby for producing the index.

Much of the drafting of this book was made possible by a semester sabbatical leave from the University of Louisville. I am grateful to the university for this support, and more directly to Susan Griffin, who as chair ensured that I received that support. I am grateful to the University of Louisville College of Arts and Sciences for a grant to cover the costs of indexing; to Glynis Ridley, Susan Griffin's successor as department chair, for her support for this grant; and to both Glynis and Susan for their support with many other tangible and intangible costs incurred during the writing of this book.

I am grateful to the following journals and presses for granting permission to reprint material from journal articles and book chapters in this book:

- *JAC*, for permission to reprint material from "Redefining Work and Value for Writing Program Administration," *JAC* 27.1–2 (2007): 163–84.
- National Council of Teachers of English, for permission to reprint material from "Rewriting Composition: Moving beyond a Discourse of Need," *College English* 77.5 (May

2015): 450–79. Copyright 2015 by the National Council of Teachers of English. Reprinted with Permission.

- Rowman and Littlefield, for permission to reprint material from "The WPA as Broker: Globalization and the Composition Program," *Teaching Writing in Globalization: Remapping Disciplinary Work*, ed. Daphne Desser and Darin Payne (Boulder, CO: Lexington Books, 2012), 57–78.

Thanks to Min-Zhan Lu, John Trimbur, Marilyn Cooper, and Donna Strickland for their patience in reading through earlier versions of the book manuscript and for their criticisms and suggestions. My thinking about ideas presented in this book is also better for conversations with innumerable colleagues, among whom I thank especially Anis Bawarshi, Patricia Bizzell, Deborah Brandt, Suresh Canagarajah, Christiane Donahue, Dylan Dryer, Viv Ellis, Keith Gilyard, Juan Guerra, Jeanne Gunner, Cynthia Lewis, Constant Leung, Theresa Lillis, LuMing Mao, Paul Kei Matsuda, Vivette Milson-Whyte, Weiguo Qu, Cynthia Selfe, Brian Street, Kathleen Yancey, Vershawn Ashanti Young, and members of my University of Louisville reading group, especially Megan Bardolph, Nancy Bou Ayash, Joy Karega, Carrie Kilfoil, Tika Lamsal, Amy Lueck, Brice Nordquist, Hem Paudel, Shyam Sharma, and Vanessa Kraemer Sohan. The formulation and revision of ideas presented here also benefited from discussions at Dartmouth College, Emerson College, Fudan University, Indiana University, Kings College London, Miami University, Michigan Technological University, the National University of Singapore, Northeastern University, Oxford University, Penn State University, Shoreline Community College, Simon Fraser University, Sun-Yat Sen University Guangzhou, the University of Illinois Chicago, the University of Maine, the University of Maryland, the University of Massachusetts Amherst, the University of Minnesota, the University of New Hampshire, the University of Pittsburgh, the University of the West Indies, Virginia Technological University, and Western Washington University.

The generosity of Margaret Lu and Jerry Zhu and the rest of my "Seattle family" made it possible for me to complete this book during difficult times. I am thankful to my parents for teaching me what work can mean, and to Yvonne, Paul, Kai, and Lee for giving me frequent and important reminders that there is more to life than work.

This book would be unthinkable without Min.

REWRITING COMPOSITION

Introduction

This book contests the meanings commonly assigned to specific terms that have emerged as key in the dominant professional discourse of what in this book I continue to call composition: terms of *language*, *labor*, *value/evaluation*, and *discipline*, as well as *composition* itself. My purpose is to identify the conceptual and effective limitations set by the inflections given these terms in that discourse. These limits shape and give direction to our work—what we do, what we think we do, and what we think about what we do in taking up the work of composition.

Like my previous book *Terms of Work for Composition*, I align myself in this book with the tradition of cultural materialism and the larger Marxian tradition it exemplifies. The tradition of cultural materialism takes as a given the materiality of the "conceptual," as well as the "conceptuality" of the seemingly purely "material." So, for example, while in one sense this book is a book of "theory," *theory* is here to be understood as "a process in society," as Stephen Resnick and Richard Wolff put it, the aim and point of which is not to identify "the essence of anything" but rather "the particular social intervention every theory makes" (2, 3). Theorizing is thus not opposed to or discrete from material social practice but instead constitutes a particular—material, social—form of practice itself.

In saying this, I am, of course, engaged in a kind of special pleading to justify, not merely explain, the potential value of the work I take up here. Readers who do not accept this argument will find the book frustrating to the point that, I suspect, they will soon stop reading. Those who do accept it may still dispute its points and mode of intervention, but as fellow participants in that process of intervention. Part of the broader aim of the book, however, is precisely to intervene in conceptualizations *of* the conceptual as distinct from material social practice, and thereby to further recognize the significance of all the work of composition, whether designated ordinary or esoteric, commonplace or foreign, theoretical or practical.

In keeping with this, the approach taken here challenges dominant cultural claims and representations of what is normal, significant, and, of course, what is not, recognizing all these as historical in the Marxian sense of being contingent, the ongoing products of human history, and therefore always subject to change and in constant need of (re)production rather than existing as stable, timeless entities. The hegemonic, likewise, is understood not as total but as always subject to change and contest and thus also always in need of reproduction. As Raymond Williams observes, a lived hegemony "does not just passively exist as a form of dominance. It has continually to be renewed, recreated, defended, and modified. It is also continually resisted, limited, altered, challenged by pressures not at all its own" (*Marxism* 112–13). This is not to deny the reality of hegemonic pressures but to refuse their claimed status as not merely the hegemonic but hegemony total in its reach, and to acknowledge the possibility and reality of agency exercised whether in maintaining or challenging such pressures. Seen as part of lived, historical reality, what is claimed as hegemony can be recognized as in fact merely hegemonic, its status an ongoing product of its claims to be, instead, hegemony.

It follows that the terms of exchange offered by the dominant to name our work, or dominant inflections of these terms—such as *composition*, *language*, *labor*, *value/evaluation*, and *discipline*, as well as such terms as *theory*, *practice*, *modality*, *pedagogy*, *research*, *knowledge*, and *writing*—are in this book put under scrutiny both for what they keep us from noticing and for the work they themselves do to affect our work—the ways these are put into play as, in fact, terms of exchange to name, define, and set the value of composition.

The larger concomitant circumstances in which the work of this book aims to intervene, it will quickly become apparent, include a globalizing economy; the rise of fast-capitalist, neoliberal ideology; the globalization of English; the diminishing role of labor and of the professions, as conventionally understood; the turn to a "knowledge" or "information" economy; and the privatization of higher education. But the intervention aimed at in this book has to do not with these as discrete entities with which composition must contend but, rather, with how the relation of composition to these is imagined, thought, and enacted. The intervention attempted is thus likely to be perceived as at a distinct remove from these. This is not to deny their significance but to address the fact that our very conceptions of these and of the relation of composition to them stand in the way of effective interventions in them, hence the need to intervene in these conceptions themselves. For example, a recurring thread in the argument of this book is that dominant conceptualizations of our work in composition direct us to accept not only what dominant ideology has already defined as our work and its significance, but also what it has defined as the alternatives to it. To accede to these conceptualizations is to participate in dominant ideology and the relations of power it maintains, even and especially when we accept as alternatives to the dominant what it prescribes for us as its alternatives.

To those who would ask, perhaps rhetorically, what difference considerations like those presented here make, I answer that these considerations may help us rethink what constitutes "difference" and how it is made so that we may learn to recognize change where none is thought to occur, and the sameness permeating what we have learned to herald as different. The method, to give a glorified name to the practices represented in this book, is to rethink some key terms in contemporary composition discourse by considering the work specific inflections of them do. The "development" of the book from chapter to chapter may seem less like an argument than a passacaglia presenting successive reworkings of a common theme. For there is a recursiveness to the chapters as each (re)iterates, from a somewhat different beginning vantage point, a rethinking of composition, language, labor, value, and discipline in their relations to one another. Part of what the book argues is that every reiteration inevitably produces a difference. Whether the chapters are persuasive in demonstrating the production of difference through reiteration is, of course, something readers will have to decide for themselves.

Chapter 1 identifies in the problematics of composition and its definition the imbrication of debate on composition in dominant conceptualizations of "composition" and of what is "alternative," "new," and "different" to it, conceptualizations in terms of which arguments to "end" or "move beyond" composition and to improve it are caught (and caught up). These preclude more substantive engagements with the problematics of composition by participating in a "discourse of need" by which composition itself is defined as deficit, something either to be abandoned, replaced, or added to as cure for what's missing. In the arguments made by David Smit to "end" composition, and by Sidney Dobrin to move "postcomposition," I trace the contours of that discourse and the alignment of arguments like theirs, despite the apparent opposition of their arguments to one another, with hegemonic fast-capitalist values. In calls to somehow improve composition by linking it to the study of rhetoric, or rename and reshape it as "writing studies" or add to it considerations of "multimodal" composition, I identify further permutations of that discourse of (composition's) need, a discourse within which "composition" serves as inadequate foil to what the dominant has defined for us as "new," "better," "different," all evidence to the contrary notwithstanding. I counterpose the strategies of the critiques of composition these deploy to the efforts of J. K. Gibson-Graham and Theresa Lillis to change, respectively, "capitalocentric" economic discourse and the sociolinguistics of writing. Rather than working within the terms set by the dominant (about capitalism and "the economy," and about sociolinguistics) and arguing for abandoning or moving beyond these, these scholars work to productively rethink such terms. James Slevin's argument for composition as intellectual work, I suggest, illustrates a comparable rethinking of terms such as *writing*, *intellectual*, and *pedagogy* by which the problematics of composition may instead be productively engaged.

Chapter 2 takes up the term "language" and its predominant permutation "English," arguing that dominant conceptions of both as discrete, internally uniform, and stable sets of forms abstracted from practice (*parole*) have been adopted uncritically in composition, with the consequence that language difference and the potential for change arising from composition's focus on language production has been stymied. Efforts to valorize language difference, for example, take for granted "sameness" as the norm of language, thereby reinforcing the ideological valuation of what is claimed as standard language/English even in the attempt to argue for the legitimacy of language practices identified with subordinated groups, deemed "different": difference in language remains, in such efforts, identified as deviation from the norm of the same, and agency is identified with abstractions of language rather than with users' engagement in communicative practices. Drawing on Alastair Pennycook's notion of language as a "local practice," Louis-Jean Calvet's conception of language as the always-emerging outcome of practice, and studies of uses of English as a lingua franca ("ELF") that highlight ELF as the ongoing accomplishment of its users, I articulate a "translingual" approach as an alternative that treats language, and English, as the ongoing accomplishment of its users, and composition as a key site for the work of rewriting English.

If chapter 2 defines language as the ongoing always-emerging result of practices, chapter 3 identifies the labor of composition with those practices: the ongoing labor of (re)writing language. Such labor is part of the necessary, ongoing work of social relations, relations that themselves constitute a productive force. Dominant frameworks for understanding labor (and work) do not recognize (that is, ideologically *mis*recognize) social relations as a productive force, hence composition's perduring labor problem. English-only monolingualism's treatment of English as commodity represents the specific manifestation of this misrecognition, and composition's complicity in the ideology of monolingualism—its treatment of English, or Standard Written English, as a discrete, stable, and internally uniform entity for transmission as a means of ensuring the friction-free movement of goods, services, and information—ensures the perpetuation of its labor problem, taking form in the criteria for hiring and evaluating writing teachers as well as in assessment of student writing and writing programs.

In chapter 4, I take up the ways that recognition has been and might be brokered by composition—the language practices by which it represents the value of the labor of composition—focusing on three sites of tension in such representations: the value of the work of composition teachers, often understood in restricted senses of "labor issues" in terms of workload and compensation in the form of pay, job security, and benefits; the evaluation of the work of writing program administrators (WPAs) for promotion and tenure; and the value of coursework in composition as defined in "articulation" agreements between schools that assign specific academic credits and terms for the exchange of credits for those students transferring from one school to another. In the dominant terms for the negotiation of these, compositionists typically participate in the commodification of the work of composition, a commodification that operates to the detriment of its value in the economies of academic professionalism, tuition credits, and skills transmission in which those commodities circulate. This commodification is accomplished through elision of both the concrete labor of the individuals under evaluation and denial of the productive force of social relations, in alignment with the increasing privatization and, concomitantly, "internationalization" of U.S. higher education leading to demands for the "smooth" exchange of stabilized/standardized credits (for academic professionals and teaching/learning). As an alternative, I consider how WPAs and others pursuing improved working conditions for composition teachers serve as academic "brokers" of the value of the work accomplished by WPAs, teachers, and students in composition programs, and I suggest ways by which such brokering might challenge standard terms of evaluation of work in composition.

Chapter 5 reviews dominant valuations of composition within the academic institutional economies of academic disciplinary professionalism. I identify in several quite different but prominent valuations of composition as a discipline an alignment with the commodification of disciplinary knowledge. By eliding the labor necessary to knowledge "mobilization," such valuations contribute not to composition's advancement in the hierarchy of professional academic disciplines based on such commodifications but, instead, to its further marginalization, given composition's inevitable identification with concrete labor practices necessary to such knowledge mobilization. As an alternative, I argue for a return to, and emphasis on, those practices, not as a rejection of "scholarship" but as a return to a root sense of the discipline of composition as practice.

In its remove from the seemingly immediate, perplexing difficulties those in composition confront in their work as students, teachers, program administrators, and scholars—any litany of which would include, at a minimum, the continuing exploitation of contingent teachers, the lack of institutional support and autonomy for writing programs, continuing denials of the professional academic disciplinary legitimacy of composition scholarship and (therefore) the lack of support for such scholarship—the difficulties taken up here, at least in the form they are taken up, may well seem maddeningly peripheral to what is needed: better working conditions for teachers, more institutional support and autonomy, free student tuition, academic disciplinary status, or at least a plan to achieve these. Moreover, in its questioning of current arguments to achieve these, this book may seem not merely peripheral but counterproductive, even regressive. It therefore may be in order here to affirm that none of the arguments presented in this book should be construed as opposing rigorous scholarship, the right to collective bargaining and the need for better working conditions for composition teachers, linguistic rights, free tuition and living stipends for students, and a broader and more secure claim for composition on curricular space. Nonetheless, it is also in order to question the terms under which pursuit of these is undertaken. For the frameworks set by those terms often enough render those pursuits futile. Or, worse, they might well change the course of those pursuits, leading us to arrive all too successfully at places we had no intention of going. In short, we need to question the terms under which pursuit of these is undertaken lest, in accepting those terms as a condition of achieving such aims, we put at risk the project I argue we must recognize as composition. In rewriting composition, as we must, the terms of exchange make all the difference.

1. *Composition*

Composition is an ongoing historical project: the name given to work done in colleges and universities, mostly in the United States, by students and teachers as they engage and mediate differences in written language. That is the definition I am willing to offer, knowing that it is at best only a beginning, and necessarily incomplete.

The difficulty in defining composition arises in part out of the tension built into the term itself as a referent for both an activity and the product of that activity. Composition is the name given not merely to what students produce (as in "write a composition of 500 words") but also to the activity of production. But composition also refers not only to what is now understood to be the composing process(es) of individual students or groups of students (or other writers) but to the full panoply of material social conditions and practices out of, and within, which such processes and products appear—the "field" of composition, composition programs, and the history of these. Hence by "composition" one may refer to a kind of text, the authors of such texts, the means by which such authors produce such texts, the courses in which such means are deployed to produce such texts, the programs responsible for such courses—their design, staffing, and maintenance—and the professional academic disciplinary participation in and study of the programs, courses, students, texts, and activities by which those texts are produced in relation to one another—"Composition" writ large.

The undeniable location of the work of *this* Composition in material social history (compare, for example, "biology") distinguishes the difficulties besetting it—its lack of academic institutional status and the working conditions and perquisites attending such status—from the difficulties of definition and purpose experienced by other disciplines as they revisit, redefine, and defend their terms, aims, procedures, and value (see, for example, Burawoy; Firth and Wagner), in keeping with their own location in material social history. For while every discipline faces on occasion the challenge of self-(re)definition (think of the range of scientific fields that have arisen in the last century), few are *defined* in terms of their material social location within academic institutions or identified with that location, as composition is. Instead, following the ideology of professional academic disciplinarity, most disciplines deny that location in defining themselves.[1] In short, the term *composition*, unlike the names of other academic disciplinary fields, brings with it the specific material social conditions of its historical and, especially, institutional location—one reason for the difficulty those "in" Composition have explaining their work to those engaged in what might otherwise appear to be allied work outside the United States, such as the fields of *la didactique de l'écrit*, or academic literacies (cf. Björk et al.; Dauney; Donahue, "Writing"; Ganobcsik-Williams; Janković-Paus; Schmied; Thaiss et al.). While it is wrong to claim that there is nothing like Composition outside the United States, it is also the case that what may be *like* Composition outside the United States is nonetheless distinct in light of the specific material social conditions obtaining in other locations (see Anson and Donahue).

Dominant efforts to respond to the very real difficulties of those working in composition (as students, teachers, scholars), rather than engaging composition's location and character as material social practice, have followed the lead of these other fields. In so doing, they have accepted dominant culture's limited conceptions and valuations of composition as low, limited, preparatory, illegitimate. Such efforts produce and maintain a "discourse of need" about composition itself, defining it as lacking what dominant culture identifies as legitimate disciplinary characteristics and therefore as in need of either abandonment or supplement.[2] So, for example, graduate programs to prepare teachers of courses in "composition" are themselves dubbed not programs in composition but, instead, in "Rhetoric and Composition," "Writing Studies," "Writing, Rhetoric, and American Culture," "Rhetoric, Composition, and Literacy Studies," "Critical Studies in Literacy and Pedagogy," "Language, Literacy, and Rhetoric," or "Composition and Cultural Rhetoric" (cf. Hesse, foreword xii; Horner and Lu, "Working" 472).

Clearly, there is use in exploring interrelationships between composition as I have defined it above and work identified with these other terms. Nonetheless, it is worth questioning the assumptions driving the demand to represent or change the work of composition as something other or more than what *composition* might represent. At issue is whether these demands accede to what the dominant has assigned to be the meaning and value of composition, and thereby reproduce and reinforce those dominant views, in both their (implicit or explicit) denigration of composition and in their quest for and heralding of alternatives. At further issue is whether, in their pursuit of what we have learned to recognize as the new, alternative, better, or different, they accede to dominant cultural demands for and definitions of the "new," "alternative," "better," "different." For acceding to such demands and definitions can lead us to overlook the value—realized and potential—of the actual work that may take place under the guise of the seemingly pedestrian term "composition."

This is not to deny deeply problematic, limiting characteristics of work in composition, or of the dominant official charge for that work—to produce universally applicable writing skills in students, for example, or ideal citizens or employees (or all of these). But it is to refuse to treat these ascribed meanings and values for composition as either fully adequate or equivalent to the work actually accomplished in composition. Just as labor officially deemed "unskilled" is anything but (see Kusterer; Rose, *Mind*), and regions deemed economically "depressed" are more than simply gaping pockets of need (see Gibson-Graham, *Post-Capitalist*), so work in composition inevitably is and does more and other than what either its official proponents or its critics may claim or appear to recognize. The work of theory, in composition as elsewhere, is precisely to challenge such official, dominant ascriptions rather than, by pursuing ostensible alternatives, merely reproduce them (see Gibson-Graham, *End*).

This is difficult work to be sure, insofar as it entails engaging dominant representations to call them into question: to think both the existing terms of our work and also the terms we would exchange them for differently, lest we unwittingly lapse into accepting what the dominant predisposes us to recognize as the "new," "alternative" and "different" *as* new, alternative, and so on (and as preferable) to what the dominant predisposes us to (mis)recognize as the old and inadequate, and thereby to operate within the very terms of exchange set *by* the dominant. It is difficult insofar as it requires that we acknowledge both the effectivity, on the ground, of dominant representations (and their officially designated alternatives) of composition work and, simultaneously, their inadequacy. Given these difficulties, it is not surprising that calls for changes to composition can often fall short: mistaking the alternatives proffered by dominant culture with the new, different, better; mistaking the existing "traditional" work of composition with the limited and worse; mistaking addition or expansion for significant change. Finally, this work is difficult insofar as those of us engaged in it are disposed, by the conditions enabling our participation in that work, to conceive of both our task and the subject of our task in immaterial terms: theory and critique as working from a privileged space outside the spatiotemporal dimensions of the material social realm.[3]

To illustrate these difficulties and ways past them, I first turn to the treatment of writing, theory, and pedagogy in two seemingly opposed calls appearing in the last decade for ending composition as we know it—David Smit's *The End of Composition Studies* (2004) and Sidney Dobrin's *Postcomposition* (2011). From seemingly quite different perspectives, both books argue for ending, or for the end of, composition and, instead, for something else. Whereas Smit calls for an end to composition studies in light of its apparent failure to fulfill its official institutional charge of writing-skills transmission, a failure for which he proposes a particular curricular remedy, Dobrin argues for moving "postcomposition" to break from pedagogical concerns—the "pedagogical imperative"—altogether. Thus, the two represent the poles of what has become a well-worn debate on composition's identity as what Joseph Harris has called a "teaching subject." But for my purposes here, what is especially compelling about the appearance of these two works is their alignment, despite their opposition to one another, in accepting the dominant's definition of composition and hence their joint participation in a discourse of need, demonstrating its reach across apparently sharp divides. Together, both books illustrate the difficulties of thinking the work of composition outside the terms set by the dominant, for they end up reinforcing dominant notions of both composition and alternatives to it. Both rely on notions of work in composition and alternatives to such work that are removed from material social history, and notions of writing, theory, pedagogy likewise removed from the material social realm. And both reinforce dominant, if different, terms of exchange in their heralding of, respectively, either "good writing" or "writing" and "theory."

The apocalyptic rhetoric found in these two works brings into sharp relief the assumptions and moves driving not only their arguments but, as I will show, seemingly less apocalyptic, but increasingly pervasive, calls to expand or move beyond or supplement or rename composition in light of its perceived lack—the participation of all such arguments in the same discourse of need. All such arguments require both a debased, if prevalent, understanding of composition work as foil to the alternative that is proposed, and a removal of both that work and the proposed alternative from their location in time and (social) space as material social practices. Thus ideological misrecognitions (in Bourdieu's sense) of both composition work and the proposed alternatives that are aligned with dominant culture are achieved, as evidenced in the gap between representations of either and actual practices and locations: the ongoing history of composition work and, as well, other kinds of work in the United States and elsewhere of students, teachers, scholars. And, thus, both the promise and ongoing daily accomplishments of work in composition go unrecognized, while unpromising alternatives occluding those accomplishments are heralded. Commodifications of knowledge and learning are substituted for the ongoing work of knowing and learning, and dispositions of flexibility in keeping with fast-capitalist dictates are pursued as ideals. As counterpoint, I suggest ways by which we might redefine common terms for the work of composition and their relationships to one another—pedagogy, rhetoric, writing, modality, theory—ways we might rewrite these terms to counter both the limits of dominant conceptions of these and the false claims of what those conceptions define as solutions to those limits.

The discourse of need can be identified by the following interlocking assumptions and moves:

- Writing, at least as practiced in composition, is treated as a stable, internally uniform entity
- Teaching is treated as the transmission of the ability to produce that stable entity "writing"
- Power relations are treated as set rather than subject to and in constant need of reworking, with hegemonic relations of power what the argument is either resigned or aligned to, leading consequently to
- Change being understood in apocalyptic terms as tragic resistance, revolution, and/or violent breaks with the past

- The past itself is treated as a known, finite, and stable entity discrete and different from what is claimed to be the current/new
- Difference is understood as deviation from a norm of sameness rather than an inevitable characteristic of all writing, including writing that is conventionally identified as "the same"
- Theory is treated as an escape from practice rather than a practice itself with material social effects, encouraging blindness to the alignment of theoretical practice aimed at the "different" with dominant ideology and its reinforcement of that ideology

These assumptions govern efforts to understand and address composition's difficulties, shaping not just the solutions various such efforts provide but also the definitions of the problems to be addressed. As I will argue, these assumptions thereby perversely reinforce the very difficulties prompting these efforts. Drawing on the strategies deployed in J. K. Gibson-Graham's critique of "capitalocentric" discourse in economics and Theresa Lillis's critique of the treatment of writing in sociolinguistics, I outline an alternative approach to addressing real limitations in disciplinary discourse, using James Slevin's argument for composition as intellectual work to illustrate such strategies.

It's worth emphasizing that the challenges facing those working in composition to which the arguments considered here respond are real, hence there is genuine exigence for the efforts they represent, whatever questions arise about the specific directions those efforts take. These challenges include, among many others, the perduring poor working conditions for those teaching composition; highly questionable staffing of course sections and student placement and exit procedures; conservatism in program administration and pedagogy; and the seeming impotence of those working in composition to withstand institutional and larger sociopolitical pressures on the definition, conduct, conditions, and valuation of their work. But, ironically, the discourse of need ends up leaving these unchallenged: understood at best as "problems" rather than problematics. Alternatively, I argue for engaging the ongoing, necessary, inevitable rewriting of composition, a possibility that appears once we recognize its always emergent, varied, and changing character.

Composition as Failed Delivery of Marketable Writing Skill

Smit's *The End of Composition Studies* offers one permutation of the discourse of need. In his book, Smit defines composition strictly in terms of pedagogy, understood as the transmission of knowledge of how to write to students, in the form of general writing skills, in a first-year composition course, that will be applicable to future challenges students face elsewhere: "Broadly speaking," he asserts,

> the goal of composition studies is to promote the use of writing: to help people acquire the knowledge and skill they need to convey what they want to say when they put pen to paper or fingers to the keyboard. (1)

However, given the apparent inability of research to date to demonstrate any general writing skills and the apparent tendency of writers only to "acquire" skills at writing in particular ways through immersion in specific communities of practice, Smit concludes that composition needs to end. In other words, the work of composition is understood in terms of the official charge assigned to it by institutional and other authorities, a charge that it appears unable to meet and so should resign from attempting; instead, Smit argues, it must redirect its energies toward facilitating the kind of acquisition of skill in writing in particular ways, in specific disciplines, that Smit thinks does occur.

Curiously, Smit bemoans the lack of consensus about the teaching of writing, yet invokes just such a consensus in his argument for changed writing instruction. On the one hand, he argues that

> writing and writing instruction will always be confounded by contradiction and paradox, a range of possibilities, or bound by the use of certain concepts that occur over and over again in the thoughtful literature on these matters, concepts such as "complexity," "indeterminacy," "dialogue," "dialectic," "heteroglossia," and "negotiation." (12)

On the other hand, he argues that "what we *do* know [about writing instruction] suggests some broad principles [about writing instruction] that the field has yet to act on" (11).

This is among several contradictions in Smit's argument.[4] As I've suggested, on the one hand, he claims a lack of consensus about writing but then invokes just such a consensus about writing ("broad principles") to argue for the kind of change to the writing curriculum he advocates. And while he claims that "we are at the 'end' of what we can know about [the] nature of writing, learning to write, composing processes, writing as a social practice, writing as thinking, and the process of transferring learning from one context to another," he also argues that composition studies "needs to go back to basic questions, such as these: What is writing? How is writing learned? Can writing be taught, and if so, in what sense? And if writing can be taught, how should it be taught?" (2).

Writing, in Smit's book, is used in two contradictory senses (part of what enables and produces the contradictions identified above). On the one hand, he uses it in the singular as a noncount (mass) noun condensing all activities and products associated with the term into a single, uniform entity: writing *tout court*. This is the meaning he invokes in the "basic" questions about what writing is (cited above). On the other hand, he also uses *writing* to refer to a broad range of highly differentiated practices and products—what scholars of writing (including "composition" scholars) have for some time now documented (see, for example, Lea and Street; Thaiss and Zawacki). He defines composition as tied indelibly to the first understanding of writing (despite the fact that composition scholars have been at the forefront of those contesting it), hence the need for composition to come to an end. In other words, because he defines pedagogy as the transmission of a single codified and fixed set of skills and knowledge, whether through explicit instruction or through scaffolding or some other means, the inability of researchers to identify a universal set of these for writing (or, conversely, researchers' findings of myriad shifting kinds of skills and knowledge involved in writing) leads him to the conclusion that composition is at a (dead) end: there appears to be no single set of forms and skills, or even knowledge about these, to transmit, and worse, even if there were, they don't seem to "transfer" to sites beyond first-year composition (FYC).[5] He frames the pedagogical question thus:

> In teaching our students to write, what is it that we want them to know, what is it that we want them to be able to do, and how should we go about helping them to learn what they need to know and practice what they need to be able to do? And what sort of evidence would we accept in order to demonstrate the efficacy of a particular kind of instruction? (139)

The apparent inability of researchers and teachers to answer these questions, at least so far as writing conceived as a noncount, uniform entity is concerned, leads to the end of composition. In other words, assuming a transmission model of pedagogy and a uniform concept of writing at odds with what compositionists in fact recognize paints him (or the field) into a corner: as he puts it, "no one ever learned to write primarily by completing a two-course sequence in writing at a college or university" (182). So he proposes a "Writing in the Disciplines" (WID)–like alternative as the only viable option.

Smit's concluding position is aligned with an acceptance of status quo power relations, exemplifying what Lea and Street have identified as an "academic socialization" model of academic literacy, which they distinguish from both what they call a "study skills" and what they call an "academic literacies" model. Lea and Street characterize the academic socialization model as being

> concerned with students' acculturation into disciplinary and subject-based discourses and genres. Students acquire the ways of talking, writing, thinking, and using literacy that typif[y] members of a disciplinary or subject area community. The academic socialization model presumes that the disciplinary discourses and genres are relatively stable and, once students have learned and understood the ground rules of a particular academic discourse, they are able to reproduce it unproblematically. ("The 'Academic Literacies' Model" 369)

As Smit himself puts it,

> Writing is a process of *socialization*, of novice writers learning to use writing as a tool in order to accomplish particular tasks that they find meaningful and useful or in order to belong to social groups who can use writing as a means of participating in the group. (61, emphasis in original; see also 182)

For Smit, the ideal pedagogy is the "tutorial or a master-apprentice relationship" (142). Omitted from his consideration, significantly, are the actualities of power relations and contingencies of value operating in the material social realm—the features attended to in the "academic literacies" model Lea and Street advocate. Lea and Street distinguish the academic literacies model from an academic socialization model by its view of

> the processes involved in acquiring appropriate and effective uses of literacy as more complex [than the socialization model represents them to be], dynamic, nuanced, situated, and involving both epistemological issues and social processes, including power relations among people, institutions, and social identities. (Lea and Street, "'Academic Literacies'" 369)

Avoiding these more complex features of literacy acquisition, Smit's academic socialization model aligns him with what social theorist Anthony Giddens has identified as a normative functionalist reading of institutions and social practices that ascribes functional normativity to specific academic literacy practices: things are as they are and operate as they do because that is what their appropriate function is.[6] In this reading, official accounts of apprenticeship models are taken as both the full and normative representation of them: the conditions and practices that we should aspire to even if, inevitably, they fall short in some ways. Such an approach ascribes to institutions and institutional processes the value of what they officially claim, and thus reinforces status quo relations of power and the practices maintaining these. While the institution and institutional practices of composition are defined as dysfunctional, work in disciplines outside composition and outside the academy is treated as functional, its processes and contours right—functioning normatively—by virtue of being as they are.

Perhaps the most troubling consequence of the alignment of Smit's position with a normative functionalist perspective can be found in his invocation of the (free) market as the criterion against which we can judge writing and its teaching. So, for example, he contrasts classroom instruction in composition (defined as dysfunctional) with the expert-novice model. In his representations, whereas all writing in the composition classroom is merely an exam (147) or "practice" (165) for what might come later, in the novice-expert socialization process,

> novices are immersed in a social system; they learn genres and how to apply them through reading these genres as an integral part of their daily life and producing them themselves as the need arises. They receive help in writing as they need it or want it, or it is forced on them. If they have a particular problem with writing, they will find out about it all too quickly and "naturally." They will not accomplish with their writing what they set out to accomplish. Their boss will

> send back their memos for revision because they have not adequately addressed the issues they were assigned. Their editors will reject their essays because they have not been sufficiently literary or insightful. The city commission will reject their petitions because they have not been sufficiently persuasive. The members of their community will provide the responses, the feedback, the criticism they need. They will learn how to write because they want to, because they have to, for the same reason that young children gradually learn to talk. (148)

Here the invisible hand of the (free) market is implicitly invoked as an explanation for why some writers and writing receive praise and others don't. In this fantasy, writing simply is or is not persuasive, literary, insightful, effective, as determined by its "buyers"/consumers: bosses, the public, editors, those whose authority to know what is and isn't good writing goes unquestioned, like that of purchasers of stocks and other commodities; the market, here as elsewhere, decides, and its decisions are by definition right in determining the value of what is purchased. Or, as Smit claims, "the only way to determine whether novice writers write adequately is to see if their writing accomplishes their purposes outside the classroom in the larger 'marketplace'" (156). Smit follows this claim with a demurral—"not all writing must accomplish real effects in the world analogous to a company selling a product"—but then reasserts the rightness of the marketplace: "without the constraints of that larger marketplace, how do instructors go about determining what students need to know in order to become better writers?" (156).

In keeping with this free-market fantasy, students themselves are also identified as the free agents of that marketplace: the consumers who by definition are always right and whose desires are both fixed and entirely their own:

> Students are responsible for their own choices, their own goals, their own values, and we are bound to respect those choices, those goals and values. . . . We cannot set ourselves up as experts in ends, in what students might choose to do with their lives. We can only offer our judgment of means. . . . give them as much help as possible in choosing the ends they wish to pursue. (192)[7]

Hence Smit argues for course descriptions that "specify the purpose of the writing required in the course, the theoretical or ideological framework of the course, and the discourse community to which the course is designed to introduce students" (192). But while it seems inarguable that course descriptions should not deliberately mislead students, and that students, like their teachers, should have their current views acknowledged and taken seriously (not to be confused with being taken uncritically), it is also patently obvious that no course description can fully represent what students, or their instructors, will encounter or produce in a course, and that student desires, views, and beliefs, like those of other humans, are inevitably diverse, in flux, often contradictory, and not fully or readily available either to them or their instructors for inspection—but vulnerable to and always in need of being reworked.

It is Smit's free-market fantasy model that requires a transmission model of pedagogy, which in Smit extends to the demand for a "truth in advertising" of course descriptions whereby teachers must tell the student consumers what those enrolling will be getting, and, of course, teachers must then deliver what's promised, and students are assumed to know what they want and will need. This is the assumed model behind the current wave of demands for (school) accountability, requirements for statements of "learning outcomes" for all courses, and so on. It is a model that elides the overdetermined character of any educational work in favor of a simplistic model of learning as information/skill transfer, and of knowledge as commodity. As in those demands, Smit treats the complexity of such work not as a problematic but as a problem, something to be avoided or eliminated rather than engaged. Thus, while Smit makes the occasional nod toward the possibility of change and difference resulting from student apprenticeships with the discourse communities they have somehow chosen to join, his general argument is to make writing instruction more efficient in delivering specific writing skills demanded by employers and therefore, it is assumed, desired by the students, conceived of primarily as future employees. Having established for himself that no general writing skills exist to be transmitted, he argues for transmission of writing skills specific to particular disciplines and worksites and is disturbed at the extent to which composition courses fail at this task, asking rhetorically,

> If school genres lack sufficient context to help students grapple with all of the rhetorical constraints they will confront in the world at large, just how useful are they in preparing students to write for

> that world? . . . What sort of "real-world" genres are writing classes supposed to be training students to write? Or what sort of skills are school genres supposed to be honing that will transfer to writing outside of the classroom? (148)

The fact that "what students write in college does not sufficiently prepare them for writing in the workplace or in other nonacademic settings" (153) is seen as a flaw in composition pedagogy to be corrected, not an inevitability to be engaged, explored, embraced.

We thus see in Smit's argument a treatment of writing as a stable entity and pedagogy as (ideally) the means to transmit skill in producing it efficiently, in alignment with status quo power relations and hegemonic ideals. Composition's past, and its knowledge, are treated as knowable and known; difference is understood not as the norm of writing but as deviation from a norm of sameness, with varieties of writing as each internally uniform rather than in flux and in fluctuating relation with one another. Practice is something following research and theory rather than in dialectical relation with it: classrooms are where theory and research are to be applied rather than the site of theorizing and (real, vs. a simulacrum of) research.

Composition as Hegemony in Student Training and Management

As I've already suggested, Sidney Dobrin's *Postcomposition* would seem, on its surface, to represent the complete counterargument to Smit's *End of Composition Studies*. While, for Smit, composition is at an end because of the failure of composition pedagogy to meet the needs of the dominant, Dobrin calls for composition studies to break with the "pedagogical imperative" (as well as the "administrative" imperative) and with student subjectivities altogether in favor of pursuing writing/theory. For Dobrin identifies composition as defined (limited, hobbled) by its commitment to pedagogy and the administration of pedagogy and of student subjectivities. As he puts it, the difficulty with composition is its "inability to articulate an intellectual focus *beyond* the training of teachers, an activity set in service of the continued management of student bodies rather than in pursuit of understanding of writing in the formation of the signifier 'student'" (18, emphasis added). Given a view of composition as defined by its commitment to pedagogy, and a view of pedagogy as "training" and "management," composition, for Dobrin, is not worth keeping to. In place of composition so defined, Dobrin argues for the study of writing, defined as a "producing machine" of subjects/subjectivity, a study which will "reconfigur[e] the subject as posthuman, non-autonomous agent" (17).

At various moments in *Postcomposition*, it appears that Dobrin's project is meant to spur rethinking of the terms defining composition in ways aligned with the project of this book. For example, Dobrin explains that postcomposition is not "no-student" but, rather, "post-student as student is currently conceived," and that postcomposition is meant to enable us to "think 'differently' about writing than disciplinary limits have previously allowed or encouraged" (15, 189). In such statements, there is the potential to rethink conceptions of "student" and, by implication, pedagogy (and, of course, writing). But that potential is undercut by Dobrin' acceptance of dominant conceptions of pedagogy. For in the same breath as he argues for being "post-student as student is currently conceived," he insists that postcomposition is "certainly postpedagogy." This acceptance of dominant conceptions of composition pedagogy is confirmed by his call for the work of theorizing writing. That work is defined as "not the work of a teaching subject nor dependent upon the role students play in making writing an object of study" but as something that "is—and must be—bigger than the idea of students" (15).

Thus, while Dobrin's argument is clearly opposed to those like Smit's concerned with producing a more efficient composition pedagogy for students, and would seem to share the aim of my argument to rethink the field's discourse, his argument, like Smit's, assumes a debased view of the work of composition—most prominently, pedagogy and work at the pedagogical scene. His argument differs from Smit's only in choosing to abandon that work rather than replace it with WID. And so, while he offers no idealist/fantasy portrait of how writing pedagogy should work, what he does propose is no less idealist—that is, removed from material social history—than Smit's proposed "solution." In place of composition, with its "neurosis of pedagogy," he advocates what he terms "writing studies." But it is a "writing studies" largely removed from the material social realm.

We can see this removal by comparing Dobrin's articulation of what writing studies might be to seemingly similar calls for a shift from "composition studies" to "writing studies" by others (see, for example,

Bazerman, "Case"; Trimbur, "Changing"; and discussion below). What Dobrin seems to mean by writing studies appears oblivious to large swaths of scholarship that can already lay claim to such a name, and he dismisses much of the theorizing of writing affiliated with composition while conflating particular writing practices associated with digital communication technologies with writing *tout court*. For example, given Dobrin's hearty "Amen" to Charles Bazerman's argument to broaden composition's focus to attend to the full panoply of writing practices (Dobrin 25–26), we might expect that Dobrin will consider at least some instances drawn from the hefty reams of scholarship in literacy studies focusing on these practices.[8] But in fact, no such instances make any appearance in *Postcomposition*. Instead, writing studies appears to be imagined as only just emerging *ex nihilo* in the work of a handful of theorists: something new and at odds with all that has come before—one reason Dobrin postulates for the difficulty of the work of theorizing writing. Like early colonizers of what came to be known as the Americas imagining the "new lands" (new to them, anyhow) on which they had set foot as spreading open, vacant and inviting, before them and for them, Dobrin appears to see writing studies as a yet largely unexplored and uninhabited vista, all evidence to the contrary notwithstanding. Likewise, Dobrin dismisses from consideration theorizing writing in terms of such matters as "ideologies, politics, subjectivities, agencies, identities, discourses, rhetorics, and grammars" insofar as these are issues "composition studies has come to be so invested in," suggesting that talk about such issues serves merely to enable composition theorists to talk "about the things that other theorists in English studies talk about" and thereby "gives claim to legitimacy" (25). This dismissal effectively clears the field of theorizing by deeming (at least some) extant theorizing something else. That is, while we must theorize writing, not all theorizing counts as such. The theorizing of writing in which writing students engage, for example, remains invisible.

At certain points, Dobrin acknowledges the corner into which he's painted himself, complaining of the frustration and difficulty of "trying to identify writing as independent from other phenomena and the dangers in trying to essentialize writing as a scientific (positivist) thing devoid of ecological/textual/network connection to other phenomena" (24–25). Encouragingly, he rejects the idea that "the phenomena of writing can be/should be identified in an a-contextual, vacuous state not related to other phenomena." But he then insists that we cannot understand writing's relationships to these until we "understand what the phenomena of writing are and, in turn, how writing functions to produce other phenomena"—in other words, writing as distinct first cause (25).

Dobrin attributes his frustration and difficulty to "a discursive encampment in the boundaries of composition studies" (25). But I would argue that it is his theoretical framing that leads to his troubles, if not exactly of essentializing writing "as a scientific (positivist) thing," then of seeming simultaneously to grant to "writing" a purely abstract significance, like God, on the one hand, and, on the other, to anchor it in what has already become a stale set of beliefs about the role of global digital communication technologies in redefining what constitutes "writing" and "what the phenomena of writing are" (25). On the one hand, writing is posited as beyond representation (except as "writing," like "God" for God). "Writing," Dobrin asserts, "resists metaphor as a means of explanation both in its complexity and in its instability" (134). For

> writing is unique in its systemicity in that theorizing it does not require a metaphor to explain what it carries or represents, as what it carries or represents is either not as important as writing itself or else writing does not carry or represent anything beyond or outside itself. (150)

Except, of course, that identifying "writing" as complex, as systemic, as unique, engages Dobrin precisely in representation, even in his efforts to deny that possibility. On the other hand, the one reference to writing as material practice that Dobrin reiterates identifies writing specifically with the "current hyper-circulatory condition of writing," a condition that, he claims, "now demands more complex theories than composition studies has previously provided," such as "ecological or posthuman rhetorics" (142).

The contradiction between Dobrin's call for writing studies and his failure to acknowledge or build on the plethora of extant work in writing studies points to a significant limitation in Dobrin's theorizing. Dobrin offers postcomposition as a response to real, often seemingly intractable, difficulties and limitations of pedagogical and administrative work in composition. However, theory is treated as a means of leaving behind such seeming difficulties and limitations rather than as a considered practice by which one might rethink (and change) them and that is itself in need of continual rethinking. This is in sharp contrast to, for example, Lynn Worsham's description of theory as "the never-ending work of making 'really free' places, lives, and identities," "a deadly serious matter" that, in composition, takes the form of "both the writing that scholars in composition studies must do and the writing that we must teach," "driven by a passionate political consciousness . . . that seeks the conceptual tools, the explanatory frameworks, to engineer social change," "coming to terms with the real world" by bridging "the chasm between the actual and the possible" ("Coming" 104; cf. Resnick and Wolff 37; Gibson-Graham, Resnick, and Wolff, "Toward" 19). Likewise, in "Toward a Theory of Theory in Composition," James T. Zebroski sees theory as a practice to be engaged *through* teaching, observing that characterizations of composition as at best the object of critique by Theory (*sic*) fail to do "justice to the complexity of thinking that occurs when a composition teacher works with a student on the production of a text" (31). For such writers, theory is not an escape from places, lives, and identities, but imbricated in and a means of acting on these. Conversely, as Dobrin himself puts it in his postscript to *Postcomposition*, "Postcomposition moves forward, *not* bound by *rethinking*, *reassessing*, or *reworking* the past but by looking to *new frontiers* for composition theory" (210, emphases added). Pedagogy, rather than being rethought, is simply left to its own (old) ways, ostensibly at best as the site for the application of research, in exchange for the new, relatively unexplored and hence relatively unknown world of "theory." While aligning himself with Freire's famous critique of the "narration sickness" of banking pedagogy, Dobrin does not, as Freire does, rethink and rework pedagogy (for example, by exploring a "problem-posing" pedagogy) but, instead, washes his hands of pedagogy altogether, advising us to "stop talking about teaching" (190).

Given the thick layering of references in *Postcomposition* to the work of figures enjoying currency in the heady realm of contemporary high theory (Badiou, Baudrillard, Bauman, Deleuze and Guattari, Derrida, Foucault, Haraway, Hardt and Negri, Hassan, Hayles, Jameson, Lyotard, Soja, Ulmer, Žižek), it is tempting to see Dobrin as, in fact, hoping that composition might exchange the economic capital associated with pedagogy and administration that he sees composition earning (as a "cash cow" [75]) in the economy of academic institutions—largely under the "service" category in traditional academic valuations of work—for production of cultural capital earning a higher rate of exchange in the economy of academic status: that associated with the production of high theory. This would help explain why Dobrin's admirable desire to better understand the "phenomena of writing," and his entirely legitimate argument that a focus on writing and the teaching of writing limited to writing conducted under the auspices of "composition" is narrow in the extreme, do not lead him directly to the enormous body of scholarly work in literacy studies focusing on, well, phenomena of writing (see footnote 8). For that work, like work in composition, is too closely associated in the public and institutional academic imaginary with education.[9] Hence, it is accorded lower status than "pure" theory.[10]

This disdain for attending to actual literacy practices is in accord with Dobrin's metaphors of moving "forward" to "new frontiers," and his identification of his abstracted theorizing of "writing" as "open complex system" with what he repeatedly identifies as the "hyper-circulatory nature of writing and the drastic technological shifts we are witnessing regarding the (re)circulation of writing" (160; see also 83; 133; 137; 142; 185). These land Dobrin's project of moving postcomposition firmly in the ideology of dominant discourses heralding a communicative globalism aligned with fast-capitalist ideals of constant and rapid change, flexibility, complexity, and, above all, the inevitability of these, whatever the cost to those on the ground.[11] So, for example, Dobrin insists that "in fact, the whole world—or, more specifically, writing—*is* in the Web because the Web/writing is (in) the whole world, whether an individual or society is consciously aware of it or not" (144).[12] Citing approvingly Mark C. Taylor's warning that "those who are too rigid to fit in rapidly changing worlds become obsolete or are driven beyond the edge of chaos to destruction" (Taylor 202; qtd. in Dobrin 168), Dobrin explains that "as the complexity of networks with which we interact increases and as the speed of network-changes accelerate, the ability to adjust to rapid shift becomes necessary" (168). And later, Dobrin approvingly cites Margaret Syverson's warning that "as contexts and technologies for writing continue to change at an ever accelerating pace, we cannot cling to our familiar, comfortable assumptions about writers, readers, and texts, or we will find ourselves increasingly irrelevant and even obstructive" (Syverson 27; qtd. in Dobrin 177). In fact, Dobrin warns, in only a decade after Syverson's warning, "the situation of writing has changed even more dramatically/radically than even Syverson suggests" (177). We are, we are told, reaching a "tipping point" (177, 185) that has rendered common ways of thinking about writing "outmoded" and that requires "creative destruction," "wiping the slate clean and starting anew" (188). Those who resist will be doomed as "obstructive," "outmoded," "obsolete," "irrelevant," and therefore quite justifiably "driven to destruction." To *this* (technological) imperative, we are told, There Is No Alternative.

Dobrin does follow these imperatives with a kind of demurral, admitting that "there is little possibility or need to decimate composition studies and start from a completely blank slate; we can't really be free of our past, nor do we want to be" (188). But he nonetheless then calls for the "destruction of composition studies," albeit a destruction that occurs as a "deliberate, slow reinscription of the objectives of the field and the spaces that composition studies occupies," a kind of conversion or "mutation into a different form" (188–89). But this model of change is in contradiction to the violence he deems necessary to the accomplishment of such change, signaled by the language of violence and destruction he deploys. That language follows, as I will discuss below, from the landscape of hegemony in power relations and global forces that he imagines us to inhabit.

For example, to return to the question of the "hyper-circulatory nature of writing and the drastic technological shifts we are witnessing regarding the (re)circulation of writing," it is of course futile to deny changes to communication technologies, the pace of these changes, and the need to attend to them, any more than we should deny the fact of "market pressures" on writers. However, it is nonetheless important to insist on also acknowledging (1) the ongoing, incomplete, varied, and uneven distribution and "development" and direction of development of these; (2) the simultaneous presence and interaction of other, competing technologies with these; and (3) consequently, the indeterminate character of the effect of these changes on writing and culture more broadly, with, as complexity theory itself insists, unintended, even unimaginable consequences as these technologies interact in overdetermined ways with other phenomena. In short, it is to refuse to accept pretensions of the hegemonic to hegemony.

It is Dobrin's acceptance of such pretensions that aligns his argument to those like Smit's, for it leads to his participation in the same discourse of (composition's) need. For example, Dobrin's argument, like Smit's, accepts dominant definitions of and the official charge to composition of writing skills transmission. His argument differs from those like Smit's only in wanting to move beyond or escape from rather than better meet that charge, while accepting as inevitable the need to follow the path for writing officially set by hegemonic notions of technological change. Writing, for Dobrin, remains a singular, if abstract and complex, entity; pedagogy continues to be understood as student management; hegemonic relations of power and their directions for cultural change are treated as known and set; difference is postulated as a break from the norm rather than as the norm itself; and theory is treated as an escape from the material social realm rather than a participant in that realm.

Rethinking Terms of Disciplinary Discourse

By way of illustrative contrast to the strategies found in Smit and Dobrin, I turn briefly to the strategies deployed in two disparate critical projects: J. K. Gibson-Graham's project against capitalism and Theresa Lillis's project for a sociolinguistics of writing (*Sociolinguistics*). Both projects, like Dobrin's and Smit's, respond to significant limitations in an existing field (economics and sociolinguistics, respectively). Both can be characterized as intensely theoretical. However, in these works, theory (and research) are taken up not as alternatives to but engagements in and with the material social realm. Or to be more precise, these projects theorize in order to rethink, re-represent, rewrite, and change, rather than escape from, end, or leave behind the terms (and practices) of the disciplines they critique for something new.

In a series of papers and in two books whose titles eerily echo those of Smit and Dobrin—*The End of Capitalism* and *Post-Capitalism*—Gibson-Graham seek not so much to escape capitalism *per se* but, as the full title of *The End of Capitalism* suggests, change the way in which capitalism is known: to put an *End to Capitalism (as We Knew It)* so that "capitalism *per se*" can be known, and thereby responded to, differently.[13] (The subtitle, *A Feminist Critique of Political Economy*, suggests the kind of difference that will be made.) Toward that end, Gibson-Graham reject the terms in which capitalism is traditionally thought by both its apologists and its critics: as not only dominant but total in its hegemony. Arguments operating within such governing terms, including those opposed to capitalism, participate in but also thereby contribute to "capitalocentric" discourse that reinforces capitalism's hegemonic position. As Gibson-Graham observes of her own earlier work opposing global capitalism, "The image of global capitalism that I was producing was actively participating in consolidating a new phase of capitalist hegemony" (*End* xxxix). To intervene in this dynamic, she explains that, without eschewing acknowledgment of the dominant position of capitalist formations currently, she had instead to take a

> theoretical option . . . that could make a (revolutionary) difference: to depict economic discourse as hegemonized while rendering the social world as economically differentiated and complex. . . . to understand capitalist hegemony as a (dominant) discourse rather than as a social articulation or structure. Thus one might represent economic practice as comprising a rich diversity of capitalist and noncapitalist activities and argue that the noncapitalist ones had until now been relatively "invisible" because the concepts and discourses that could make them "visible" have themselves been marginalized and suppressed. (*End* xl–xli)

What dominant discourse had represented (and thus perpetuated) as the full story of the economy could be counterposed to alternative representations of (economic) activities. Failure to do so, as Gibson-Graham go on to demonstrate, acquiesces in, and thereby perpetuates belief in the legitimacy of, the terms of argument postulating capitalism as not merely hegemonic but hegemony, total in its reach (see *End*, chapter 1).[14] In such arguments, even alternatives to capitalism are defined in advance within its terms as always already capitalism's "*feminized* other . . . lack[ing] efficiency and rationality . . . its productivity . . . its global extensiveness, or its inherent tendency to dominance and expansion" (7). It is thus that dominant discourse, including, importantly, discourse opposed to capitalism, is, as Gibson-Graham put it, "capitalocentric." Gibson-Graham combat this by "cutting capitalism down to size (theoretically) and refusing to endow it with excessive power" (*End* xxiv). So, for example, they

> recontextualiz[e] capitalism in a discourse of economic plurality [to] destabilize its presumptive hegemony. Hegemony becomes a feature not of capitalism itself but of a social articulation that is

> only temporarily fixed and always under subversion; and alternative economic discourses become the sites and instruments of struggles that may subvert capitalism's provisional and unstable dominance (if indeed such dominance is understood to exist). (*End* 15)

In *Post-Capitalist Politics*, Gibson-Graham further this project, exploring the specific challenges and strategies for the intellectual/affective work of rethinking political economy through reconsiderations of their own action research projects.

The subject of Theresa Lillis's argument for a *Sociolinguistics of Writing* is more recognizably related to questions of composition. I take up specific points in her argument later in this and subsequent chapters. Here what are most relevant are the strategies by which Lillis calls for a significant departure in, or readjustment to, the focus, assumptions, and practices of sociolinguistics, a change that radically repositions writing, rather than only or primarily spoken language, as a legitimate and significant area of sociolinguistics. The challenge of making this argument, like the challenge Gibson-Graham face in rethinking capitalism, resides at least in part in dominant conceptualizations of writing in sociolinguistics, for it is those conceptions that have relegated writing to the margins of sociolinguistic research. These include the notion that writing is primarily concerned with codifying and maintaining specific standard varieties of language use; that it exists in binary opposition to speech; that it is permanent, monomodal, formal, lexically dense, distant, context independent, monologic, detached, and impersonal whereas speech is transient, multimodal, informal, grammatically complex, local, context dependent, dialogic, involved, and personal (*Sociolinguistics* 8–10). As Lillis observes, it is this framing of writing (and speech) by dominant discourse in sociolinguistics that needs to be rethought, its "paradigmatic imaginary" that defines "what its objects of study are, and importantly, can or should be" (10). So, for example, "The focus on writing [in sociolinguistics] in processes of standardisation and codification hides other ways of noticing and understanding what writing is and does in social context, thus potentially limiting our understanding of 'everyday' writing" (8).

While Lillis refers to empirical evidence to demonstrate the invalidity of how writing has been framed in sociolinguistics, such research alone is inadequate insofar as it can easily be accommodated to the dominant terms. For instance, when examples of speech are presented that have characteristics assigned to writing, dominant discourse in sociolinguistics does not rethink its framing of speech and writing but, instead, dubs these examples to be not "genuine" speech (and writing with attributes associated with speech are dubbed "speech-like") (*Sociolinguistics* 9). Hence Lillis must retheorize the binary framing itself to enable as legitimate a sociolinguistics of writing.

The projects of both Gibson-Graham and Lillis are motivated, like Smit's and Dobrin's, by dissatisfaction with "the field." But unlike either Smit or Dobrin, Gibson-Graham and Lillis proceed not by declaring the field to be at an end, nor by abandoning the field in pursuit of some other "end" or new "frontier," but by pursuing ways of thinking that field differently: for Gibson-Graham most obviously, rethinking the hegemony of capitalism; for Lillis, rethinking the position of writing in sociolinguistics. And both Gibson-Graham's and Lillis's projects are explicitly located in a wide range of ongoing research and theory, rather than pretending to leave behind the old, as at an end, in order to seek out and produce something entirely new. So, for example, Gibson-Graham do not propose to abandon political economy (or the study of capitalism) for some other pursuit, or declare these fields to be at an end, nor does Lillis propose abandoning sociolinguistics. Instead, they theorize—find ways to think—the governing terms (*economy*, *capitalism*, *sociolinguistics*, *writing*) differently. Following their example, we might see that the difficulties Smit and Dobrin wrestle with are not to be understood in terms of pedagogy vs. theory, or FYC vs. writing studies or WID, but, rather, how *pedagogy*, *theory*, *FYC*, *writing studies*, *WID* have come to be understood and practiced. Theory, for example, far from being a monolith, beneficent or maleficent, in tension with an equivalent monolith of "practice," itself denotes an enormous range of emergent practices taking an enormous range of forms, some that we might want to encourage and some not. The same can be said of teaching, administration, FYC, and so on. But it would be wrong to conclude from what we deem to be poorly theorized/practiced theory, pedagogy, administration that we should abandon work identified by such terms for something else, since to do so would accede to the impoverished definitions shaping that work in a futile effort to leave behind composition as material social practice. What is needed instead is a reworking and rewriting of theory, pedagogy, administration, etc., with what constitutes "better" rewritings of these of course inevitably a matter of debate and, well, work.

It might be argued (though I will not) that the consequences of the rethinking of a field's key terms of the sort Gibson-Graham and Lillis engage in are not as "revolutionary" as the consequences envisioned by either Smit or Dobrin. But ironically, to argue thus would in fact be to remain subject to the very terms, conditions, and criteria set by the dominant for what counts as, in fact, "revolutionary." I have already suggested that Smit's envisioned change amounts to little that is different from WID curricula already on the books, inflected with dominant free-market ideology.[15] Dobrin's envisioned change, insofar as it promises to abjure composition as a "teaching subject," would seem to be more radical. On closer inspection, however, his proposed escape to the beyond of composition is fully resonant with a dominant discourse of fast capitalism.[16]

That Dobrin's desired move to escape what seem to be the limit-situations of composition should land him so unwittingly in a far more problematic position illustrates the role of "hegemony" in maintaining the hegemonic. Composition studies, for Dobrin, is represented as an undifferentiated and stable monolith (identified as and with "the WPA") to which he ascribes an all-encompassing power: not merely hegemonic but hegemony.[17] And, accordingly, the only route out would appear to be the same apocalyptic (impossible) escape imagined by opponents of capitalism who accord it a similar identity. It is no wonder, then, that, faced with such a conception of composition, the only option and hope would appear to be "violence" (113), "total revolution" (188), or at the very least the appearance of some heroic "critical wpa," someone who is not merely being critical but who disrupts (114). For, as Gibson-Graham warn,

> Once we have created a theoretical monster and installed it in the social landscape, our thinking and politics will tend to orient themselves around its bulk and majesty and our emotional outlook will reflect the diminished likelihood of displacing it. (*Postcapitalist* 199; cf. Chaput, "Fear")

Nor is it surprising that Dobrin's proposed alternative lands him so firmly in a position aligned with a dominant discourse of globalism condemning to destruction all those who resist its good intentions. Thus, just as the treatment of capitalism as monolith, as Gibson-Graham warn, leads to it "be[ing] seen to operate as a constraint or a limit . . . that to which other more mutable entities must adapt" (*End* 14), so Dobrin's and Smit's treatments of composition perforce render any efforts in response, theirs included, merely accommodative. Indeed, we can best understand claims to the violent, revolutionary, or disruptive character of such efforts as rhetorical ploys to obscure their actual status as adaptations, their acquiescence to the terms governing thought.

In place of such adaptive strategies we can, following Gibson-Graham's and Lillis's strategies, work to re-cognize, in order to break from the hegemonic misrecognitions of, the governing terms of arguments and the established frameworks for those terms. In the case of composition, this would involve challenging commonplace distinctions (iterated in both Smit's and Dobrin's arguments, albeit from ostensibly opposed perspectives): that between intellectual work and pedagogy; that between a concern with what the dominant identifies as material concerns, such as labor and administration, on the one hand, and, on the other, theory; that between writing and composition. It would involve relocating all work intersecting with composition studies, including theoretical work, in the material social—including the academic institutional—realm so as not to stake out as "new" territory fields that are, in fact, already long under cultivation. And, following Raymond Williams, it would require refusing to accede to the hegemonic's false claims to being not merely hegemonic but "hegemony": the exclusive, total story. For, as Williams warns, "*no dominant social order and therefore no dominant culture ever in reality includes or exhausts all human practice, human energy.* . . . [Rather] they select from and consequently exclude the full range of human practice" (*Marxism* 125, emphasis in original). In line with this, instead of treating composition, or composition studies, in the singular, we would need to recognize composition as both (1) multiple, and (2) always emergent, contingent. We can cut "Composition" down to size, theoretically and practically, by refusing to assign it status as an all-powerful, stable monolith and rejecting the accuracy of dominant representations of its work. Just as Gibson-Graham found they had to contest "the tendency to constitute 'the' economy as a singular capitalist system or space rather than as a zone of cohabitation and contestation among multiple forms . . . and . . . to lodge faith in accurate representation that guaranteed and stabilized the prevailing substantive framings" (*Post-Capitalist* xxi–xxii), so those who would counter dominant and problematic characteristics of work in composition must resist the tendency to constitute "composition" as "a singular . . . system or space rather than as a zone of cohabitation and contestation," and reject the accuracy of dominant representations of that work. As Bazerman has observed, "Just because [compositionists] have been funded with a reductionist notion of our task has not meant that we have been bound to follow through in a reductionist way" ("Response" 252).

Composition as Intellectual Work

James Slevin's critique of dominant work in composition and representations of that work, and his heralding of different work in and for composition, provides a useful contrast to efforts like Smit's and Dobrin's. Like Dobrin, Slevin rejects conservative "academic" discourse, such as demanding conformity to community norms through deployment of terms like "engagement," "collaboration," and the "common good" (*Introducing* 235), identifying such discourse with the project of colonization (*Introducing* 6). Slevin identifies intellectual work as by definition opposed to such discourse: as "the critical examination of the truthfulness of knowledge created, received, and exchanged" (*Introducing* 235). However, whereas both Dobrin and Smit locate intellectual work outside the material realm—for Dobrin, part of its appeal as escape from the merely "academic," for Smit, the basis for rejecting it—and whereas both Dobrin and Smit see intellectual work as at most operating on but not produced at the scene of pedagogy, Slevin locates intellectual work insistently in the material social realm, including the academic institutional realm and, most notably, the scene of pedagogy. So, for example, Slevin argues that

> *teachers of writing* . . . can bring into being a radical reorganization of the professional hierarchy. The very concerns that locate us at the base or bottom of the prevailing power system need to be elaborated, so that we can alter both the theory and practice of English studies. Our aim, then, should be not simply to resituate ourselves within institutions but, in doing so, to *reconceive* and *reconstruct* those institutions. ("Depoliticizing" 10, emphasis added)

And he identifies the pedagogical scene as the site of intellectual work, crediting the emergence of a "writing movement" not to theorists or researchers but to "the presence and intellectual energy of *students* who questioned the hegemony of received ways of reading and writing" (*Introducing* 2, emphasis added).

In seeming alignment with both Smit and Dobrin, Slevin rejects "promoting the 'field' of composition studies and within it composition specialists," but he identifies such promotion not with composition *per se* but with "current *representations* of composition" (*Introducing* 3, emphasis added). Hence his aim is not to retreat from, put an end to, or move beyond composition represented thus, but, rather, to offer "a different way of representing the work and workers of composition, not as a field one works 'in' but rather as a set of activities and practices one works 'with'" (*Introducing* 3). Such reconceptualizing, he suggests, "refines the meaning of disciplinary work to include teaching and learning and broadens the meaning of workers to create alliances of literacy teachers *and learners* across conventional educational boundaries and even beyond educational institutions as ordinarily conceived" (3). So, whereas Dobrin calls for bringing the attention of "intellectual and scholarly inquiry and speculation" to writing phenomena "beyond composition" because "writing is more than composition (studies)" (2), and whereas Smit argues for abandoning such inquiry altogether in favor of settling for what is officially on demand by disciplines and workplaces, Slevin argues for expanding those recognized as fellow scholars engaging in the intellectual work of composition to include not only college writing teachers and students, but all those engaged with composing, including seven-year-olds composing thank-you notes (*Introducing* 50–51). Instead of aiming to meet composition students' ostensible disciplinary and vocational needs, as Smit insists, Slevin argues for composition to make "other needs imaginable and their realization possible" (*Introducing* 239). Thus, whereas both Smit and Dobrin work within established academic institutional categories and hierarchies to extend, end, or move beyond the present "field" of research in what are ultimately quite familiar ways, Slevin calls for making composition a "*movement* for institutional change within and among all levels of education and many different fields of study and learning," one "concerned not with remediating lack but with examining and understanding differences as they enrich education" (*Introducing* 52, emphasis in original).

This is a far cry from either Dobrin's view of attention to students and the management of curricula as at best a way to "attract the attention of local resources, garner support from local administrations, and often solve local problems" (26), or Smit's view of these matters as service to those higher up in the academic and social hierarchy and the marketplace. That Slevin's proposals appear to have garnered significantly less attention than Smit's and Dobrin's can be accounted for by the very familiarity of the thinking to be found in Smit and Dobrin, notwithstanding their rhetoric, and the difficulty of recognizing the thinking of the former, given the deviation of Slevin's proposals from the frameworks of dominant, hegemonic discourse in composition.[18] Familiar terms—theory, pedagogy, service, writing, composition—are in Slevin assigned quite unfamiliar meanings and thus pose genuine difficulty, the difficulty of thinking composition differently.

This is not to say that Slevin's own arguments are beyond dispute—an impossibility for any argument—but rather that his efforts to rewrite composition, like Gibson-Graham's efforts to rewrite economics and Lillis's to rewrite sociolinguistics, work against dominant representations of these fields rather than accepting (and thereby promoting) the legitimacy and/or inevitability of dominant definitions and valuations of these. And, unlike Smit and Dobrin, Slevin locates composition firmly in the material social realm—in academic institutions and the work of students, teachers, and scholars—as practices in, with, and on these as "intellectual work"—a phrase paradoxical in the root sense of that term. Difference, for Slevin, is not something to be pursued in lieu of or as a means to end composition but rather as an inevitable, pervasive, and defining feature of composition as a material social practice, located in space and time.

Composition as Foil to Rhetoric, Writing Studies, and "the Multimodal"

If Smit and Dobrin argue from the position of an ostensible present of composition to a prospective future beyond, or following the end of, composition, others have attempted to resolve the difficulties of work in composition by aligning it with, or broadening its reach to include, traditions, forms, and materials seen as other than or additional to the practices traditionally identified with the work of composition: rhetoric, (new) media, cultural studies, literacy studies, or (as we have seen) by renaming it "writing studies." But, as in Smit's and Dobrin's arguments, these moves assume (again) either that composition itself is inadequate to describe the work that we do, or that the work we do is inadequate to what we should be doing—hence the need to rename composition, or add something else on to composition. And the assumption underlying that is that dominant definitions and valuations of the work of composition *qua* composition, definitions and valuations in terms of which composition is judged to be lacking, are themselves adequate, reliable, valid.

While adopting far less apocalyptic rhetoric than we find in *Postcomposition* or *The End of Composition Studies*, arguments for these changes are aligned with them in assuming a deficit in composition for which the presumed addition or substitution is offered as solution. Traditional frameworks and definitions of composition, pedagogy, academic disciplinarity, and value are left unquestioned—the very frameworks and definitions by which composition must be seen as lacking—and the solutions or improvements that are offered as correctives are aligned with and work within these frameworks and definitions. I'll focus here on three of the most prominent of the efforts at changing composition: efforts to identify, or link, composition with rhetoric; efforts to rename composition "writing studies"; and efforts to change, or add to, the forms and materials students are to work with and produce in composing, most commonly by insisting on what is termed "multimodal."

One difficulty in assessing these efforts is that, in one sense, many of the proffered changes call for doing what in fact is, and long has been, already part of traditional work in composition but that dominant conceptions of that work have blinded us to. Hence we might agree with the appropriateness of the activities called for while rejecting the claim that engaging in them somehow constitutes a radical break. Simultaneously, however, the performative effects of these dominant representations of composition as lacking, in need of something else that's "new" or "alternative," cannot be denied: the hegemonic may not be total or exclusive, but it is by definition hegemonic. This complicates efforts to retrieve what it denies and to learn to recognize, in forms and practices we are predisposed to understand in limited ways, the accomplishment of more and other than what is claimed: to see, for example, in traditional "compositions" the multimodality and engagement in writing study we have learned to identify only with activities taking specific other forms. In other words, we have to contend not only with dominant ways of conceptualizing composition, but with dominant conceptualizations of the alternatives to it as, in fact, alternative.

Composition and Rhetoric

There is by now a long tradition of both linking and debating the linkage between rhetoric and composition (see for example Braun; Coleman and Goodman; Fulkerson, "Composition"; Gage; Horner and Lu, "Rhetoric," "Working"; Kopelson; Mulderig; Murphy; Swearingen; Winterowd). As Min-Zhan Lu and I have argued elsewhere, at issue in these efforts is the definition of each term and its relation to the other—for example, composition as merely rhetoric manqué or as insurgent force for sociopolitical change; rhetoric as a kind of textbook (in a composition course) or a hoary tradition extending from before Plato to the present (Horner and Lu, "Working"). While both rhetoric and composition are often treated as interchangeable and as equivalent to a set of other terms—*English, literacy, writing*—they are each also typically treated as discrete, stable, and self-evident in meaning and as either mutually exclusive or in hierarchical relation to one another, in alignment with a set of other binaries: scholarship/teaching (service), theory/practice, intellectual/practical, past/present, authors/students (Horner and Lu, "Working" 471–73, 482). So, for example, my own current institution identifies the program responsible for teaching a required array of undergraduate courses the "Composition Program," directed by the "Director of Composition." However, the graduate program whose students teach most of those courses, and with which their teachers (like me) are affiliated, is the "PhD in Rhetoric and Composition." (Both are housed in "the Department of English.")

In the most cynical readings, the pairing of composition and rhetoric represents no more than a marriage of convenience: compositionists adding "rhetoric" to the name of their field in order to purchase the cultural capital associated with rhetoric as a scholarly tradition with an ancient pedigree, and thereby to improve their institutional academic disciplinary status, and "rhetoricians" identifying themselves as being in "rhetoric and composition" merely to improve their chances in the current academic job market, with its demands for people who can teach, or supervise the teaching of, courses in composition. It would be wrong to conclude that such marriages, by definition, cannot produce valuable progeny (just as the common practice of hiring those identified with "creative writing" to teach composition courses can lead, and has led, to engagement in productive work in those courses, by students and their teachers). Good things often begin inauspiciously.

Nonetheless, what is at stake is how we might otherwise imagine the relationship between composition and rhetoric to work against, rather than within, existing frameworks of status and value that would see the pairing in just such cynical and dismissive ways. In such frameworks, composition is commonly defined as an untheorized set of institutional practices whose shape and purpose are determined by dominant institutional and cultural forces, and hence as in need of rhetoric understood and defined as a tradition developed over millennia of the study and art of investigating arguments concerned with social and civic discourse. That tradition, understood as discrete from composition, is thus imagined as necessary to composition if it is to think itself out of its current ways. Andrea Lunsford, for example, identifies rhetoric as providing "the intellectual and theoretical grounding for" composition (qtd. in Ratcliffe para. 9); Crowley sees rhetoric as something with which to "inoculate" composition ("Composition" para. 3). Indeed, for Crowley, any trends in composition that would appear to be aligned with rhetoric's ostensible concern with social and civic discourse are the result of some comparable inoculation from outside: if not from the study of rhetoric, then, she suggests, "Marx and neo-marxist theorists such as Gramsci and Althusser, or . . . the brand of cultural studies associated with the work of Raymond Williams and Stuart Hall" ("Composition" para. 6).[19] Composition in and of itself, in other words, is no more than a patch of inchoate experience lacking a theory to understand and think its way out of its troubles, which it therefore must import from elsewhere.

Such representations reiterate the theory/practice, thought/experience binaries out of which the cynical readings of the relationship between rhetoric and composition described above arise. But while the dominance of these binaries makes it difficult to imagine alternative frameworks for relations between the two, and while, for example, it seems indisputable that many compositionists find many such traditions of theory useful in helping them articulate their experience (present company included), it is also the case that experienced contradictions may themselves lead us to rethink the terms of those binaries—including theory, practice, and even experience. So, for example, while Crowley's formulation assumes politicization to be something to be imported to composition from either rhetorical or Marxian theory, Elspeth Probyn has observed that there is an epistemological level, and not only an ontological level, to experience that "impels an analysis of the relations formulated between the articulated and the lived" enabling experience to be used "overtly to politicize the ontological" (22). Such a process is suggested in Mina Shaughnessy's account of those who devoted themselves to the teaching of basic writing. That experience of teaching, she attests, "pedagogically radicalized" these teachers by helping them "come to know, through [their] students, what it means to be an outsider in academia," leading them to "reject in [their] bones the traditional meritocratic model of a college" ("The Miserable Truth" 114). But such an explanation is, of course, at odds with dominant academic models of the relationship between theory and practice, whereby knowledge resides in the former and is then executed in ("applied to") the latter, rather than seeing the relationship between practical experience and theoretical knowledge as dialectical (see Lu and Horner, "Problematic" 259).[20]

This suggests that rather than seeing composition as the passive receptacle for inoculation from rhetoric—the recipient of the theoretical insights as well as prestige of rhetoric transmitted to and informing student (and teacher) subjects and their writing—we can recognize the "pedagogical" scene as itself already the site of and for rhetorical theorizing and action (Freire's action-reflection), in other words, for reworking any ostensible "insights" rhetoric—understood as a single, stable, and discrete body of scholarship—might be offering to gift composition with.[21] Leaving aside for the moment significant limitations in common definitions of "the" tradition of rhetoric as a single, stable body of Western theory (see Baca, Mao), we can rethink rhetoric as a tradition as one necessarily (in need of, and always in any case) being reworked by composition students and teachers in their work writing and studying writing.

Of course, such a possibility would require redefining the pedagogical scene as something other than a site for the transmission of stable, commodified knowledge (including knowledge as skill) sourced elsewhere: in this case, a commodified knowledge of "rhetoric." Such a redefinition of the pedagogical scene would set such work entirely at odds with the "rhetorical axiology" that Fulkerson saw dominating composition teaching, at least as of 1980, an axiology that puts a premium on accommodating the demands of the audience in a manner congruent with Smit's concern about marketplaces. Instead, it would have students pose such models of "the rhetorical approach" against other conceivable rhetorics one might deploy, question what some writers (on "rhetoric" and not) might argue, and experiment and arrive at (inevitably always) tentative conclusions in light of these activities. To put it another way, students might engage in the work of composing rhetorics, rather than attempting to compose according to a selectively defined, reified "rhetoric." Likewise, graduate programs might consider offering courses not in the history of rhetoric but in the composition of such histories; not teaching rhetoric but the rhetoric(s) of teaching and of composition (and composition programs), and of theory.[22] That is, rather than reinforcing stable and discrete definitions for and hierarchical relations between rhetoric and composition, we can disrupt these by redesignating them as activities cutting across the locations assigned them in traditional binary frameworks.

Composition and/as Writing Studies

Some might well see in these recommendations something equivalent to arguments for some version of "writing studies" as an alternative to composition. I discuss Dobrin's call for "writing studies" earlier in this chapter. Here I consider two other, quite different, arguments for renaming composition "writing studies." One set of such arguments makes the case for writing studies as a way to incorporate consideration of the full range of writing practices, in and out of school and at all levels and places, into composition scholars' conception of writing. So, for example, Charles Bazerman makes the case that the range, diversity, and ubiquity of writing practices across time and space are a legitimate focus for writing studies as a "major discipline," and that those of us affiliated with composition are well placed, by our commitment to the study and teaching of writing, to provide the foundation for such a discipline ("Case"). Susan Miller, echoing Bazerman, has argued for writing studies as a way of "gather[ing] many varieties of intellectual work around the discrete questions about relations between writers and texts that first formed composition as a field," and questions promoting "attention to the production of texts over their interpretations" ("Writing" 42, 41). Both Bazerman and Miller present writing studies almost entirely as a scholarly project—"studies" in the sense of an area of scholarship.[23]

A different set of arguments conceives of writing studies as an alternative to, or at least a new direction for, undergraduate pedagogy and curricula. Most prominently, Doug Downs and Elizabeth Wardle have advocated for a "Writing about Writing" ("WAW") pedagogy in which students in first-year composition ("FYC") courses read scholarship on writing and write about that scholarship. Others have argued for a writing studies major involving students in the study of writing. Downs and Wardle argue for a WAW pedagogy partly as a means of "righting misperceptions" that the public at large, and students in particular, have about writing, misperceptions uninformed by decades of composition/writing studies scholarship. And they also point out that a course focused on composition/writing studies scholarship provides teachers of composition courses with a "content" about which they have, or should have, expertise, and that they can help students explore. Further, they argue, defining FYC as WAW can justify insisting on hiring only those teachers who do, in fact, possess such expertise—teachers who, because of their greater qualifications, would presumably be able to negotiate better working conditions (or have better working conditions negotiated for them). Thus, a WAW pedagogy for FYC would (1) improve the public's perception and knowledge of writing, (2) give composition a disciplinary "content" about which it might claim expertise and ownership for students to explore, and (3) help resolve the perduring shameful practices in staffing FYC courses.

Arguments for a writing studies major, while sharing the aim of giving curricular space to the disciplinary content of the field and improving staffing practices in writing programs, call for shifting the focus on FYC to a "vertical" focus through imagining a curriculum of both beginning and more advanced courses in writing as a distinct major. As Libby Miles and her colleagues claim in a response to Downs and Wardle, asking "the first-year course do all our educational work. . . . would [itself] demean the intellectual integrity of the discipline" insofar as it would suggest that the discipline can be fully addressed in a single course (505).[24] And so they advocate a vertical curriculum including not only courses at the first-year level geared directly at achieving aims of general education but also a range of subsequent courses enabling, and meeting students' need for, "recursion, for repeated exposure and practice, so students can cycle back to reconsider what they've learned in earlier coursework" (Miles et al. 507). The aim of this curriculum, they emphasize, is not to produce writing scholars but, instead, "intellectuals with a deep understanding of rhetorical situatedness and a multivaried portfolio of their written products in a wide range of situations, with academic and non-academic writing carrying equal weight" (Miles et al. 508).

The distinction Miles and colleagues make between producing not "writing scholars" but "intellectuals" points to an unresolved tension in both purpose and pedagogy. Is the aim to produce more scholars of writing (and more writing scholarship) or to produce a difference in writers and in the writing they produce—a difference often described in terms of quality, as in "better"? If the latter, what is the role of "content knowledge" of writing provided by, say, scholarship on writing in producing such differences?

In an early review of the "writing studies" movement, John Trimbur couches the issue in terms of two different questions composition has asked itself: "Can writing be taught?" and "Should writing be studied?" and he suggests that composition's answers to the first have prepared the groundwork for taking up the project of the latter question ("Changing"). The first, and earlier, question was a pedagogical question, Trimbur notes, and it was resolved by changing the question to "How is writing learned?" This enabled composition teachers to identify and justify pedagogies that, it was claimed, provided the conditions under which writing was learned. The assumption behind the change in the question (from "Can writing be taught?" to "How is writing learned?") was that content knowledge was of negligible or no value in learning writing—in other words, that writing cannot be "taught," but it can be "learned" through engagement in particular practices arranged by knowledgeable teachers: lots of writing and rewriting, with frequent response of certain ("facilitative") kinds—coaching, "workshopping," and so on.[25] Trimbur identifies this approach with taking "writing" as a participial rather than a noun: writing is something you do, and one "teaches" writing by having students do it.[26] Trimbur distinguishes this from writing as a noun—that is, as "the material manifestations and consequences of writing as it circulates in the world" ("Changing" 18).

Taking writing as participial, Trimbur argues, is aligned with the "pedagogical imperative" understood as the imperative to engage students in practice (as in preparatory work) directed always at "improvement": making students "better" writers. From this perspective, asking students to study more ephemeral forms of writing—such as grocery lists—is a waste of time. As Trimbur reports, students who are asked to study such forms of writing complain that they already know how to make shopping lists: they need and expect from their teachers help with how to write, say, essays for their history course, or lab reports, or how to write them better. Taking writing as a noun rather than participial also clashes with a pervasive sense among many in composition that writing is not a "field of study that *belongs* in the curriculum but a practice that *pervades* the curriculum," starting with FYC and continuing through WAC/WID ("Changing" 21; emphasis in original), and that composition not only is but should be a "service" to the university, the mission of which would be compromised, a "scandal," by any prospect of becoming merely yet another in a string of area studies programs ("Changing" 22).

But it is possible to frame the issue differently. Rather than a choice between service and scholarship, pedagogy or theory, it is possible to see the pedagogical scene as itself the site of writing study—not just by teachers, but students as well.[27] And doing so need not take the form of inducting captive FYC students into the profession's ranks as budding writing scholars, at least not as conventionally recognized. The issue is (mis)understood this way because of the forms in which we have learned to recognize "study" and "scholarship": academic journal articles and book chapters, or prototype versions of these, or the crude efforts to engage in methodologies of, say, the case study or ethnographic fieldwork. Both the argument for a WAW pedagogy and the argument for writing studies majors tend to conflate the study of writing with the production of such forms, hence Miles and colleagues and Downs and Wardle end up debating whether teaching students to produce recognizable "writing scholarship" is appropriate for an FYC course. Alternatively, following Slevin's argument, we could argue that students in composition courses (as well as elsewhere, within and outside school settings) are always already studying writing; it's just that their practices in doing so do not follow methodologies, nor lead to the production of textual forms, conventionally recognized as manifestations of "writing studies."

The seemingly separate argument for composition as "writing studies" would appear to escape from composition's "pedagogical imperative," at least insofar as that imperative is defined as the demand to somehow "improve" students' writing. Instead, the simple impetus for and aim of writing studies would seem to be the centrality of writing to past and contemporary human culture, like the impetus for and aim of the study of language by linguists: a "scholarly" imperative to study phenomena because, well, they are there, in spades. Any prescriptive or evaluative interest about writing would, in these arguments, be extraneous to the concerns of the discipline of writing studies, just as linguists have ruled prescriptive grammar out of order as a professional concern.

Susan Miller, for example, has suggested that "writing studies might tell a less evaluative story," undertaking writing studies instead as the extension of "justifiable curiosity about textual production, not to judge curious locutions" ("Writing" 44).

Without discounting the need to set aside judgmental dispositions, however, there is underlying writing studies so defined an inevitably evaluative role—just not necessarily the role of prescriptive grammar the public might expect. Lillis, drawing from Deborah Cameron, notes that the question a sociolinguistics of writing faces is not whether to be evaluative—to engage in writing studies as anything more than an apolitical act of benign curiosity—but rather the question of which values are to be advanced through writing studies. As Lillis observes, the "identification of function [of writing] is powerfully bound up with practices of evaluation," with a common, if implicit, "slippage towards a normative evaluative stance" (175). So, for example, she notes the evaluative stance both in writing scholars "celebrating the explosion of all forms of writing and production activity . . . as well as researchers expressing doom about such—unregulated—activity" (175). Thus, rather than emulating the pretension to value-free "study," we might instead directly engage with questions of value. As Cameron notes, linguists might "persuade people that there are other values and other standards that might underpin the use and the teaching of language," such as values of utility, aesthetics, and morality (Cameron, *Verbal Hygiene* 82, cited in Lillis, *Sociolinguistics* 10).

To do so, however, would seem to return us to issuing imperatives. But this is merely to say that it returns us to pedagogy—both as conventionally understood and located in courses and classrooms and as located in the teaching-learning that occurs at other sites, such as academic research, academic/nonacademic interchanges, or ostensibly purely "public," nonacademic sites (see, for example, *Code Switch*). When conflated with and understood as the site of pure hegemony in the sense critiqued above, pedagogy appears to be anathema to, well, academic values of disinterestedness, hence the use of the term "imperative" as a pejorative attachment to pedagogy: the imposing by teachers on students of particular views on what constitutes "better" writing, and the dominant cultural and institutional imperative that teachers do so. Understood, alternatively, as the site of the inevitable and ongoing reworking of writing and the ascribing and production of specific values to writing practices, by students and teachers (and countless others), pedagogy becomes the (inevitable) and therefore appropriate site for the work of writing study.[28] There is, then, a false if dominant distinction between the teaching, or learning, of writing in FYC and a "writing studies" curriculum vulnerable to reproduction and reinforcement in the design of FYC and writing studies curricula. But we should not confuse that very real potential for what is possible for either.

I am suggesting that the debate on WAW and writing studies (as either a "field" or a degree program with its own curriculum) hinges on false distinctions between an evaluative and a disinterested stance, and between following a "pedagogical" and following a "scholarly" imperative (to study to understand phenomena), and between a participial and a nominative understanding of writing as (singular) activity or thing. Against such frameworks, I propose seeing the interrelations between what are otherwise set as opposed: that we might think both pedagogy and scholarship differently; that what Dobrin refers to as the "phenomena [*sic*] of writing" are/is activities and artifacts continually subject to reworking in the activities of students and teachers (among countless others), and that the "learning of writing" and the producing of writing is (therefore) an ongoing activity for which composition is one important site. This understanding does not resolve specific debates on what a writing studies curriculum might look like. Several writers have argued not for a full-blown and traditional "major" offering either pre-professional training for prospective professional (technical, business) writers or students with greater discursive and practical knowledge of writing but instead for an array of composition courses spread through the undergraduate career that would allow additional occasions for students to do the kind of intellectual work that Slevin calls on composition to undertake.[29] I wouldn't discount any of these aims, and I would acknowledge that any one of these does not exclude others from consideration. But as suggested by Trimbur's caution that "writing studies" might be seen by some as a "scandal," a degree of wariness is, well, imperative. The danger, as my argument so far would suggest, is not that pursuit of a writing studies program would eliminate composition's "service" mission. Understanding composition as mere service accepts the limited charge dominant academic institutional and public culture has assigned composition—an imperative to enact a highly restricted kind of pedagogy. Rather, the danger is that this work, and the "content knowledge" of composition, will be reified and transformed into the now "naturalized" dominant understanding of an academic discipline as "a bounded field of knowledge expanded by research" (Slevin, "Disciplining" 159). As Slevin warns, adopting such an understanding, in fact, "makes every effort to change things—even just to see things clearly—impossible" ("Disciplining" 158).

In this respect, I find promising Miles and colleagues' insistence that their curriculum is one that students themselves will be expected to participate in (re)designing, and Downs and Wardle's identification of students as active participants in the project of writing study, insofar as these suggest both the emergent character of writing and the role of students in its ongoing emergence. If, as Slevin suggests, "our discipline is about the encounter of ordinary people with different ways of reading and writing" ("Disciplining" 159), then composition's focus on the teaching and learning and study of writing by adults might make it particularly appropriate as a "home" for writing studies so reconceived, as opposed to the many other fields in which work otherwise identifiable with the study of writing might find a home—Bazerman notes work in fields that include applied linguistics, linguistic anthropology, psychology, sociology, cultural history, political science, education (32–36); Lillis draws on work in semiotics, multimodality, "discourse and genre studies, stylistics, new rhetoric and contrastive rhetoric(s) and on academic literacies" (15). Given the presence of something identifiable as "writing studies" in these other fields, one might question the need for composition to claim writing studies for itself as instancing another denial of the material social location of work in writing studies in disciplines and departments outside composition—another version of blindness to the fact that the "field" of writing studies is, in fact, not a new frontier but an area already long under cultivation by others. But without discounting the presence and value of such (ongoing) work and workers, composition might nonetheless be considered a particularly ideal site precisely because of its commitment to not merely "studying" but reworking writing, and its engagement with nonprofessionals (adult students) as well as "professional" academics in other "fields" as colleagues in that project. In other words, it brings as a strength its familiarity with the inevitable tension between writing as participial and noun, which can be understood not as discrete stages following a fixed sequence in the field's development toward the status of being a mature field but, rather, as composition's refusal to accept the governing terms for determining the appropriate trajectory of an academic disciplinary "field," and its acceptance of the Marxian dictum that the point, and inevitable consequence, of our work is not merely to interpret but to change the world.

Composition and "Multimodal Composition"

In acknowledging students' participation in the ongoing emergence of writing, I would seem to be aligning myself with arguments that composition needs to expand the range of types of composition considered to include "multimodal" composition insofar as composition students are commonly figured as already engaged in such practices. To do so would, from these accounts, constitute a radical refiguring of composition. Simultaneously, to do so would also seem to be yielding to an imperative like the imperative Dobrin invokes, one issued by rapid changes in the communicative technologies dominating contemporary (and, it seems, future) culture, locally and globally, that demand we adjust to or risk being annihilated by.[30]

However, framing the issue as a "new" technological imperative either to resist or embrace assumes both the radically new, yet somehow also known and knowable, character of what is coming to composition (or has arrived) and the limited character of what has been: assumptions that merit interrogation. Leaving aside historical research revealing that composition teaching that has been consigned to a monomodal dustbin has been anything but (Palmeri), and the remediation of "old" technologies in the "new" (Bolter and Grusin), more to the point is the problematic question of ascriptions of modality altogether. Both reactionary (sometimes coded "resistant") and celebratory responses to modalities ostensibly new or different than those ostensibly characteristic of composition until "just now" or "just recently" mistake dominant ascriptions of the modalities of particular forms with the full, actual and potential modalities engaged in with those forms. For, as John Trimbur and Karen Press have recently observed,

> Multimodality itself is not new, nor is it a break from the past. Multimodality is new as a *term*, a *conceptual terrain* that surfaced at a particular historical conjuncture, goaded by the need to understand dramatic changes in the means of communication. (Trimbur and Press, emphasis in original)

Likewise, "monomodality" is not an accurate characterization of print texts but, rather, a set of "ideological claims" about such texts (Trimbur and Press).

Part of the difficulty here is that, as Lillis warns, "definitions of mode vary, as does the specific level or layer of mode invoked," depending largely on "the specific interests of the researcher" (*Sociolinguistics* 22). This explains, for example, how Gunther Kress can state that writing is in danger of losing its privileged position by "the increasing prominence—dominance even—of the visual in many areas of public communication" (182), while Cynthia Selfe can identify print writing *with* the visual and in need of supplement by attention to the aural ("Movement" 621–23 and passim). Such seemingly contradictory claims from two such eminent scholars of modality illustrate how the full panoply of actual and potential sensory engagements with the material objects representing a particular form—here, writing with pen on paper—can be obscured by a focus on one dominant ascription of that form as either visual or in competition with the visual. All such ascriptions are correct so far as they go, yet none are adequate, hence the appearance of contradiction. The sense that writing with pen on paper is in competition with visual modes or, alternatively, is itself primarily a visual mode is the effect of a practice of selection from the full range of possible engagements with writing. For, as Raymond Williams warns, what we have to work with are not "works" as "objects" at all but "notations" "which have then to be interpreted in an active way" (*Problems* 47). Following this, ordinary forms of writing—say pen markings on paper—are "activated" into work through specific reading and writing practices with these, any one of which, significantly, neither exhausts nor entirely excludes from apprehension the full spectrum of sensory engagement with such notations. So, for example, barring pathological impairment, encounters with ink writing on paper for most of us engages the senses of sight, hearing, touch (including kinaesthesia), smell, and even (especially for the younger set, or those using the wet-finger technique to turn stuck pages) taste. And this is aside from the wide range of personal and cultural associations individuals have developed, about and through the senses, for the practices of reading (and writing), let alone the reading and writing of particular texts and types of texts, that shape their engagements with such objects. As Kress elsewhere observes, "none of the senses ever operates in isolation from the others—other than in severe pathologies. That, from the beginning, guarantees the multimodality of our semiotic world" (184). As a consequence, "no text can exist in a single mode, so that all texts are always multimodal" (187; see also Shipka 11–13). Further, we need to attend to the "social mediating factors that give meaning to" specific forms. Those ignoring this tend to slide from attention to a selection from the material qualities of a particular medium—for example, sound, light—to a "determinism" that ascribes specific "affordances" to these, now treated as functioning autonomously to produce specific effects. What is needed to counter this, as Street cautions, is an "ideological model of multimodality" ("Future" 31–32)—that is to say, a model that attends to modality as an ideological construct, which of course returns us to questions of power and value and, hence, pedagogy. "Mode," like "language," is a representation made of a practice, and such representations are inevitably selective, an exercise of power over practices and those engaging in them.[31]

I am suggesting that the difference in modality to be sought in composition is not a difference one must import or add to composition or the composition classroom. For the limitations in composition to which those advocating importation of other modalities or "multimodal" compositions as somehow new phenomena into composition (teaching and study) in order to correct it are not so much the monomodality of writing, even of the most conventionally recognized forms. Rather, they are limitations in our representations and, consequently, perceptions of the modality(ies) of that writing as, say, visual or not, akinetic, disembodied, etc. So, just as composition has long engaged in recognizably "multimodal" forms of composition (see, for example, Coles, *Plural*), it's also the case that even in its focus on seemingly monomodal forms, composition has always already been "multimodal"—just not in the ways that dominant ideology leads us to recognize as such through its representations of mode and composition.[32] It is that ideological (mis) recognition that needs to be resisted: otherwise we simply reproduce that misrecognition in our insistence that "multimodality"—as something new, better, different than the "old"—be imported into composition, which dominant ideology leads us to misrecognize as, in fact, limited in modality, lacking, in need, and that such insistence reproduces and reinforces (cf. Prior, "Moving"; Wysocki 15–17). That is an ideology complicit with the insistence on newness, the obsolete character of whatever was (until a moment ago) current, belief in the necessity of the "creative destruction" advanced in neoliberal fast-capitalist discourse, and above all, flexibility in adapting to and providing what is demanded. Modality becomes no more than a set of predefined choices among ostensibly new (and "improved!") commodities for teachers to permit student-consumers to select from, rather than an open question and subject for inquiry, experimentation, and reworking.

To break with that ideology, rather than attempting to import what passes for multimodal composition to composition, we can teach, learn, and study the typically overlooked multimodality *of* composition, in whatever form—taking what Cindy Selfe, Tim Lockridge, and I have come to term a "transmodal" approach to modality (Horner, Lockridge, and Selfe). Precisely because of the difficulty of recognizing the multimodality of traditional forms of composition (for example, typography; layout; use of charts, diagrams, and photographic illustrations, paper weight and color; binding materials and techniques, as well as the wide range of sensory engagements in the production and reception of any of these), given dominant representations of mode and of composition, these merit special attention (see, for example, Bernhardt; Trimbur, "Delivering"; Trimbur and Press). Of course, it would seem to be the case that we can often better learn to recognize the multimodal character of traditional forms of composition to which dominant ideologies of those forms have blinded us by confronting the more easily recognizable multimodal character of nontraditional forms of composition (just as one often learns to recognize grammatical and phonetic characteristics of a familiar language as one learns another). This would seem to be the historical trajectory in the discovery of multimodality in composition and literacy studies more broadly. But the purpose of that trajectory would not have to be the replacement or expansion of one set of compositional forms with others, but rethinking and reworking those with which we had thought we were already familiar: composition as we (thought we) knew it.[33]

Such a project would break with moves being called for to develop writing studies curricula as pre-professional training in deploying what are recognized as a variety of different modes and media insofar as such curricula would seem to assume an additive model of modality akin to the additive model of multilingualism.[34] Such curricula are in part an effort to give more curricular space to all that composition might entail, rather than attempting to fit that into the space of a one- or two-semester sequence of required courses.[35] But instead of pursuing verticality in composition curricula as a means of either "improvement" or adding range, we can see the greater curricular space as, in fact, providing more time for fuller consideration, reflection on, and revision of understandings of modality in (academic, and other) writing rather than, simply, a means of expanding the repertoire of what are seen as discrete modalities that students are to develop skill in deploying.

There is, of course, a different argument against the development of such curricula as yet another instance of a failure to locate the work of composition in the material social realm—here, the academic institutional realm of already existing disciplines, departments, and programs of study in the visual and performing arts (including film), graphic design, journalism and public relations, communication studies, and so on. The curricular "space" of such work is, it seems, once again, already fully occupied by others, many of them with strong claims to providing, and being better prepared to provide, pre-professional training (*sic*) for prospective producers of "texts" in specific media. Likewise, just as there already exist scholars in a variety of fields that might lay claim to "writing studies" at least as conventionally defined, scholars in these fields can also lay claim to having some grasp of—even expertise in—the interrelationships between modalities in forms of expression—music, painting, graphic design, etc.—that dominant ideologies of multimodality fail to acknowledge.[36] From this perspective, composition's claim to new territory can appear as yet another instance of the colonizers' willful blindness to the presence of others already inhabiting the territory they tell themselves is vacant and ripe for settling.

Alternatively, we might both acknowledge the presence of these others and consider what composition might bring to that work. Anne Wysocki, for example, in an argument for writing new media, suggests that "new media needs to be informed by what writing teachers [already] know" ("Opening" 8). While it is always presumptuous, if not dangerous, to tout one's own accomplishments as a gift that others need, what composition can provide is curricular space and time, even in its existing traditional array of courses, for thinking "how agency and materiality are entwined as [writers] compose" (Wysocki 6). In this sense, the very qualifications of existing programs for offering pre-professional training in the production of specific forms of expression—graphic design, journalism and public relations, music, film, "creative" writing, etc.—may make it more difficult (though of course not impossible) for them to engage in such reflective action. (Conversely, to the extent that composition accepts its assigned "mission" of providing [ersatz] pre-professional training in composition of all available types, it gives up its potential for just such action-reflection.)

But composition's location in the academy argues for further narrowing of the range of aims it undertakes to reflection/action on *academic* composition: not as service to the other academic disciplines, by claiming to prepare students to undertake without difficulty the writing tasks assigned in other disciplines, but, again, as occasion for reflection on and transformation of academic writing practices—preferably at multiple "levels." That is, rather than seeing composition as a reductive form of academic writing, we need to understand academic writing as a species of the broader realm of composition, and to recognize the location of the writing of students *qua* students in courses as, by definition, academic writing, *whatever* the forms and purposes that writing takes. After all, composition teachers, students, and scholars have been in the forefront of those who have revealed limitations in what other disciplines' engagement with writing—and arguably, limitations resulting from their close engagement in specific forms of disciplinary writing—has led them to believe and claim about that writing (as verb and noun).[37] This would enable composition to make use of its actual material social location in academic institutions and bracket the issue of the inevitable limits, and differences in the limits, of access to particular digital technologies that a focus on multimodality understood in terms of those technologies alone otherwise puts composition in the position of always chasing. Modality would be a question, not a proposed solution.

Addressing modality as a question would work against acceding to what I have been terming the technological imperative. That imperative would align us with the dominant ideology of neoliberalism, with its characteristic values of (worker) flexibility ("teamwork!"), efficiency, multiskilling, integration (with a concomitant collapsing of jobs), speed, and pursuit of market share—as when Johndan Johnson-Eilola advises compositionists to rethink composition in light of new technologies in order to "gain broader influence and relevance" (7). Pursuit of that ideology's attendant values would direct composition toward preparing students to be flexible and more marketable in their compositional work by virtue of the large portfolio of technical skills at their disposal for projects, in ignorance of independent traditions of practices with media, and in pursuit of technical pseudosolutions to social problems. We can see pursuit of such values in a project Jennifer Rowsell describes. In that project, students in impoverished neighborhoods are to be "helped" not by attempts to understand or combat the structures responsible for their impoverishment but, instead, by technologies to enable the students to take virtual field trips to museums while remaining locked in those same neighborhoods: "allow[ing] children to benefit from the riches and affordances of cutting-edge technologies in their own neighbourhoods" (75). The aesthetics and values of Apple here stand in for a questioning of design aesthetics and values. But rather than acceding to those aesthetics and values, composition might instead take up such questioning of them. And while this might entail experimentation with specific engagements with specific modalities, questioning of these would move beyond exploring the "aptness" or "fitness" of these for specific purposes to question the purposes themselves, and the conditions and people for which they might be purposeful.

* * *

I have argued in this chapter that dominant, limited conceptions of composition have governed efforts to respond to the very real difficulties in which those working in composition (students, teachers, scholars) have found themselves. Those conceptions have produced a "discourse of need" not only about students but about composition itself, defined as lacking and, therefore, in need of either imports or abandonment. I have argued instead that what is needed is not something ostensibly new or different, either as alternative or supplement to composition, but a new understanding of composition: a rewriting of composition as something other than either service bound or gaping need. Such rewriting requires rethinking the terms used to define, and limit, composition: writing, pedagogy, theory, modality, and composition itself. To fail to do so, I have argued, is to align oneself with dominant ideological constructions of these that consign composition to mere service or worse, and of what might constitute legitimate alternatives to or "improvements" of them. It is these constructions, not composition *per se*, that threaten to keep composition shackled. We need to break with the misrecognition of both composition and the proffered alternatives and improvements to it in order to give full play to all that might and does get accomplished in the work of composition.

As this suggests, we need, if not a new language, then a different way of inflecting the existing language to rewrite composition—a politics of language. This will entail rewriting language itself as a term key to composition that I have yet to address. It will be the burden of chapter 2 to take up that task.

2. *Language*

Language is the ongoing outcome of practices. Writing is one such practice. Representations of language, like the one you are reading, are themselves language practices contributing to the ongoing social accomplishment that is language.

I begin with this stark (re)presentation of language, entirely (if inevitably) unoriginal, as a marker against which to place dominant representations of language with which composition must inevitably contend.[1] Precisely because of its undeniable status as material social practice, composition, I will argue, is ideally situated to contribute usefully to meaningful reworkings of language, understood in the terms presented above, through intervention both in language practices as ordinarily understood and in practices of representations of language. To do so, however, requires rethinking the terms of language shaping our practices with language as these are manifested in our teaching, scholarship, and institutional arrangements. And as argued in the previous chapter, such rethinking requires that we work against both dominant conceptualizations in composition and what hegemonic ideology represents (within its terms) as that which would be alternative, new, or different from the dominant, lest we end up pursuing as different, new, or alternative what in fact is fully aligned with the hegemonic.

I begin by considering the prevailing equation of *language* with *English*, both treated as mass nouns, and the alignment of this equation with the English-only variant of the ideology of monolingualism. Efforts to work against this that herald difference in language, I then show, tend to accept monolingualism's representations of language difference that locate difference outside the spatial temporal realm, representations that serve as the dominant's prescribed alternatives to English-only monolingualism that leave unchallenged the tenets of monolingualism that support practices against which those pursuing these alternatives are directing their efforts. As a model counter to these, I pose a translingual orientation to language and language relations, an orientation that starts with recognition of the role of language practices, including practices in representing language, in constituting and shaping language and language practices, thus understood as always emergent and in co-constitutive relation to contexts and users of language. Such an orientation, I show, cuts through the horns of dilemmas a monolingualist orientation poses of having to choose between "one's own" and a "standard" language, while relocating language and languages, by virtue of their character as always emergent, as that which we are always necessarily (re)learning and rewriting. The emphasis of this orientation on the location of language in time—as "local practice," in Pennycook's phrase—also helps to address the difficulties and tensions in studies of language "beyond" the sentence: genres, situated literacy practices, activity systems, and those besetting current debate on "transfer." By relocating these in time and thus as always emergent and subject to and in need of (re)production through practices, and thus recognizing difference as the norm of language practice rather than a deviation from the norm, a translingual orientation makes possible recognition of the labor and agency of language "users" in the ongoing (re)production of language(s) within and beyond the sentence.

English/Language

References to language in composition illustrate conceptualizations of language hegemonic within the academy and the larger public sphere. On the one hand, *language* seems to name a primary concern of composition: the production of "proper," "correct," or (somehow) "more effective" language in writing—the concern that leads laity to express the need to "watch their language" when within earshot of composition teachers. At the same time, in its teaching and scholarship, composition operates almost entirely within the framework of only one assumed language—English—making language in this sense invisible. Of course, the term "English" often appears in the ordinary discourse of composition teaching (as in the course "Freshman English" taught by "English" teachers). But *English* in such usages is understood not as itself *a* language in relation to other languages (say, "Freshman French," "Freshman Arabic," "Freshman Chinese," etc.) but, instead, simply as language *tout court*. This is in keeping with the practice in U.S. colleges and universities of allocating to the purview of "English Studies" areas of study far beyond those areas of study assigned to departments identified with the study of languages other than English (French, Arabic, etc.). These include not just the study of the history and practice of spoken and written English but all writing ("creative" and not) and often the study of mythology, genre and genres (poetry, drama, fiction), and so on, cultural "texts" and critical theory of all kinds, even linguistics. Understood not as *a* language but as language *tout court*—a term capable of application (like "text") to all manner of modes and media (think "body language," "the language of clothes," "the language of medicine," "the language of film," etc.)—nothing would seem to fall outside the purview of "English." At the same time, this treatment largely elides the understanding of English as a linguistic practice comparable and in relation to and interaction with other such practices, such as French, Chinese, etc. *That* sense of English as a language among others evaporates in the heat of understanding "English" *as* language, hence, paradoxically, English studies is the site where, typically, English itself is not studied.[2]

In composition, this peculiar status accorded English is evident in the use of only English as the language of instruction, readings, and writing despite the obvious fact that, historically and currently, composition as a practice globally engages a wide variety of languages. This restriction to English only, however, is the assumed rather than explicit framework of work in composition, the unsaid which need not be specified. In fact, if and when students or teachers do write, speak, or read in languages other than English, it is seen as somehow outside the boundaries of composition proper ("What's with the *tout court*?"), to be dismissed as either erroneous, exotic, or fatuous.

The dominance of monolingualist ideology and, relatedly, the dominance of structural linguistics help to account for this paradoxical state of affairs. These contribute to a disembodied sense of language as system removed from language practices, which by definition are located in the material social realm, in time and space. Monolingualist ideology (a.k.a. "monolingualism") posits languages as stable, internally uniform, and discrete entities indelibly linked with the social identities of their users, thereby rendering users' language practices mere reproductions, adequate and accurate or faulty, of the language: the "parole" in structural linguistics distinguished from and in distinctly subordinate relation to "langue."[3] More generally, monolingualist ideology, manifested in the United States by a tacit policy of English Only, accounts for both the lack of study of English as *a* language and for the peculiar position of departments of English and the boundaries of "English studies" in U.S. colleges and universities (and in secondary schools) vis-à-vis departments named for other languages. For that ideology treats English as the assumed stable, discrete norm that itself neither requires nor merits investigation—the unrecognized linguistic ocean in which we all swim (see Horner and Trimbur, "English Only").

Such an ideology has worked in concert with much of the work in linguistics on which compositionists have attempted to draw. As two reviews of composition and language study, both appearing in 1989, indicate, linguistics—at least forms of linguistics dominant in the periods under review—ultimately have had little to offer composition (Faigley, "Study"; Crowley, "Linguistics"). As Sharon Crowley observes in her review, at least that linguistics under her consideration (1950–80) "favors an extremely narrow, noncontextual notion of what it means to be a user of language. Thus compositionists must recognize that linguistically based pedagogies necessarily operate as though texts are constructed in a cultural vacuum"—clearly a problematic assumption limiting its applicability to composition (Crowley, "Linguistics" 499). Lester Faigley, in his account of the relationship between the study of language and the study of writing, likewise sees much of the linguistics dominating North America during the period under consideration to be too limited to be of use insofar as it focuses on (ostensibly neutral) form, to be understood scientifically, to the neglect of meaning altogether (243–44). Given this approach in (this) linguistics to the study of language, its lack of use for the study of writing appears self-evident.[4]

The institutional "division of labor" separating the teaching of English as a Second Language (hereafter, "ESL") and the study and teaching of second language writing from "composition" proper constitutes a further manifestation of the effects of monolingualism on both areas of study.[5] For that division rests on the presumptions that monolingualism is the norm rather than the exception; that languages are stable and discrete rather than interrelated and in flux; and that writing serves as mere transcription of speech, rather than constituting a material mediation necessarily subjecting the "language" written to transformation.[6] Languages, in short, are located outside the material social realm as disembodied, discrete, atemporal entities, hence they appear to remain impervious to, while serving as ideals/norms against which to measure, efforts at their material "expression" (in either speech or writing).

Despite all this, *language* remains a pervasive term in composition. As Faigley observes, "The study of writing must be at some level the study of written language" ("Study" 240). But as Faigley's overview also shows, by and large language has been studied at the level of syntactic form, register, and "style"—features identified as characteristics of language as a universal, noncount ("mass") noun rather than as *a* language produced through selection from among an enormous range of differentiated and fluctuating practices. At best, difference in language is associated with different styles and discourses—the "language" of science, business, and so on. But as this suggests, "language" in such discussions no longer appears to serve as a useful category in itself, hence the study of writing may proceed without attention to the study of language, at least in any sense other than as style or discourse, for which terms such as *style* and *discourse* can do just as well or even better than *language*.

Likewise, there is a tradition of addressing the study of language in writing in terms of differentiated modalities—writing vs. speech—usually understood as distinct and in hierarchical relation to one another.[7] But as discussed briefly in chapter 1, approaching writing as a mode distinct from speech typically entails drawing questionable inferences of far larger characteristics of the uses and meanings of each, usually in contrast with one another, on the basis of selected material characteristics of specific media. The selectivity of the characteristics invoked accounts for the contradictory claims made for either writing or speech. So, for example, writing is often treated as more permanent and therefore acontextual than speech (Lillis, *Sociolinguistics* 9), but, seemingly in contradiction, writing has also been argued to be more fleeting, because it is revisable, than speech (Barthes, "Writers"). This contradiction is "afforded" by selecting specific features of the media deployed in the practice of either and conflating these with all practices with either—all speech as evanescent sound (never mind audio recordings) *or* as irrevocable (hence permanent) sound; writing as permanent visual markings on a surface *or* endlessly revisable (and deletable), unlike the irretrievable emissions into air of speech. Or insofar as speech (including "signed" speech) is (barring pathological impairment) a technology available to all humans, it is seen as more democratic, spontaneous, and natural than writing, viewed as more elite and unnatural because humans do not come biologically equipped with technologies for its production or training in their use. Or speech is a tool of the elite in its command of the soundscape (think deafening rock concerts), resisted by surreptitious writing (James C. Scott's "hidden transcripts" of powerless peasants) escaping the public character of (some) speech. In these treatments, historically and socially specific cultural practices in the production and circulation of spoken and written language and assignment of their status are mistaken for the full range of such practices (for example, ignoring, in treating writing as elite in relation to speech, the historically low status of scribes and written texts vis-à-vis oral testimony throughout much of European history [see Clanchy]). Specific values are conflated with specific material social practices with one or the other mode and then attributed to that mode itself, leading to arguments to somehow improve the one mode through importing to it attributes thought to characterize the other (see, for example, Elbow, *Vernacular*). The problematics of ideological, social conflict—say, between subordinate and dominant groups—is thereby reduced to and conflated with an abstracted medium, and to a "problem" susceptible to purely technical solutions, for example, through tweaking or broadening the range of (allowed, taught) communicative technologies.[8]

Representations/Practices of Language Difference

Of course, significant attention has been paid to language difference in composition teaching and scholarship appearing both prior and subsequent to, for instance, Faigley and Crowley's 1989 accounts of the relationship between the study of writing and the study of language (coded "composition" and "linguistics"). So, for example, language difference has been at the forefront of work in "basic writing" scholarship as a way to account for the difficulties, and differences, of basic writers from other writers; there is a longstanding commitment by professional organizations with which composition is associated to honor language differences, represented most prominently by the Conference on College Composition and Communication (CCCC) Statement on "Students'

Right to Their Own Language" (hereafter SRTOL); and there is a burgeoning literature on the language differences of students appearing in composition courses and on the possibility of a rapprochement of composition studies with scholarship in the Teaching of English to Speakers of Other Languages (TESOL).[9]

Insofar as this literature, in contradistinction to what English-only ideology purports, acknowledges the fact of language differences (even in the United States!) and the possibility of linking such differences to differences in writing, it represents a significant advance over perspectives that read language difference in writing as, in fact, not a difference in language at all but in cognitive development (for example, "egocentrism"), cognitive "style" (field dependence/independence); brain "hemisphericity," location on an oral-literate divide, or even moral integrity ("laziness!") (see Rose, "Narrowing"). After all, if languages, including language varieties, are viewed as each having their own internal logic and integrity (a big "if"), and if writing is seen as a somehow different language ("grapholect") from oral language—or if academic (written) English is seen as a different language from other varieties of language, written or spoken—then the difficulties students experience in producing academic writing at the "college level" can be understood not as evidence of cognitive or cultural deficiencies but, instead, as the inevitable difficulties accompanying the learning of an additional language. Even "errors" can be understood as evidence of writers' production of an "interlanguage" representing an approximation of the "target," with all the inevitable overgeneralizations and mistakes attendant on such approximations by those new to that target language, by application of models of second-language acquisition to the learning of writing.[10]

Given the continuing denigration and persecution of students and others for differences in their written and spoken language (see Mao, "Interdependence," Lippi-Green), and given the real advantages in pedagogy to which approaching writing from studies of second-language learning has led, redefining difference in these terms constitutes a significant, hard-fought, and still highly tenuous advance to be neither dismissed nor taken for granted: language "rights" remains a real issue for those living under monolingualism. At the same time, however, many of the basic terms by which this scholarship frames the issue to be addressed bring with them, and thereby reinforce, debilitating monolingualist assumptions responsible in the first place for the denigration of writers that their efforts aim to combat: not just *language* but terms such as *language variety*, *language practices*, *native speaker*, *second language*, *language competence*, *multilingual*, and of course *English*.

It would be foolish to attempt to remove such terms from the lexicon. Leaving aside the futility of attempting to do so, constructs such as specific languages and language varieties do have a strategic utility for particular groups, as Suresh Canagarajah has recently observed in arguing for a translingual perspective on language. However, as Canagarajah also observes, at least from the translingual perspective he advances and with which this chapter is aligned, they nonetheless do not have "ontological status" but instead "are always open to reconstitution and relabeling" (*Translingual* 16; see also Lu, "Living"). In short, just as terms like *composition*, *pedagogy*, *theory*, and *modality* are not to be abjured but rethought (as discussed in chapter 1), so terms like *language*, *multilingual*, *language competence*, *language difference*, *language practices*, and *English* need to be subjected to reworking, and (thereby) thought differently.

This is not a theoretical (abstract, immaterial) point but, rather, a necessary and inevitable part of composition's ongoing material work in and on language and literacy. Louis-Jean Calvet observes that, on the one hand, "*languages do not exist*; the notion of a *language* is an abstraction that rests on the regularity of a certain number of facts, of features, in the products of speakers and in their *practices*." But, on the other hand, he observes,

> Coexisting with these practices there are *representations*—what people think about languages and the way they are spoken—representations that act on practices and are one of the factors of change. They produce in particular *security/insecurity* and this leads speakers to types of *behaviour* that transform practices. (241, emphases in original)

Thus it is that "*the invention of a language* and consequently the *way it is named* constitute an intervention in and modify the ecolinguistic niche" (248, emphases in original). How we think language and language relations shapes the practice of these—that is to say, language and language relations understood as practices.[11]

Two of the most damaging effects of adopting terms of reference like *language*, *multilingual*, *language competence*, *language difference*, *language practices*, and *English* uncritically are (1) the perpetuation of the relegation of some writers to the cultural periphery by virtue of their ostensible language difference, and (2) the reinforcement of ideological norms of a stable, pure, "mainstream" language ("English"). That is to say, within the framework of those advocating for as well as dismissing some students from consideration, difference (in language/culture) continues to be understood, if not as deficit, then as deviation from a norm of sameness. Conversely, an idealized notion of English—a.k.a. "Standard English" or "Standard Written English" (hereafter SWE)—remains unchallenged in status as the norm against which other forms (*sic*) are understood and judged. As a consequence, agency perversely comes to be associated only with formal deviations from the ostensible norm, deviations that only some writers are authorized to produce. These are thus fetishized and heralded to the neglect of more substantive kinds of difference writers accomplish in their writing.

What distinguishes these efforts, radical in appearance, from those that might truly counter monolingualist ideology is their "additive" framework. That is to say, in response to English-only monolingualism's assumption of only one legitimate, stable, internally uniform, discrete language, these efforts call for acknowledgment of equivalent additions to that language—either as specific practices granted the status of legitimate, stable, internally uniform, and discrete languages themselves, or as distinct varieties of English (and other languages)—Appalachian English, African American Vernacular English, and so on, each likewise granted equivalent status as distinct, discrete, stable, internally uniform, and legitimate versions alongside, say, "Standard" English and SWE. Having the status of being a language is equated with being sociopolitically legitimate, logical, and having an internal integrity and distinct character associated with a specific population (and often, geographic region).

Given the long and ongoing history of refusals to grant logic, integrity, and legitimacy to the language practices of specific groups—most prominently in the United States, African Americans, Native Americans, Asian Americans, and Latino/as—and given the long and ongoing history in the United States of institutional authorities using perceived or attributed language practices of subordinated groups as the basis of discrimination against them (as in the continuing refusal of some schools in the United States to allow students to use languages other than English in school), insisting that language practices identified as languages or language varieties are legitimate, logical, and so on, and that people have a right to express themselves by engaging in such practices, is crucial.

At the same time, those same terms can hobble serious work on language in composition, as illustrated by the paucity of effect on composition teaching arising from SRTOL despite the controversy surrounding the appearance of that statement.[12] This suggests that the terms in which that and aligned arguments were framed allow for continuation of business as usual. Monolingualism continues as the reigning language ideology, but now in a pluralized form, and thereby in some ways more insidious because more difficult to resist. For all the controversy surrounding the granting (to students) of language rights, it turns out that doing so comes with very little cost, and that a focus on which language or language variety to allow may well have distracted us from more substantive concerns. As Bourdieu warns, "Social acceptability is not reducible to mere grammaticality," for

> the competence adequate to produce sentences that are likely to be understood may be quite inadequate to produce sentences that are likely to be *listened to*, likely to be recognized as *acceptable* in all the situations in which there is occasion to speak. (*Language* 55, emphasis in original)

The granting and winning of language rights, then, can be accomplished without radically changing existing social relations: "Speakers lacking the legitimate competence [to produce sentences that are likely to be *listened to*] are *de facto* excluded from the social domains in which this competence is required, or are condemned to silence" (55). From this perspective, the difference in how people speak is itself a matter of *in*difference in its effect on existing social relations.[13]

Calvet's argument for recognizing both that (1) language is the ongoing product of practices, and that (2) representations of language, as practices themselves, participate in shaping that ongoing practice and its product, can help here in its acknowledgment of both the power of representations of language and the situated perspectives motivating and delimiting them. Representations of some language practices as merely deficient or broken forms of a language (for example, "bad English") are problematic in failing to recognize the logicality, legitimacy, social value, and rhetorical efficacy of just such practices and their users. That failure then leads to the kind of self-doubting about one's language practices, and traditions of such practices, deleterious to engagement with these—the feeling of being "tongue-tied" (see Blanchet, "Quels" 187–88; Confiant); equally damaging, discrimination against some people, now falsely deemed justifiable on the basis of their use of "bad" English; and finally, a false justification of the privileges of some people on the putative basis of their ostensible use of "good" or "standard" English, and perpetuation of the ongoing production of vacuous discourse deemed acceptable because of its ostensibly "standard" linguistic features. Given these effects on language practices, it behooves all language teachers and scholars, compositionists included, to counter such representations.

But in their efforts to do so, it would be equally problematic to represent language(s) as, in fact, discrete, stable, internally uniform entities—monolingualism pluralized. For while such representations would seem to make it possible to grant students the "right" to engage in a practice represented as just such a language, doing so reinforces simultaneously the legitimacy, stability, and discrete and neutral character—and, therefore, in a word, the "rightness"—of another set of practices also deemed a language (variety), a.k.a. "English" or "Standard English" or "SWE." Operating within that framework restricts us to posing the question of which language to "allow" our students to write in, a question that assumes the stability and significance of the languages to be chosen, and it poses the false dilemma of having to choose between the language that will supposedly grant (academic and economic) survival and the language that is somehow more "authentic" but condemned by institutional authority as "inappropriate." When all practices are abstracted into reified systems, then measuring one against the other (the "dialect" against the "standard") is near inevitable, as is the measurement of practices against the abstraction of these into "language" (*parole* vs. and subordinated to *langue*, again) (see Milroy). Such a framework attributes agency not to users but instead to the abstracted features of the (abstracted) language (as system)—for example, the "power" language for teachers to somehow "give" to those lacking it—while ignoring the actual agency of users and the necessity of their contribution to the ongoing (re)production of language. Thus it is, for example, that SRTOL, in adopting an approach to language varieties as stable and discrete entities, ultimately allows those accepting its argument to continue with business as usual of teaching and insisting upon the production of a purported SWE, now with the qualification that, of course, students have a right to their own languages, too, for use in specific, discrete domains. Finally, such representations, by retaining the monolingualist identification of each specific language and language variety with a specific social group as "its own," attribute to students, like "their" languages, stable, internally uniform, and discrete identities from which they stray in their language at peril to their ostensibly uniform selves.[14]

In short, many of the responses directed at combating the ill effects of English-only monolingualism work within the terms set by that very language ideology: terms that define languages and language varieties as stable, internally uniform, discrete entities operating on the material social realm from a location somehow outside it, rather than as the always-emerging products of practices. English, or Standard English, is granted a status it has never earned, rendered into yet another theoretical monster against which, ultimately, it is impossible to win within the given terms for exchange.

Thus, developing effective alternatives to monolingualism requires that we rethink, rather than reinforce, by multiplying, monolingualist conceptualizations of language, language competence, language users, and language relations. And one significant difficulty in doing so is that the very terms deployed—*language*, as should be clear by now, chief among them—carry monolingualist inflections difficult to slough off, hence efforts can get derailed or subsumed under monolingualist frameworks. A further difficulty is that we are (pre)disposed by the ideology of monolingualism to define "newness" in terms set by that ideology, for example in terms of the production of recognizable forms of glossodiversity, or in terms of "new" students. This can lead to ignoring the potential of actual alternative practices not already marked by monolingualism as, in fact, alternative, and to leaving assumptions about "mainstream" students and writing unchallenged.

Practices > Languages

If monolingualism posits languages as atemporal, discrete, and disembodied, each identified with a discrete category of users, then a countermodel will require that we relocate languages as temporal, in flux, and embodied. And if monolingualism locates language difference only spatially—in terms of the degree of proximity or distance between the stable, set territory of one language and another—then a countermodel must redefine difference as temporal, to be found not on borders but in every utterance, the norm rather than the exception to the norm. This countermodel gives primacy to practices with language over abstractions of language, locating language only in such practices, and attributing agency to the producers of language—those whom monolingualist ideology has taught us to think of as mere "users" of (a single) language.[15] In Calvet's formulation, "languages exist only in and through their speakers, and they are reinvented, renewed and transformed in every interaction, each time that we speak" (7).[16] Thus, language can now be understood to be always temporal, contingent, emergent. And insofar as language is always only temporal—"a local practice," in Pennycook's formulation—difference in language is also an inevitability, the norm rather than exception. Hence from this perspective, the question facing writers (and their teachers) is not which language to use (or permit), "mainstream" or "different"—but, instead, what kind of differences to attempt to make through their writing with and on language, how, and why.

As this suggests, such a perspective—one that my colleagues and I and others have come to call "translingual"—does not so much give different answers to the same questions as change the questions to ask.[17] Thus, rather than being locked into a battle with another theoretical monster—here, "English" or "Standard Written English"—defined in a way that dooms the combatant to fight for what the dominant has identified as different against what it has likewise defined as "English," "English" itself can be theoretically cut down to size as less than what was imagined or claimed, and difference itself understood differently.[18]

Adopting such a tack does not require abjuring English (or other languages) or, for that matter, celebrating language differences as conventionally defined but, instead, finding ways to rethink both of these. And while this is difficult work, it is also work in which we can justifiably enlist all our students (whatever their ostensible language backgrounds and repertoires). For if languages are not discrete, stable, internally uniform and disembodied entities, and if language users are not locked in discrete, linguistically homogenous territories, then transmission models of pedagogy, understood as transmitting knowledge of such entities to students (whether directly and explicitly or through drill or immersion or apprenticeship) assumed to lack such entities, no longer apply. English thus is to be understood not as a language one writes "in" but, instead, something "always in translation," as Pennycook puts it, and hence an "entity" one must always face the challenge of (re)writing: a challenge in which collaborators will always be welcome and, indeed, necessary, and one that a composition course is ideally situated to take up.

This is not to deny the historical fact of continuities in language practices, including practices writing English. As Canagarajah observes, "Language practices lead to sedimentation of certain forms/patterns via repeated situated use over time, and their gradual shaping into grammars, norms, and other products" (*Translingual* 16). However, as he immediately warns, "these norms and products are constituted by practices and are always reconstructed to be meaningful . . . always changing, variable, and constructed" (*Translingual* 16–17). There is, then, not a denial of such sedimentation or continuity but a different perspective on how it is to be understood. First, it's worth noting that claims of what is, or has been, common practice are always both selective and interested, typically formulated to deny the selectivity of the process and the interests served by that selectivity.[19] Second, and in alignment with the first point, such selections typically neglect the ongoing, contingent, and contestable status of the sedimentation process. That is, the extension of "continuity" into the present, and thus its vulnerability to change, is typically elided in claims about "common" practice, whereas it is in fact always emergent. For as Karin Tusting observes, patterns of literacy practices

> do not exist beyond the recurrent present events that constitute them. Instead, they emerge through these present events "in" time, rather than being imposed from "outside" time. Memories of these recurrent events make up a *constructed* past, which is *reconstructed* [recontextualized] every time it is recalled or drawn upon as a resource; it is through drawing upon this resource of a constructed past, drawing on memories of recurrent events, that it becomes possible to construct these patterns. And the constructed patterns are themselves drawn on in the constitution of future events. (40, emphasis added)

This sense of sedimentation as an ongoing phenomenon always contingent rather than one restricted to some somehow completed past means that writers inevitably contribute to that sedimentation process through their writing. Moreover, by locating their utterances temporally as well as spatially, we can recognize that writers contribute to that sedimentation process both when they appear to break from what we are disposed to recognize as sedimented practices and when they appear merely to "repeat" past formulations. Just as the "repetition" of a musical phrase, even if an acoustic "duplicate" of a prior iteration, carries a different significance by virtue of occurring "after" the earlier iteration, so seeming repetitions are never only "the same" but in fact also always different. Likewise, as postcolonial theory has taught us, "repetitions" by the colonized of the words of the colonizer carry a different significance in meaning and power relations, however identical the seeming "repetition." Difference is thus the norm of language practice rather than an exception to the norm, hence neither an attribute to be sought after nor avoided by student (and other) writers and teachers but, instead, one to be explored.

To further illustrate, I turn to Min-Zhan Lu's account of a student who formulated the unconventional phrase "can able to" to describe someone who has both the ability and the permission to undertake some action ("Professing"). A monolingualist perspective would simply dismiss "can able to" as an error, evidence of the student's lack of competence with SWE, supporting this view by reference to the student's identity as a "foreigner" to the United States (a Chinese woman from Malaysia) for whom English was an additional language. And in fact, in Lu's account, this is the perspective the student's colleagues initially were prone to adopt in responding to her phrase "can able to." Following an extensive discussion, however, students came to see the logic behind the phrasing and began adopting it themselves when describing comparable situations in order to highlight the distinction between having ability and having permission. In other words, they took up and began further sedimenting the phrase as a language practice part of the language, at least within the course.

The student herself, however, ultimately opted to replace "can able to" with the more idiomatic "may be able to." From a monolingualist perspective, this would seem on the face of it to represent what was mandatory, whether understood as a correction to align with the norms of SWE—following what Gilyard identifies as an "eradicationist" view—or, from a conventional view of multilingualism, a capitulation to those norms. However, from a translingual perspective, we can see the writer contributing to the sedimentation of the language, and thereby exercising agency, both when she wrote "can able to" and when she wrote "may be able to." For, understood in their temporal location, both constitute productions of difference contributing to the ongoing process of (re)shaping and (re)writing English. Thus located, for example, the student's writing of "may be able to," while appearing to be the "same" as conventional American English usage, relocates that practice, and in so doing, produces a difference in meaning by virtue of who is engaging that practice, when, where, and why.

That, of course, is decidedly not how such practices are commonly represented or understood. But as Calvet argues, how we represent such practices, to ourselves and to our students, participates in and affects those practices themselves. For example, as Lu notes, the practices of negotiation and deliberation like those through which Lu led the student and her colleagues in discussion render whatever decision the student arrives at "particularly meaningful," even when the students ultimately decide to reiterate conventional usages. Lu engaged her students in exploring the ideological assumptions (of individualism) underlying the equation of individual ability and permission expressed in the idiomatic treatment of "can" and "may" as synonymous, and, alternatively, the insistence on the effects of material social conditions on what individuals "can able to" do. Such deliberations make all the difference in the significance of students' writing decisions. As Lu explains,

> Although the product might remain the same whether it is made with or without a process of negotiation, the activities leading to that decision, and thus its significance, are completely different. Without the negotiation, their choice would be resulting from an attempt to passively absorb and automatically reproduce a predetermined form. . . . If and when [these] student[s] experienced some difficulty mastering a particular code, [they] would view it as a sign of [their] failure as a learner and writer.
>
> On the other hand, if the decision [of the author of "can able to"] to reproduce a code results from a process of negotiation, then she would have examined the conflict between the codes of Standard English and other discourses. And she would have deliberated not only on the social power of these colliding discourses but also on who she was, is, and aspires to be when making this decision. If the occasion arises in the future when she experiences difficulty

> in reproducing a particular code, as it very likely will, her reaction would be much more positive and constructive. Aside from tracing it to her knowledge and experience, she would also contextualize her difficulty in the power struggle within and among cultures important to her life. (180–81)

Though Lu's argument focuses on how to make sense of students whom dominant monolingualist ideology predisposes U.S. composition teachers to identify as peripheral to the linguistic and cultural mainstream (as inaccurate as that representation of students may well be [see Hall; Harklau et al.; Matsuda, "Myth"]), it applies equally to students those teachers are disposed by dominant culture to represent as mainstream—"the norm"—and to usages that appear to students and their teachers as "conventional" and/or "correct." For example, as Lu and I have argued elsewhere, the reiterations of the "great man" theory of history in general, commonplaces on creativity more specifically, and in particular the gridiron exploits of Billy "White Shoes" Johnson accomplished in the "White Shoes" essay discussed in David Bartholomae's well-known essay "Inventing the University" can be understood not simply as an instance of a writer somehow unwittingly caught up in these discourses but, instead, as a writer exercising agency through iteration of them—an exercise of agency for which, of course, the writer can and should be asked to take responsibility and to consider alternatives to in deliberating how and whether to revise his writing (Lu and Horner, "Translingual").

I am suggesting that language, language difference, and "English" need to be thought differently: difference not merely as an addition or import or extension to "English" (or whatever is identified as the "mainstream" or "native" language) but as the ground on which any language is produced through practices, including its rewriting, even in what is sometimes dismissed as its "re-production," and English as the ongoing collaborative accomplishment of such practices. This does not preclude the possibility and need for differences to be made to what is accepted as "English." But rather than conflating all difference with any and all differences in linguistic form alone, this perspective seeks differences however accomplished—whether through iterations of conventional forms or breaks from them—that make a difference worth making: that enable resolution of the gap between what Raymond Williams identifies as "practical consciousness" and "received forms," between "what is actually being lived" and "what it is thought is being lived" (*Marxism* 130–31). This is how Williams accounts for differences in language from generation to generation, including but not limited to "additions, deletions, and modifications" (*Marxism* 131). As he explains:

> There are the experiences to which the fixed forms do not speak at all, which indeed they do not recognize. . . . And even where form and response can be found to agree, without apparent difficulty, there can be qualifications, reservations, indications elsewhere. . . . For practical consciousness is what is actually being lived and not only what it is thought is being lived. . . . Its relations with the already articulate and defined are then exceptionally complex. (*Marxism* 130–31)

Williams is working here toward articulating a concept that itself lacks ready formulation, the concept he ultimately terms "structures of feeling." It is a term he acknowledges "is difficult" but is meant to suggest something other than the more conventional "world-view" or "ideology" and "not feeling against thought, but thought as felt and feeling as thought: practical consciousness of a present kind, in a living and interrelating continuity" (*Marxism* 132). Williams's own work in this passage to formulate his concept—giving the new term and then qualifying what it means and distinguishing it from available terms and meanings—itself illustrates both the challenges he faces and the linguistic strategies by which he attempts to meet those challenges. This is quite different from beginning with such linguistic strategies and then justifying these by conflating them with all linguistic difference, abstracted from context and purpose, with a significance on their own—the commodification of linguistic difference as in itself carrying significance. But it is often difficult to distinguish differences in meaning that appear to require differences in form from mere displays of linguistic difference as conventionally understood.

Debates on "code meshing" and neologisms such as "translingual" illustrate this difficulty. On the one hand, code meshing would appear to be not a strategy but the outcome of a strategy, the term itself specifically the result of the strategy of twisting an existing, conventional term and concept—*code switching*. From this viewpoint, *code meshing* is a neologism meant to destabilize notions of discrete codes by giving recognition to the fact that all such "codes" are, after all, meshed—the opposite of what a code is meant to be and how it is to operate. On the other hand, code meshing has also been defined as a strategy (sometimes associated with "translingual writing") for mixing "codes." Understood thus, the term *code meshing* reinforces the concept of discrete "codes" by presenting code meshing as a choice writers make—to mesh or not what are presumed to be the available, stable, and discrete codes (see Lu, "Metaphors"; Vance).

At roughly the same time as the appearance of *code meshing*, the term *translingual* has emerged, along with similar terms, suggesting the presence of a gap akin to what Williams refers to as the failure of existing forms to match practical consciousness and experience, a gap that these new terms are designed to close.[20] And in fact, much of the chapter you are now reading can be understood as an effort to explain what the official terms and received interpretations fail to represent, and hence why a term such as *translingual* is needed. At the same time, what *translingual* might itself represent is also now up for grabs. My colleagues and I see it as representing an orientation to language and language relations rather than a set of practices or a marker of some language users as opposed to others. Alternatively, there is a sense that *translingual* might refer to a specific type of writing with formal characteristics—perhaps characteristics that student writers should emulate—or that it refers to particular kinds of individuals, those who possess competence in multiple languages and are adept at mixing and working across these in their spoken and written utterances (see for example, Canagarajah, *Translingual*), or both—the writing, with specific characteristics, of specific kinds of people: *translingual* writing by *translinguals*, distinguished from monolingual writing by, well, monolinguals.

But the use of these terms to identify specific forms, or specific groups of people identifiable by their use of these forms, returns us to monolingualist treatments of language, or specific languages, outside the spatiotemporal realm. Like "Standard English" and "Standard English speakers," each of which is defined circularly in relation to the other (Standard English defined as the language of "educated" speakers, identifiable by their use of Standard English), the treatment of "code meshing" (and code meshers) and of "translingual writing" and "translinguals" abstracts a *langue* from specific practices (*parole*) and represents this as an entity existing outside material social history but which writers and speakers may choose to deploy: a tool like other languages (*langues*) abstracted from practice (for example, Spanish, French, Chinese, English).

Such moves constitute what Williams identifies as "the basic error" of reducing the social to fixed forms through "conversion of experience into finished products" (*Marxism* 129, 128). While Williams acknowledges a need for this in the production of "conscious history," he warns that when it is projected into "contemporary life,"

> relationships, institutions and formations in which we are still actively involved are converted . . . into formed wholes rather than forming and formative processes. Analysis is then centred in relations between these produced institutions, formations, and experiences, so that now, as in that produced past, only the fixed explicit forms exist, and living presence is always, by definition, receding. (*Marxism* 128)

The mistake, he summarizes, "is in taking terms of analysis as terms of substance. Thus we speak of a world-view or of a prevailing ideology or of a class outlook" (129).

Alternatively, adopting a perspective on a translingual orientation focuses on practices, with language understood as the always-emerging outcome of those practices rather than the stable realm within which practices occur. We can see this difference in Elaine Richardson's insistence that we define African American language as "survival culture" (33). For Richardson, African American Vernacular English (AAVE) includes not merely "narrowly conceived verbal surface features" but also "the broad repertoire of themes and cultural practices . . . used by many historic and contemporary African Americans . . . the totality of vernacular expression" (*African American Literacies* 33). This would thus include any and all expressions by African Americans, whether somehow "marked" conventionally as linguistic iterations of "AAVE" or not. For as Richardson explains, "extending the definition of African American language usage *beyond* (surface level) syntax, phonology, and vocabulary etc. into (deep level) speech acts, nonverbal behavior, and cultural production"—in other words, to focus on language *practice*—"requires emphasis on rhetorical context, the language users, their history, values, and their socio-cultural, political, and economic position" (34, emphasis added). We should not, then, identify AAVE strictly as and with a decontextualized and stable set of surface-level linguistic features but, rather, as an ongoing tradition of practices with language by African Americans contending with their positioning in U.S. and global culture. As Gilyard and Richardson state,

> Confronted with a pervasive racism, which is embedded in dominant texts or official discourses, most African Americans feel a need to reaffirm their African American selves, individually and collectively. This is often accomplished primarily through language, as is evident in the rich tradition of African American literacy. (40)

The emphasis that these writers give to context, it's worth noting, should be understood not purely as determinative but instead as contingent and continually (re)produced: context and language as co-constitutive rather than, as monolingualist ideology would have it, context pre-existing and determining (appropriate) language. The appearance of language practices as merely the product of contexts arises by removing those contexts from their temporal location as the (ongoing, potentially fluctuating) outcomes of those practices, what those practices work to accomplish, including the accomplishment of survival. Likewise, the language known as AAVE itself is, following Gilyard, Richardson, and Calvet, the ongoing outcome of such practices rather than an entity that groups and individuals merely speak or write "in."[21]

Practices, from this perspective, represent what Pennycook terms "meso-political" activity operating "between the individual and the social" (*Language* 28). As he explains, "Practice as the meso-political allows us to move beyond [Gee's] dichotomization of discourse (Big D/ little d) brought about by the structuralist/poststructuralist divide, and to focus instead on the meso-political practice between words (little d) and worldviews (Big D)" (*Language* 127). So, for example, AAVE, at least as Richardson (re)defines it, is best understood precisely as such meso-political practice, part of what she calls "survival culture." To the extent that AAVE includes production of linguistic forms recognized as distinct from "standard" English, these can best be understood as means by which to articulate and affirm aspects of African American experience "to which the fixed forms do not speak at all, which indeed they do not recognize" and thereby to close the gap between "what is actually being lived" and "what the official, dominant discourse claims is being lived," which is why its "relations with the already articulate and defined are . . . exceptionally complex." But to conflate African American language strictly with codifications of linguistic structures identified as AAVE removes these as specifically located practices—as cultural work—to timeless *langue*. The ingenuity and concrete labor contributing to the ongoing production of African American language—as defined by Richardson—then get elided.

Re(learning) English

In this translingual representation of practices and language, "English" is to be approached neither as the invisible ocean within which some of us swim, nor as a distinctive monolithic entity threatening or threatened by other distinct linguistic entities (French, Spanish, Chinese, etc.), nor as a mosaic of distinct (hierarchically related) varieties within one of which each "English" speaker is located. Rather, it is an ongoing collaborative project, one that composition students and teachers do, can, and should participate in rewriting. Such a project, while not opposed to expanding the repertoire of languages learned, addresses the question of language learning and language repertoires differently than in conventional models of multilingualism. Rejecting the notion of languages, English included, as discrete, stable entities necessarily complicates conventional models of language learning as a uniform, linear, predictable sequence of the learner developing knowledge of the language. Instead, the process under which learners are learning "the language" is simultaneously a process of the language itself also being continuously subjected to change, albeit (also) in nonlinear fashion. Importantly, this means that—insofar as the language is no longer a discrete and stable entity—this simultaneous development of learner and language is continuous for all "users" of "a language," whether identified by monolingualist ideology as its "native speakers" or not. We are all always language learners, including learners of the language we might think of as "ours." For the notion of mastery of a "target" language no longer obtains once we reject the stable identity of the language.

It follows that what conventional usage calls the learning or possession of "other" languages (or language varieties) is likewise an ongoing collaborative project. Those setting out to learn a language are, in the course of doing so, contributing to the ongoing process of sedimentation of that language through their iterations of that language, and hence reworking the language as they learn it.[22] The incessant borrowings of terms from ostensibly "other" languages by "English" is the obvious example of this process that our training in defining languages in terms of lexicon enables us to recognize (while the term "borrowing" is used to insist on a clear distinction between what does and does not properly belong to a language and its users, all etymological evidence to the contrary notwithstanding). Such borrowings are better understood as specific language practices, some of which become more generally sedimented, others only locally—for example, within specific families or groups or courses or histories, say—while others fail to gain traction.[23] Such borrowings are also, then, more readily recognizable means by which students "rewrite" and thereby contribute to the project of English as they "learn" it: rather than writing "in" English, they are (re)writing it. And as already discussed, this applies not only to that writing that introduces forms not common, or not heretofore recognized as common, to English but also to that writing that reiterates forms recognized as conventional English.

There are two significant points to be made about the learning of languages as a collaborative, negotiated reworking of them. First, when we recognize English as not being (re)made by individuals alone but as continually emerging and produced and (re)iterated through the myriad ongoing practices with it, we can better grasp how a composition course might be particularly well situated for this work insofar as it occasions work by a group of students focused on the rewriting of English through their writing, reading, and rewriting/revision. While this contribution by composition is recognized unofficially in occasional references in scholarship to the local version of English that often develops in and through a course (see, for example, Bartholomae's "Writing Assignments" 181, and Coles's *Plural I*), it is a rare course that identifies this work as an explicit project or projected outcome of the course. Yet that work is being done there, and with material conditions allowing it to be done with greater intensity, through a curriculum focused on writing and its revision, than in most other courses or extracurricular settings. But because this is collaborative and because the outcomes of that work are necessarily contingent insofar as the process of sedimentation does not stop at the end of the semester, it is not recognized as work at all. Such work on English is of course not restricted to the composition course or, for that matter, to the academic site. That said, it can be more consciously taken up at that site through the material resources it affords of time, space, common meetings, and so on.

Second, insofar as "English" is not a practice taken up in isolation from practices identified with other languages—Spanish, French, Chinese, etc.—then taking up this work more consciously can profit from engagement with such practices, ideally through inclusion of students with a broad range of habituated practices with these. The expectation would not, in such a course, be the "mastery" of English (or of other languages)—a chimera from the perspective of languages as the ongoing, emerging products of practices—but collaboration in its remaking. One outcome of such work would, inevitably, be the remaking of what is demarcated as other languages—"borrowings," for example, occurring in all directions in language practice, say, from "English" to "Chinese" as well as the reverse. But, again, the purpose of that remaking would not be mastery of these other languages, at least as conventionally understood. Instead the focus would be better directed at learning to work across and with differences of language, given the expectations that (1) such work is, globally and locally, the norm (even within ostensibly monolingual, say "English only," settings), (2) such work is inevitable given the fluctuating, emergent character of languages (think here of the constant changes to conventional English with which "native English speakers"—putatively possessing mastery of English—must incessantly contend). That is to say, the aim would be at developing an orientation—call it *translingual*—to language, language relations, and language differences alternative to dominant, monolinguistic conceptions and habits of approaching all these.

Microstudies of the uses of English as a Lingua Franca ("ELF") provide a model here. Contrary to dominant views of Standardized English as in fact already the de facto current global lingua franca, and contrary to efforts to codify a set of neutral forms to be used in ELF situations *as* ELF, these microstudies, typically of conversations among groups of individuals none of whom claim "native English speaker" status but for all of whom English is the one shared language, suggest instead a deliberate reworking of English and all other available communicative resources by the participants. Contrary to what monolingualist ideology would lead us to believe, communication in these situations is not marred by the absence of a commitment to, knowledge of, fluency in, and use of a standardized set of forms—"English." Instead, researchers report, users of ELF succeed in their communicative efforts by drawing on whatever diverse linguistic resources and pragmatic strategies they have, and by adopting attitudes of patience, humility, and tolerance for diversity, and strategies of cooperation, accommodation, negotiation, and letting ambiguities pass. Indeed, rather than requiring use of a uniform and static code, researchers find that "[ELF] never achieves a stable or even standardized form." And not just the forms ELF takes, but "even the enabling pragmatic strategies do not have to be the same" for its speakers (Canagarajah, "Lingua Franca" 926). ELF, they find, "is intersubjectively constructed in each specific context of interaction . . . negotiated by each set of speakers for their purposes" (Meierkord 129; qtd. in Canagarajah, "Lingua Franca" 925). In fact, as Nicos Sifakis has explained, "Variability in the communication between different [ELF speakers] renders any attempt at codifying [and teaching] the various uses of English in [ELF] situations difficult, since we would have to know in advance many things that are situation-specific and user-dependent" (155). In other words, we cannot assume a fixed set of conditions, contexts, or language use but must instead accept the emergent and co-constitutive character of all these.[24]

Further, because ELF is reconstituted in each instance of its practice, we cannot identify a particular set of practices with "competence" in it. Instead, competence itself is in need of redefinition. For, as Juliane House puts it, "[A] lingua franca speaker is not *per definitionem* not fully competent in the part of his or her linguistic knowledge under study" (557). Or as Canagarajah iterates, "all users of [ELF] have native competence of [ELF]" ("Lingua Franca" 925). Thus, teachers can assume neither the need to move students toward a state of "competence" in ELF nor the stability of that state itself. Instead, ELF is best understood and taught not as a codified set of forms but rather as a language function accomplished through adopting a particular set of dispositions toward all language (Friedrich and Matsuda). The emphasis for teachers would thus need to be not on giving students a specific set of forms to use but on "the socio-pragmatic functions of language choice" (House 558), and on "interaction strategies" (Canagarajah, "Ecology" 96). The attitudes necessary to effective engagement with ELF, these studies show, include "tolerance for variation, and a focus on mutual cooperation" (Rubdy and Saraceni, introduction 12), an understanding that "variation from the norm . . . is itself likely to be 'the norm,'" (ibid.), an orientation to issues of "process" rather than "product"; humility and a willingness to negotiate meaning, including the practice of "letting ambiguities pass" on the assumption that they will eventually be resolved (Canagarajah, "Negotiating" 204–5; "Lingua Franca English" 926, 931; "Place" 592–93); and a recognition of language "as changing rather than static" and not just "context-appropriate but context-transforming" (Canagarajah, "Negotiating" 211; cf. Khubchandani 20–21).

I am proposing that the practices of ELF revealed by these studies present an alternative but appropriate model for the "translingual" work across languages that can be and in fact is taken up in composition. To this proposal I foresee at least two objections. First, some might argue that the practices with English represented in these microstudies are all oral—speech practices—therefore inapplicable to writing, which is thought to represent and require conformity to a codified form of language (see, for example, Barbour). Second, it might be objected that the contexts in which these ELF practices occur have built into them a shared commitment among participants to a specific aim that accounts for the kind of attitudes of patience, humility, acceptance of language variation, and so on that cannot be assumed in other contexts. They are, after all, by definition contexts in which no speaker claims or is attributed expertise with Standard English, and in which a shared communicative goal has already been determined to which other interests and aims must be subordinated—for example, participants attempting to conduct a commercial transaction or, in a study Canagarajah presents, students in an advanced undergraduate/graduate course on second language writing in which Canagarajah enacted a "dialogic" pedagogy encouraging such attitudes (*Translingual* 133ff.).[25] It seems unwise to assume that similar conditions will obtain in other contexts (the examination of students' writing by faculty evaluators representing the *locus classicus* counter context).

But the latter objection contradicts the former. For whereas the first objection assumes a uniform condition for writing associated with what Brian Street has identified as the autonomous model of literacy—a condition in which all writing by itself represents a repository of meaning so long as it is properly "coded" (in the way information, as distinct from knowledge, might be coded following specific algorithmic principles)—the latter acknowledges that writing can, in fact, operate differently in different contexts.[26] And while this acknowledgement of the latter might seem to support a cloisonné model for writing that would insist on specific, if different, codified forms in specific contexts, such a conclusion would itself ignore the ways in which writing does not so much operate within given contexts as operate in co-constitutive relation to context: writing, and writers (along with readers) through their practices continually (re)produce contexts as the ongoing product of those practices. In other words, just as language is seen as emergent, resulting from interactions rather than preceding these, from a translingual perspective, contexts are understood as always emergent, exerting enabling and constraining pressures on but also being actively shaped and reshaped by individual language practices. As James Gee has observed, "Situations (contexts) do not just exist . . . [but] are actively created, sustained, negotiated, resisted, and transformed moment-by-moment through ongoing *work*," explaining that "[a] word or deed takes its meaning from a context which it, in turn, helps to create" (190; see also Fox 16).

Accepting the co-constitutive relation between writing (and reading) practice and context does not of course rule out the possibility of readers and/or writers engaging in practices producing contexts in which conformity to what are invoked as universal conventions for writing, or sets of these each designated as proper to a specific location, is privileged over, say, intellectual inquiry. The testimony of millions of students and their teachers demonstrates that, for example, the principle of *not* letting ambiguities pass is one iterated in many reading/writing practices. But recognizing the domination of this principle in engagements of student writers with teacher readers, say, is not the same as acceding to its domination as inevitable. To do so would (again) be to conflate the hegemonic with hegemony. It would participate in the dominant's neglect of the obverse practice of letting at least some ambiguities pass in responding to some writing, and of seeking out and reveling in such ambiguities in the writing of (authorized) writers. And it would overlook the always-emergent and contingent character of "ambiguity" (and "clarity") in writers' and readers' experience: a text or passage that seems at one point "clear" may subsequently become "ambiguous" and vice versa, as these are reworked by readers and writers (see Barnard).

Insofar as composition courses provide the material social conditions for engagement in conscious and intensive reflection on reading and writing practices productive of these alternative contexts—occasions for display of conformity to rules vs. occasions for collaborative intellectual inquiry through rereading and rewriting and collaborative reflection on these—they would seem especially well suited for both the study and engagement in the production of more intellectually rewarding "contexts" for writing (and reading), including the production of more intellectually rewarding representations of writing and reading, than those representations of writing prevailing in dominant culture (as, say, conduits for meaning transmission or "the dress" of thought). Rather than pretending to inculcate an ostensibly value-neutral concern with "clarity" and "efficiency" in reading and writing above all else—a concern that is anything but value-free—composition can value and work to advance writing and reading directed at intellectual inquiry. In such courses, language competence would then be redefined as a developing, always-emerging competence located not only or purely within individuals but in time and across individuals as they collaborate at engaging in more intellectually rewarding reading and writing practices and representations of these. And this competence would be understood not as a possession universally applicable but, instead, as a contingent product of specific practices located in time as well as space.[27]

Defined thus, competence, far from being utopian, can be identified as one distinctive aim and emergent outcome of at least some academic practices in reading and writing—the seeking out of difficulty, complications, problems, the questioning of dogma, and so on that are among the most rewarding of the academic habitus. Insofar as that habitus runs counter to the larger culture's valuation of the seemingly clear (cut), easy, "user friendly," *un*problematic, and even dogmatic, the academy remains a potentially powerful site for counterhegemonic work, a fact that compositionists in particular are prone to overlook as a consequence of their low status within academic institutions (it's hard to value or see potential in a workplace that provides daily reminders that you're not valued and have no potential there). But as with "English," we need to cut "the academic" site down to theoretical size so as not to grant greater uniformity and hegemony to that site than is merited and so as not to overlook the uses to which that site is and might be put.

Language beyond the Sentence

There is of course an enormous body of scholarship on language "beyond" the sentence. The move to that beyond can itself manifest an elision of the ongoing, emergent character of practices: "language," recall, is the product of abstracting from a wide range of practices a selective set of these to count as "language" (just as language-s are the product of selective categorizations and abstractions of a wide range of practices, often in the interests of nation building—see Gal and Irvine). As with "language" and "languages," there remains the risk of making the same "basic error" of "taking terms of analysis as terms of substance" in the representations effected by the terms "genre," "discourses," "situated literacies," and "activity systems" to name larger "units" of utterances (cf. Pennycook, *Language* 114ff.). A prime difficulty scholars focusing on these categories have faced is how to reconcile the bias toward timeless structure—the problem of *langue* abstracted from and thence understood as outside time and space, or material social history (*parole*)—with the temporal location of any instance of what might be identified with any of these analytic categories, that is, with practices. A further, related difficulty these scholars face is the role these categories themselves play *as* representations of practices to shape language practices. To name a particular instance or set of instances of practice as, say, instances of a particular genre, literacy, discourse, etc. is to shape both the perception of those instances and subsequent practice. The representation then comes to serve not as a heuristic but as an empirical observation against which the practice is judged: the end of rather than opening to analysis. We can see this in the diffusion and transformation of Swales's CARS ("Clear a Research Space") and the IMRD ("Introduction, Methods, Results, Discussion") concepts from terms of analysis to terms of practical prescription (see Lillis, *Sociolinguistics* 163). Attempts to get at the possible work accomplished by specific instances of practice through attention to recognized forms can also end up attributing to those forms themselves specific "functions," eliding writer agency through attributing effects to the forms themselves as commodities. More troubling, those "functions" identified with those forms then achieve normative status—a slippage from what might seem to be to what always is and even what should be.

This tension plays out in debate on the ways in which genre acts as both a constraint and an enabling resource; in the ways in which "typification" of situation with which a particular genre is associated is determined; in the disciplinary "boundary work" of genres; in the "functions" of "activity systems." To the extent that instances of these categories are granted ontological status as structures outside history, analyses can quickly tend toward structural determinism: writers writing (or, rather, written) by the designated available structures. One of the strengths of Carolyn Miller's seminal article "Genre as Social Action" is its work to relocate genre temporally. As Anis Bawarshi and Mary Jo Reiff observe, Miller "recognizes the mediated relationship between situations and responses, and therefore the social construction of recurrence" (70). Rather than granting a priori status to exigence or situation, Miller argues that "situations . . . are the result, not of 'perception,' but of 'definition'" (29). As Bawarshi and Reiff explain, this redefines recognition of a situation (one calling for a particular kind of response) as something "*defined* . . . as a situation that calls for a certain response" (70, emphasis added). Likewise, exigence for Miller is "a form of social knowledge—a mutual construing of objects, events, interest and purposes that not only links them but makes them what they are: an objectified social need" (Miller 30): hence "what we perceive as an exigence requiring a certain response is predicated on how we have learned to construe it as such" (Bawarshi and Reiff 70–71).

This returns us to practice and the sedimentation and relocalization of practice. But the identification and analysis of genres, situated literacies, and activity systems seem to require a turn away from practice to removal of potential instances of these from time—a "freez[ing] of the frame" (Pennycook, *Language* 117). This removal grants recognition to sameness while eliding temporal difference, and tends to ascribe a normative functionality to the "pattern" accomplished through this framing that itself requires either the positing of a fully rational writer-agent (addressing an equally rational reader) or, paradoxically, the removal of the writer and reader altogether in favor of ascribing agency to the identified form—the genre and what it enables, affords, does, all by itself. Activity theory, while adding to the number of actors, tends likewise to ascribe a uniformity of purpose to these: as David Russell observes, "AT [activity theory] suggests we focus on a group of people who share a common objective and motive over time, and the wide range of tools . . . they share to act on that object and realize that motive" (67). An "activity system" is then a unit of analysis that can be applied "any time a person or group (subject) interacts with tools over time on some object with some shared motive to achieve some outcome" (67). An activity system is "a functional system of social/cultural interactions that constitutes behaviour" (68). This approach tends to freeze time (out) to achieve a definitional clarity amenable to the two-dimensional diagrams frequently found in the texts of activity theory scholarship.

This approach does not preclude the possibility of change to activity systems. To the contrary, as Russell notes, "activity systems we human beings make are constantly subject to change" (71). But these changes are attributed to "contradictions within and among activity systems. . . . A change in any element of the activity system may conflict with another element, placing people at cross-purposes" (71). In other words, change and difference are not the norm but deviations from the norm arising from unassimilated (contradictory) elements within the system or the collision of two or more unaligned activity systems. Russell gives the example of a collision between the activity system of instructional design, represented by a distance-learning software program required at his university, and the activity system represented by the aims and motives of teachers in his department for using web-based teaching materials (71–72). That collision, he notes, produces pedagogical and political conflicts the teachers try to "understand and deal with as [they] 're-mediate' [their] teaching using the new software—and the new relationships with [the instructional software designers] who have a different object and motive" (73).

The practice (!) of freezing the frame necessary to producing the identification of a genre, activity system, or even "situated literacy practice" itself accomplishes the elision of the temporal location of instances of any of these—practice in the sense of actions contingent in their emergence, significance, and effects. The danger then lies in reversing this: to slip, as Bourdieu puts it, "from the model of reality to the reality of the model" (*Outline* 29), whether it be a model of a genre, activity system, or situated literacy practice no longer understood as a unit of analysis but as an entity ascribed agency in itself, so that the "action" is reduced to the status of "mere *execution* of the model (['model'] in the twofold sense of norm and scientific construct)" (Bourdieu, *Outline* 29, emphasis in original).

The most promising of work countering such tendencies looks at interactions across putatively discrete "units" (genres, activity systems, literacy practices). This shift away from a focus on the constituents within the parameters of a designated unit (genre, system, practice) to a focus on movement across these can help bring out the at best heuristic value of such designations, the enactment of agency by practitioners as acting not simply within but with and on the materials identified in research as distinct and stable forms and/or units, and, more importantly, the emergent character of these by their (re)location in time. Such a shift toward a *temporal*-spatial framework can bring out the limitations of "models" and enable us to better recognize the agency and mutually constitutive relation between practitioners and communicative materials, thereby producing revisions to these models, understood as such.

We can see such a process unfolding in *Improving Learning in College: Rethinking Literacies across the Curriculum*, a study by Roz Ivanič and colleagues, which ultimately directly addresses the problematics of such models. Ivanič and coauthors' study initially focused on the ways in which students' "everyday" literacy practices might interact with and support their learning of the literacies required in their college courses. It therefore explored the possible "interface" between and among these different literacies associated with different "domains" of students' lives (1–2), the "'border literacy practices' and 'border crossing' of literacy practices from the everyday to college" (22–23). As the study progressed, however, Ivanič and colleagues "came to see certain limits to the concepts of border literacy practices and border crossing" (169), and to question the "ways in which 'context,' 'domain,' 'site' and 'setting' are conceptualized" (23) and, as well, the associated metaphors of "boundaries and borders, and of boundary zones, boundary objects and border-crossing" (23, 24). The attention to crossing of ostensibly distinct literacy practices (and the domains assigned them) results ultimately in their conclusion that such metaphors, "inscribed in the method we had used to collect the data" about literacy practices, led to a "static two-dimensionality about the Venn-diagram representations and mapped spaces which follow from talk of 'borders' and 'border-crossings,'" rendering "the concept of 'border literacies'" "untenable" (172). These static models by definition excluded the temporal character of the literacies, border literacies included. Consequently, Ivanič and coauthors conclude the need to move to "bordering as a practice rather than identifying border literacy practices as entities" (172).

Recent work in transfer theory evinces a similar destabilizing of heretofore static models of what is to be transferred and, as a consequence, the "model" of transfer. Such models treated the knowledge ostensibly transferred, the domains from and to which it is to be transferred, and the persons engaged in the transfer as discrete entities rather than as always emergent and mutually co-constitutive. As King Beach suggests in outlining an alternative stance toward transfer, such an alternative stance understands

> continuity and transformation in learning as an ongoing relation between changing individuals and changing social contexts. Individual and contextual agency for transfer are not ontologically independent of one another. At the same time, the role of individuals is not reduced to that of social context, nor is the role of the social context reduced to a group of individuals. (103)

In this alternative model, rather than being treated as discrete, "learners and social organizations exist in a recursive and mutually constitutive relation to one another across time" (111).

Recent scholarship on theories of transfer in writing follows this destabilizing of static models of transfer. Rebecca Nowacek, for example, argues for a model of transfer in learning writing as "recontextualization" and "reconstruction" whereby "both the old and new contexts—as well as what is being transferred—may be understood differently as a result" (25). In this model, writers—particularly, for Nowacek's study, student writers—are positioned as (potential) "agents of integration," and "transfer" is understood as a rhetorical act: they work to "*perceive* as well as to *convey effectively to others* connections between previously distinct contexts" (38, emphasis in original). Thus, rather than a model of transfer by which knowledge moves inertly from one stable and discrete context to another, with the student/writer "carrier" assigned at best a mechanical role as knowledge conduit, and in which no change to the contexts, the student-conduit, or the knowledge itself is imagined to occur, all of these are seen as mutually co-constitutive and interdependent, including, importantly for pedagogy, the student's sense of self as contributing agent to the ongoing character of these contexts and the knowledge "transferred."[28]

Such models falter when, having destabilized the context and knowledge engaged in "transfer," they then attempt to grant a putative stability to the writers and, in the process, remove the site of composition work itself from the material social realm into a stage only preparatory to actual such work. We see this risk in invocations of specific dispositions, motivation, even "character" to be inculcated in students. For example, Elizabeth Wardle, in the opening to a special issue of *Composition*

Forum on "transfer," begins with an acknowledgement, in an echo of Ivanič and colleagues' conclusion regarding "boundary" literacies, that "we know the phenomenon is messier than the transportation model suggested by the word 'transfer'" ("Creative"). To get out of what seem to be the conceptual limitations that the term "transfer" brings with it, she notes proposed alternatives ("transforming, repurposing, generalizing, recontextualizing"). Yet these seem to leave important questions unanswered. As she puts it,

> Is transfer found in the individual, in the task, in the setting—or in some combination of all three? And if transfer is found in the combination of individual, task, and setting, how do we understand and explain it? How do we teach for it, study it, and engage in it ourselves?

Focusing on "why and how some people seem to continually repurpose what they know to bring their previous knowledge and experiences to bear, while others don't," she proposes the notion of dispositions, taken from Bourdieu and his work on habitus and doxa, as a way to make sense of this phenomenon, and suggests that the "problem-exploring" disposition associated with repurposing is at odds with the "answer-getting" dispositions that the U.S. educational system encourages ("Creative"). This enables Wardle to work against dichotomizing of the individual and the context and appears to answer her question seeking to understand whether or not individual students repurpose. As she puts it, "there is a dynamic relationship between the disposition of the individual and the field" ("Creative"). And yet, she concludes,

> We seem to be seeing more and more students arrive on college campuses as the products of an educational habitus that teaches immediate answer-getting and eschew problem-exploration or question asking. Why is this the case? Even if we could design our programs to teach for repurposing, how do we address the individual dispositions that disincline students from such repurposing, and the fields that inculcated such dispositions in them? ("Creative")

But here students are presented as, once again, the passive "carriers" —here of dispositions inculcated in them by an educational field. Without denying the phenomenon prompting Wardle's exploration, we can consider alternatively that what is at issue is not the disposition that students bring to an ostensibly "new" context but, rather, the agency they exercise in producing a particular kind of context in which a given disposition may appear to be aligned.[29] So, for example, students (like the rest of us) may engage in practices that work toward an "answer-getting" context, even if this runs against the practices of particular instructors directed at producing a "problem-exploring" context. Contexts, recall, are not so much stable locations to which students arrive but rather the ongoing products of practices, including student practices, hence the high degree of variability in the "outcomes" of multiple sections of the "same" course (even when being taught the "same" semester by the "same" instructor). As DePalma and Ringer observe in arguing for what they call an "adaptive" model of transfer emphasizing writers' agency in constructing both the knowledge "transferred" and the context to which it is "transferred," from such a perspective,

> students are viewed as potential contributors to an ever-changing rhetorical context rather than as passive recipients of the knowledge and conventions of a discourse of power. They are, in other words, both users and transformers of writing knowledge and writing contexts. (142)

This does not mean we should abandon the concept of dispositions but, rather, treat dispositions as likewise the ongoing products of practices, practices to which students (and the rest of us) can be asked to take (some) responsibility for producing.[30] Recognition and misrecognition are themselves the ongoing products of the work of practices that, by definition, are subject to change, as illustrated by the two student examples Wardle herself provides of students defying doxa. Wardle explains these examples as a matter of "influence," dispositions "inhabited" and "embodied" and that one brings to a context, but they can as easily, and more productively, be understood as instances of agency exercised and a recontextualization of the "fields" the students participate in, as can the counterexamples one can imagine of students accepting the doxa apparently reigning in the fields they inhabit.

As this counter possibility suggests, too, while "transfer" implies a phenomenon that involves something moving (or being moved) from one stable location to another—for example, from FYC to an advanced history seminar—we need to recognize that—understood as transformation, recontextualization, repurposing—transfer also always occurs within settings conventionally understood as *the same* in writing tasks likewise understood to be identical or nearly so. The renewing/recontextualizing/repurposing, in other words, that we tend to identify only with contexts defined as dissimilar also always occurs in contexts we tend to identify as the same or similar. The common phenomenon of a student performing quite differently in one assignment than in another in the same course illustrates the recontextualization, transformation, repurposing of the course itself as an effect of the student's ongoing practice—what we are inclined to identify instead as the student's individual "development." That the direction of that development can shift 180 degrees, multiple times, shows not the context-specific nature of dispositions but, rather, the co-constitutive relationship between practice and context. This does not preclude the phenomenon of dispositional sedimentation, but that sedimentation itself needs to be understood as an ongoing process in which students (like the rest of us) participate rather than as an agentless fait accompli. In other words, if the most promising work countering the tendency to a homogenous view of practices through "freezing" the frame for analysis has focused on interactions across putatively discrete "units," the danger of such a focus is its neglect of interactions *within* those same ostensibly discrete, internally uniform, units—situated literacy practices, activity systems, contexts, languages, and so on—leading to acceding to dominant representations of these as stable, discrete, internally uniform, and so on, and to neglect of the agency involved in iterations of those practices, contexts, and languages, and the inevitable difference such iterations necessarily produce, difference recognizable once the frame has been "unfrozen" and these have been restored to their location in time.

* * *

I have been arguing that a shift in focus from work within designated units of analysis—genres, situated literacy practices, activity systems—to work across these brings out their emergent character and the mutually co-constitutive relation between any of these and those engaging them—context, materials/resources, actors, language. The benefit to this shift in focus mirrors the benefits of a shift in debates on language from work within a designated entity—"language" or "English"—to work across different such entities—languages (and to the benefits arising from a shift of focus in debates on modality from work within an ostensibly single modality [for example, "writing"] to transmodal composition). At the same time, this shift may leave unchallenged the stability of the former. Just as a focus on "multimodality" can obscure the abstraction of separate "modes" from communicative practices, and leave unchallenged the full modal range of "traditional" forms of composition—for example, printed letters on paper—and just as a focus on multilingualism can leave unchallenged the ways in which seemingly monolingual utterances are always themselves "in translation" and "meshes," so a focus on transfer and movement across literacy practices can leave unchallenged what the dominant has led us to recognize as the normative functionality of work ostensibly within a designated genre, activity system, literacy practice. While we can recognize the work involved in working across what are designated as distinct such units, it is more difficult to recognize the work involved in what seem mere reproductions of work within such units: business as usual. That is to say, temporality is identified with what we are already disposed to recognize as movement in space (from language to language, domain to domain, genre to genre, practice to practice, system to system). The temporality of work not associated with such spatialized movement remains unrecognized. But this is a consequence of dispositional perception: what counts as "the same" space, recall, is (again), like the perception and designation of a specific situation as a recurrence, the product of a practice rather than an ontological phenomenon—the achievement of a sense of sameness and stability through denial of the presence of difference in the purportedly identical. What is needed, then, above all, is to recognize the labor involved, and the production of difference, in language we are trained to see (to designate) as simply more of the same.

To call this labor, and to call for its recognition, runs counter to dominant conceptions of language and labor and also to those conceptions of both that the dominant offers as acceptable alternatives—recognizable difference in language, and work that takes the form of language that "resists" or "goes against the grain" of the conventional. The burden of this chapter has been to challenge the alternative character of such definitions of the alternative in language. The burden of the next will be to rethink labor in language, and what the relation of the two is and might be.

3. *Labor*

Writing language is the labor of composition. That is not how labor is ordinarily understood in composition. But unless we understand the labor of composition in this way, the troubles of labor in composition as ordinarily understood cannot end. While a change in understanding will not end those troubles, working through such troubles is impossible without such a change in understanding. To say that writing language is the labor of composition is to claim for labor what is more commonly identified not with labor at all but, instead, "work." That distinction between work and labor is part of what this chapter aims to trouble. The trouble comes with language.

Labor, Work, Language, and the Social

I begin with labor and work. *Labor*, notes Raymond Williams, has an interesting relationship with the concept of *work* (*Keywords* 335). *Labor* is commonly associated with difficulty and with a particular kind of work (manual) and set of social relations (in capitalism) leading both to the denigration (and exploitation) of those engaged in labor and demands for the dignity of labor. *Work*, while encompassing labor, also includes activities not associated with difficulty at all, even activities other than those for which one is paid (my "real work" to which I devote myself when not "at work"). *Labor* once also encompassed the general sense of social activity (Williams, *Keywords* 177): in Marx's terms, "an activity which adapts material for some purpose or other. . . . a natural condition of human existence, a condition of material interchange between man [*sic*] and nature, quite independent of the form of society" (Marx, *Contribution* 36), with "material" understood to include all forms of interchange, relations, and production that take place, whether recognized or valued by dominant ideology or not. This changes in the discourse of political economy, however, when an abstract sense of labor is invoked: from labor as "all productive work" to a specialized, further abstracted sense of labor as an entity (for example, something in short or ready supply) measured in units of time, in the production only of commodities.

One of the challenges in addressing questions of labor in composition (and elsewhere) is to recuperate this larger conception of labor as, indeed, "a natural condition of human existence," "an activity which adapts material for some purpose or other." In other words, we need to recuperate for *labor* what *work* can (sometimes) still reference, rather than defining, and defending, labor within the terms and conceptual framework set by capitalism as merely something difficult and (often) unpleasant, and ideally unnecessary from which we may strive to escape and therefore for which we demand appropriate compensation in light of the degree of difficulty of the work accomplished (as "hard"): what we sell, in units, for pay, to produce commodities. For while it might seem that to raise the question of labor in a book on composition should mean simply raising questions about the poor working conditions of the vast majority of composition teachers and their exploitation by academic institutions, addressing those troubles requires that we first recognize the labor of composition in this larger, encompassing sense.[1] Specifically, recognition of the "dignity" and worth of labor in composition requires recognition of language practices—of students and of teachers with students—as also labor, in this larger sense. For to accept from the start a reductive definition and valuation of labor is to accept terms of negotiation set by capital, serving its interests. To break with those terms is the project of this chapter.

That language practices constitute a form of work (if not labor), and that we need to attend to them as work, is not new. James Gee, observing that "situations (contexts) do not just exist . . . [but] are actively created, sustained, negotiated, resisted, and transformed moment-by-moment through ongoing *work*," calls for New Literacy Studies to focus on that work and the role language itself plays in that work—what he calls "enactive and recognition work" (190–91). In that work, as he explains, "A word or deed takes its meaning from a context which it, in turn, helps to create" (190). Such work is typically recognized only when it takes the form of explicit persuasion from outside a configuration—Gee gives the example of "a sociologist of science trying to get colleagues to view work in science labs as meaningful and valuable in ways quite different from how traditional historians of science have viewed such matters" (191). But Gee notes that "we spend our lives *always and also* engaging in enacting work from *inside* the configurations we work in to get recognized in certain ways" (191, emphasis added). Similarly, Gunther Kress, anxious to emphasize "what the relations between the wider social and economic environment and the forms and means of communication might be like," observes that

> to communicate is to work in making meaning . . . [hence] any landscape, the communicational included, is the result of human work. "Human" and therefore full of affect and desire; "human" and therefore always social and cultural. To make meaning is to change the resources we have for making meaning, to change ourselves, and to change our cultures. (*Literacy in the New Age* 11)

In a root sense, and certainly from a cultural materialist perspective, to engage in language practices is to engage in labor, labor that contributes to the (re)production of the self, the social, and the world. As Williams notes, "the most important thing a worker ever produces is himself [*sic*], himself in the fact of that kind of labour" (*Problems* 35). "Productive forces," he reminds us, include not only the "base" in the sense of, say, "basic industry" but also and always "the primary production of society itself, and of men [and women] themselves, the material production and reproduction of real life." In other words, labor "produces" not merely what capitalism recognizes—the commodity—but the social relations within which the commodity can exist and have value as commodity.[2] Failure to acknowledge this, Williams warns, leads to dismissing "as merely secondary, certain vital productive social forces, which are in the broad sense, from the beginning, basic" (*Problems* 35).

It is worth observing that the fact that this labor of language practice is not recognized as labor, or as at best "merely secondary," is an ideological phenomenon in the interests of some and against the interests of others, just as designating work conventionally assigned to women as "not work" or not "real work" is an ideological strategy by which to justify the exploitation of women by men. To the longstanding tradition of hierarchies in the status of different kinds of work and, as part of the class process, the designation of particular kinds of work according to those hierarchies—for example, designating some work as somehow more, or purely, "intellectual" ("work") rather than physical ("labor") (and vice versa) and the former as therefore somehow more valuable than the latter—there is also a further, more profound and unacknowledged tradition of refusing to grant some forms of activity the status of labor (or "work") at all. This is in accord with a refusal to recognize social relations as a productive force—social relations that language practices play a significant role in maintaining and shaping. That refusal forms the basis for the current working conditions, as conventionally defined, of composition teachers: composition's "labor issue." The now well-documented "feminization" of composition work—that is, its treatment as not "real" work, manifested in the relegation of much of the teaching of composition to contingent hires assigned low pay, no job security, and typically no benefits—is in accord with this failure to recognize the productive force of social relations that language practices play a significant role in maintaining and shaping insofar as composition is understood to be concerned with just such practices.[3]

It is of course a truism of language ethnography that language practices play such a role. However, the productive force of social relations these practices are responsible for maintaining and shaping is frequently ignored in discussions of labor—even "labor relations"—insofar as economic activity, and the sphere of "work," are understood as distinct from the social in this broader sense. Instead, the only labor recognized as labor is that identified with the production of commodities. However, that is changing insofar as the "new" economy is increasingly impinging on those spheres of life previously demarcated as private and outside the sphere of recognized (paid) work and insofar as (1) the activities assigned to the realm of the private are increasingly recognized as necessary to economic production, and (2) the "real" economy is increasingly recognized as linguistic-cognitive in character rather than a matter of the production and exchange of purely physical goods. This is not to say that language practices are now a form of labor that they previously were not. Rather, it is to say that language is increasingly recognized as a form of labor even in the production of exchange value. Just as the emergence of different technologies of writing has rendered visible the materiality of all forms of writing—pen and paper as well as keyboards and screens—as technologies, so the "new economy" is forcing recognition of language as a productive force, albeit if only in the production of market value.

We can see this recognition, for example, in economist Christian Marazzi's analysis of current financial market operations revealing "the centrality of communication, of *language*, not only as a vehicle for transmitting data and information, but also as a *creative force*" (27, emphasis in original). As he puts it more broadly, "in the New Economy language and communication are structurally and contemporaneously present throughout both the sphere of the production and distribution of goods and services and the sphere of finance" (14). Michael Hardt observes that Marazzi's argument treats language not only as a "model" for contemporary capitalist economy. Instead, Marazzi argues that linguistic conventions are also the means by which the world of finance functions. Further, and more directly pertinent to the argument of this chapter, "the newly dominant forms of labor are produced through language and means analogous to linguistic performance" (Hardt 8).

Nor is this merely an acknowledgment of the shift to a "service" economy, in which language plays a central role. For economists like Marazzi are recognizing the degree to which "language and communication are crucial for the production of ideas, information, images, affects, social relationships, and the like"—a revision, by expansion, of Marx's notion of "General Intellect" (Hardt 10; see also Virno). While Marx's notion referred primarily to the ways in which knowledge inheres in machines as "fixed capital," Marazzi argues that "the productive force of knowledge resides . . . also, and increasingly today, in linguistic communication and cooperation. . . . Our brains, linguistic faculties, and interactive skills have taken the place of fixed capital" (Hardt 10; see also Lazzarato, "Immaterial").

This growing recognition of the productive force of knowledge and its location in linguistic practice would, in one sense, seem to offer hope of a broadening acknowledgment of the importance of the labor of all language that Gee and Kress have remarked on (as noted above), and a break from dominant conceptualizations of labor set by capital. For example, Hardt suggests that this recognition "indicates the increasing autonomy of living labor from capitalist control, since, by embodying General Intellect, it is ever more independently able to deploy and manage the productive forces of knowledge and language" (10). On the other hand, current manifestations suggest an effort at expanding capitalist control:

> Worktime has generally increased, and, in fact, the traditional barriers that divide work-time from nonworktime, that divide work from life, are progressively breaking down. . . . Labor produces social life and, in turn, all of social life is put to work. (Hardt 10)

And as Marazzi observes, there has in fact been an "explosive increase in the linguistic-communicative-relational time of living labor, the time that in the New Economy involves inter-subjective communication or value-creating cooperation" (54).[4]

What might be turned to account is the contradiction experienced in this "new" economy arising from a failure to accept the productive labor of (ordinary) language practices outside the official sphere of "work" (practices which of course have been ongoing throughout human history). Marazzi explains that insofar as we face an "attention" economy, the less time workers have to devote to consuming informational goods (through "paying attention"), the higher the cost of getting their attention, which leads to further expanding their worktime and consequently further decreasing their attention time: "By putting to work even nonoccupational skills and resources, by eliminating non-productive time, the post-Fordist transformation of the world of work has reduced the quantity of attention time necessary to absorb the total supply of informational goods" (Marazzi 67). This dynamic is exacerbated by the increasing precariousness of employment itself in the post-fordist economy, since this forces workers to "dedicate more attention to looking for work than to consuming goods and services" (Marazzi 68).

In that seeming contradiction there is hope: namely, recognition that "the workforce is not only a producer, but also a consumer of attention, not only salary cost, but also income" (68). In an information/knowledge economy, consumption of information itself constitutes a form of labor—the transformation of information, through "paying attention," into knowledge and meaning through the labor of language. It is in this sense that the workforce produces income through "consumption."

As economist Yann Moulier Boutang argues, this seeming contradiction in the understanding of the workforce will ultimately be resolved (if it is) only by breaking with the ordinary wage contract (in which social security is based on employment) in exchange for "a guaranteed social income (also known as citizenship income or universal income)":

> Instead of basing social security on employment, it will sooner or later become necessary to generalize what is already happening experimentally at various levels, in order to ensure that . . . nomadic employment enjoys a social protection that is guaranteed, universal and as unconditional as possible. (Boutang 134; see also Marazzi 125; Virno 266)

In other words, recognition of the labor of and with all language practices and of the productive force of the social relations these contribute to the construction of poses a significant break from the terms in which labor (and capital) are commonly understood, necessitating concomitant breaks with traditional wage relations altogether.

Monolingualism and Labor in Composition

While the immediately foregoing discussion might seem like a significant detour from "the labor issue" in composition (or "the realities of the labor issue"), I want to argue that the perception of it as detour is itself a consequence of the ways that (labor) issue has been framed and understood by the dominant. First and foremost, the labor issue is typically understood in terms of individual or collective effort and merit (and comparisons among individuals and groups), effort and merit that are (in composition, as elsewhere) not being properly remunerated: that is, in terms of an exchange of abstract labor for pay. Negotiations, when there are any negotiations, typically focus, at least for faculty, on pay in compensation for teaching and other duties (service, administration, research), course load (class size, number of sections per semester), employment security, and benefits (health insurance, retirement) (see Rhoades; Boutang 135). So-called "contingent" faculty (only so-called because their history of employment often suggests a presence anything but contingent) negotiate, when they can, in more piecemeal fashion the same kinds of exchanges: teaching load, class size, pay per section, benefits and employment security (or, more commonly, the lack thereof) (see Flaherty). Insofar as faculty are thought to engage in work that is more "intellectual," they have historically enjoyed greater success in claiming more merit and, hence, pay for their work than contingent faculty, deemed to engage in work defined as less intellectual and therefore of less merit, hence deserving less pay.

There is in this framing clearly defined sets of activities that constitute work and individuals who are workers potentially meriting compensation for that work, understood as "labor" in the limited sense described earlier in this chapter, and a specific location of work—the "workplace" (especially for the contingent workers.) The terms of negotiation set by this framing dominate, and despite the limited success of labor's negotiations within those terms, it is assumed, even in the face of evidence to the contrary, that (once again) There Is No Alternative. As Boutang notes in discussing current conflicts between the "cognitariat" and the "proletariat,"

> At a time when alliances could arise on bases that are really common—such as that of guaranteed income, or of working models for intermittency, or of the attachment of social rights to the individual and not to the job (that poisoned legacy of industrial capitalism)—a misunderstanding of the nature of our current capitalism likes to dig deeper the divisions between the new classes and the old. Let us recall, for the record, the absurd defence of jobs at any price, even the most unskilled, including in industrial plants that poison the atmosphere, a protectionism that is catastrophic for the Third World, and an absurd praise of labour value and of the value of work. (135)

The strongest opposition to notions of a guaranteed social income and the like, Boutang notes, often comes from those classes most closely tied to the "old industrial capitalism," including what remains of the labor movement, which accept neoliberal ideology's definitions of what constitute the "economic fundamentals" according to which, and by which, labor is inevitably dependent on capital (134; cf. Virno 268).[5]

All this said, in prevalent but unofficial accounts, we can see the beginning articulations of alternative, emerging notions of composition's labor (at least for faculty, tenure-stream and not). There is, for example, widespread recognition that the contract period for tenure-stream faculty bears at best a fictional relationship to the time spent on the labor they are contracted to perform: most obviously, their need for "time off" during the summers to do the research and course preparation that is expected but for which there is no time during the regular academic "school year."[6] Likewise, the legally contingent status of contingent faculty means that attention they might otherwise ordinarily "pay" to "retooling," a.k.a. professional development in the interest of better performing the teaching labor they are (hoping to be) contracted for, is for many instead necessarily "spent" searching for jobs, hence the need, sometimes articulated, that they be provided greater job security not only for their own sake, as a matter of social justice, but for the sake of the students they teach.

But even these arguments remain within the framework of ordinary terms of exchange of labor for pay to ensure "productivity" (whether defined in terms of the number of publications or the number of processed student credit hours). Give us the tools, they argue, so that we may better perform our labor ("better" as in "more productive" of such commodified entities). It is, of course, sometimes possible for labor to work those terms of exchange to its advantage, either through exploiting the inevitable gap between explicit contractual terms and concrete labor or through an insistence on performing its concrete labor according to a narrow (seemingly "literal") interpretation of those terms (that is, by "working to rule"): doing only what is literally stated. But these are at best tactics of reaction and resistance operating within the dominant('s) framework (cf. Rhoades). As understandable and necessary as such tactics may be in specific instances and locations, they are also by definition necessarily limited in effect, ceding as they do to management what is negotiable, and how.

A full analysis of academic labor is well beyond the scope of this book (and commonly, attempts at addressing academic labor from the standpoint of a single set of laborers in a specific department or field quickly run up against the heterogeneity of "academic" labor practices and conditions, not least of all between tenure-stream and contingent faculty, and between "teaching assistants" and "research assistants" [see Watkins, "Managing" 899]). Keeping, then, to composition, here I will point to a telling omission in most discussions of labor in composition: students. Students, when they appear at all in such debates, are cast as the recipients of labor in composition (ideally its beneficiaries), whose labor outside the academic realm (holding down full- or part-time jobs and taking care of family members, etc.) interferes with their ability to be such recipients. Students are almost never cast as fellow laborers in composition—our colleagues, as it were, rather than our clients, customers, or products. The primary exception proving this rule is, once again, Slevin, who, as a kind of thought experiment, proposes that we imagine that

> the moment a student walks into our classroom, the first day of class, the student would be seen—and see himself or herself—as a full participant in the work of the discipline. *Just for showing up.* She would not have to *negotiate* entry; she would not have to *earn* the right to speak and participate. She has already entered and by definition has that right. The discipline includes her as a *given*, and the intellectual work of the discipline includes her work and our work with her. (*Introducing* 44–45, emphasis in original)

While Slevin makes this proposal in the course of arguing for a reinvention of the discipline of composition, I note here that its imaginative rendering does away altogether, and explicitly, with dominant understandings of disciplinary labor as a position one earns and is then contracted for, suggesting instead that the student's mere presence be recognized as an index of her position as a fellow contributor to the work of the discipline "as a full participant." Thus students (along with faculty) would be recognized as always already participants, meriting, as residents of the academic realm, the equivalent, at least in standing, of "a guaranteed social income" or "citizenship income or universal income" awarded unconditionally.[7] Such a recognition would break with the traditional conception and politics of class, which rely on the stable class identities assigned by capitalism, according to which students are not laborers at all, language is not a productive force but commodity, and composition teaching is the transmission—efficient or not—of writing skills to students, understood as at most the products of that labor.[8] This break is thus resisted by those committed, from whatever position in such politics, to such identities—a commitment that accepts, in advance, the terms of exchange set by capitalism, in its interests, and hence a commitment to a commodified notion of language, a transmission model of writing pedagogy, and monolingualism.

Alternatively, if the labor of composition is writing language, then seeing students as full participants in that labor means seeing them not as writing *in* a language but, rather, as fellow writers *of* language. And to see them as fellow writers of language requires that we see language as (always) in need of such (re)writing. To do that requires a turn from the ideology of monolingualism according to which language is merely something one writes in, has, or acquires—language as commodity (in the service of production of other commodities: a tool to make goods for market exchange). I'm arguing, in other words, that the longstanding exploitative working conditions for composition instructors are sustained by monolingualist ideology—in the United States, "English only" monolingualist ideology specifically—that treats language (and skill with language) as commodity. For that ideology occludes the necessity and contribution of readers' and writers' concrete labor to the (re) production of what is termed simply "English." Monolingualism thus renders insubstantial the labor of both composition students and their teachers: teachers are imagined to engage in the purely remedial task of enabling students to produce what, by rights, it is thought they should already know how to produce; students are seen as inexplicably behind in their development as users of English, hence cognitively deficient or substandard (and hence the low status of working with them); and both teachers and students are positioned as lacking agency to do more than passively reiterate "English"—that is, there is no possibility of "production" attributed to their attempts at the "reproduction" of English. Given all this, it's no wonder (within dominant economic logics) that so little financial reward should be assigned to those laboring in composition.

To explain the ways in which monolingualism affects composition's "labor issue," I begin by reviewing monolingualist ideology's assumptions about language and its development, using "English only" as the specific instantiation of that ideology in the United States.[9] First, that ideology assumes linguistic homogeneity among readers and writers to be the norm for members of a nation-state: all readers and writers within the nation-state are supposed to be speakers of the same, and single, language (Matsuda, "Myth"). Indeed, the civil status and patriotism of those residing within the nation-state who do not speak that language, or who speak other languages, is seen as suspect. For, as Gal and Irvine observe, "if language and political identity are seen to be inherently, essentially linked, than [*sic*] multilingualism and shifting language use must be an icon of equally shiftable, therefore shallow, political allegiances and unreliable moral commitments" (982).[10]

Second, monolingualist ideology assumes languages themselves to be stable, uniform, and discrete—"codes" that can be readily taught and learned. This accounts for the notorious failure of proponents of "English Only" legislation in the United States to define what in fact constitutes "English": English is assumed to be self-evident, stable, and discrete from other languages. Conversely, mixing of English with other languages, and by extension mixing of English speakers with speakers of other languages, is seen as a potential threat to the purity of the language and the English-speaking polity. Difference, in short, is suspect.

Third, in line with a notion of languages as stable, internally uniform, and discrete, monolingualist ideology assumes knowledge of a language to be likewise stable, uniform, and discrete: one knows English (or any other language) or doesn't, or knows it "imperfectly." Hence the impatience of those advocating an English Only policy with those whose "command" of English is different than their own, their unwillingness to fund programs of English-language instruction, and their support for discriminatory laws against those whose speech patterns differ from their own. These speech patterns are said to constitute either "speaking with an accent," unlike oneself, or speaking poorly (for example, following speech patterns characteristic of subordinated, statistically more impoverished groups, such as residents of Appalachia and other rural areas, African Americans, Southerners). Given a view of English as stable, internally uniform, and finite, it follows that individuals should simply choose to speak English rather than something else, and that there is only one correct way to speak (and write) it.

Fourth, a conduit model of communication is assumed as the norm, whereby efficiency of communication is lauded and imagined to be achievable through use of a common code. In this model, differences in language present static interference in what would otherwise be a frictionless, transparent, effortless transfer of information from sender to receiver. This is contrary to cultural anthropologist Anna Lowenhaupt Tsing's findings that mobility (of goods, ideas, etc.) across cultures is in fact made possible by, rather than achieved despite, "friction." Thus, against common views of the global "flow" of goods, money, and people proceeding "entirely without friction," Tsing notes that "motion does not proceed this way at all" (5). As she reminds us: "Friction is not just about slowing things down. Friction is required to keep global power in motion. It shows us . . . where the rubber meets the road" (6). And as she subsequently explains, as universals "travel across difference," they "are charged and changed by their travels" (8). This charging and changing is the labor of translation—an apt characterization of all communication: "communication between languages," Pennycook notes, "presents not so much the central process of translation but rather a special case: all communication involves translation" ("English" 40). And as translation theorist Michael Cronin observes, contrary to facile (if common) notions of translation, translation involves "the effort, the difficulty and, above all else, the time required to establish and maintain linguistic (and by definition, cultural) connections" (49). Attempts at translation that overlook these, Cronin warns, lead not to transmitting knowledge at all but simply to the "physical transfer of information" (20). It is just such attempts that are advocated by English Only advocates, who herald and defend the global spread of English as contributing to the smooth flow of capital (though see Dor). In these arguments, aligned with neoliberal ideology, the standardizing of English ensures the steadiness of that flow of capital by eliminating the possibility of differences in interpretation (see Lu, "Essay").[11]

All these assumptions contribute to the treatment of language as a commodity. Marx explains that a commodity is produced when "the labour expended in the production of a useful article [is presented] as an 'objective' property of that article, i.e. as its value" (*Capital, I* 153–54). Through commodity fetishism, "the products of the human brain appear as autonomous figures endowed with a life of their own, which enter into relations both with each other and with the human race" (165). English-only ideology treats English and its value not as the ongoing accomplishment of those engaged in its production through their concrete labor as speakers, listeners, readers, and writers but, rather, as something with a life of its own with specific, objective properties that must be preserved and defended. The labor of those using English, and their contribution to its (re)production and value, are thereby occluded, as are the various and variable effects of their labor. Thus it is that we imagine writing English to be not writing English but merely "writing *in* English" (see, for example, Bean et al.). This reverses Calvet's dicta that "it is practices which constitute languages . . . [for] languages exist only in and through their speakers, and they are reinvented, renewed and transformed in every interaction, each time that we speak" (6, 7).[12]

The commodification of English and other languages as "autonomous figures" elides the history of the "invention" (and ongoing reinvention) of specific languages and the identification of putatively stable varieties of these with specific nation-states and collectivities: French, English, German, Chinese, etc. (see Gal and Irvine; Makoni; Qu). These views link social identity with linguistic identity, both of which are understood as singular, discrete, and stable rather than plural, overlapping, and in flux. Those adopting these views must dismiss as aberrations, deviations, failures, or at least annoyances the actual heterogeneity, complexity, and fluctuating character of language practices and social identifications on the ground. Likewise, they treat language learning (in speech and writing) as a matter of natural, singular, and unidirectional "development" toward "mastery" of a singular, uniform, and static language. Understood thus, college writing instruction is reduced to a transmission model whereby teachers attempt to give students knowledge of what is imagined as a fixed, correct, uniform, singular language "code" for them to follow and that, as adult writers, they should have mastered but, inexplicably, have failed to.[13]

This assumption is illustrated in the tendency among early scholars of "basic writing" to explain writers' difficulties by characterizing the students as either equivalent to (or even the same as) second-language learners or as being somehow "stuck" at an earlier stage of cognitive development (see Shaughnessy, *Errors*; Hays, "Socio-cognitive"; Laurence; Lunsford, "Cognitive"; Horner, "Mapping"). Both accounts posited a uniform, unidirectional, linear model of cognitive and/or linguistic development that students were expected ordinarily to follow unless hindered through some extraordinary circumstance. Thus students' difficulties were located outside the ordinary path of development as abnormal, a straying or dislocation to be somehow rectified through administration of the appropriate pedagogy. And thus, not surprisingly, the pedagogy most often recommended was a skills and "mechanics" transmission model (see Bartholomae, "Basic Writing").

To be sure, those pedagogies treating basic writers as equivalent to second-language learners have had the advantage of being more palatable ethically and practically, insofar as they recognize (1) the intelligence of students, and (2) the normality of language difference, signaled by the recognition that students might well know more than one language. From this perspective, for example, errors are understood as evidence of students' inferences about "academic" language and of their development of an "interlanguage," rather than evidence of faulty wiring in the brain or impeded cognitive development causing an inability to "de-center" (Laurence 31; see Kroll and Schaefer 209; Bartholomae, "Study"). At the same time, those models of second-language acquisition on which basic writing teachers have drawn in taking this approach tend themselves to reinforce, while simply pluralizing, the treatment of languages as discrete, uniform, stable entities. For example, these models retain the notion of a "target" language and of "native" fluency as the ideal aim for second-language instruction. To the putatively monolingual, fluent native speaker of one language these models simply propose adding native fluency in a second, separate language. Indeed, as François Grosjean has argued, bilinguals are commonly, if incorrectly, understood to be two monolinguals in one person (Grosjean). This preserves what, in sum, is the monolingualist model of language and language learning: a model that links one uniform, stable, and discrete social identity for an individual with one stable, discrete "target" language the development of mastery over which is thought to proceed in a uniform and linear manner.

A growing body of scholarship attests to the inaccuracy and inadequacy of this model as a representation of either language or language learning and its relation to identity. English "itself" has been shown to be neither singular nor stable but plural and fluctuating: there are multiple competing "world" English*es*, the identity and constitution of each of which fluctuates and is subject to contest (Brutt-Griffler, Kachru, Parakrama), and notions of a "standard" English, "native English speakers," and languages as discrete entities have been shown to be largely ideological (Coupland; Gal and Irvine; Kramsch, "Privilege"; Makoni; Paikeday; Parakrama; Singh). The growing majority of speakers of English know English as a second or additional language (Crystal), in keeping with the statistical norm of multilingualism, a norm that holds true globally within as well as across national borders (Khubchandani; Harklau et al.). In keeping with that norm, individuals' social identifications are not singular, nor do they correspond neatly with either a specific language used or even with a specific language affiliation (Chiang and Schmida; Harklau et al., "Linguistically").

Studies of bilingualism highlight this. The "bilingual" has been shown to be a "unique and specific speaker-hearer" rather than "the sum of two complete or incomplete monolinguals" posited by monolingual ideology (Grosjean 471; see also Auer; Martin-Jones). Thus, such features of multilingual language use as code switching, borrowing, and blending of languages, rather than representing "language interference" or incomplete mastery of discrete languages, are the norm and evidence of language competence, albeit of a kind different than that posited by monolingualist ideology—what Vivian Cook has called "multicompetence," with a focus, as Juliane House puts it, on "language use rather than on development and acquisition, and on the socio-pragmatic functions of language choice" (House 558).

Studies of uses of ELF—the use of English among speakers for none of whom English is claimed as a "native" language—encapsulate this different perspective on language and approach to language use. As discussed in chapter 2, these studies show ELF to be "intersubjectively constructed in each specific context of interaction . . . negotiated by each set of speakers for their purposes" and thus something that "never achieves a stable or even standardized form" (Meierkord 129; qtd. in Canagarajah, "Lingua Franca English" 925). Thus, while it might be possible to abstract and teach a grammar and lexicon from a particular instance of ELF, that very abstraction would work against students' ability to participate meaningfully in the multilingual languaging that continually reconstitutes ELF. And because ELF is reconstituted in each instance of its practice, we cannot identify a particular set of practices with "competence" in it.

Finally, rather than constituting a code for the smooth transfer of information among its speakers, English (like all languages) has been shown to be a language always "in translation" (Pennycook). That is to say, instead of representing a uniform, discrete, and stable code whose significance is set and can be read off by those fluent in it, English is fraught with "semiodiversity" (Pennycook), a plurality of contested meanings necessarily subject to reworking by its users.[14] And in fact, such reworking is constant, even if often going unrecognized, and even among those for whom English is "native." As countless English teachers can attest, English monolingual students regularly experience confusion in attempting to make sense of English-language texts they are assigned to read, just as the teachers themselves experience confusion in attempting to make sense of the texts their English monolingual students produce, and just as the students experience confusion attempting to make sense of their English teachers' comments on those texts. This is the norm, however disconcerting to some. From this perspective, the perpetual reconstituting of English in its uses as a lingua franca by its users simply offers a more visible representation of the labor and accomplishment of English in all instances of its use.

The apparent "friction" that is part of ELF discourse likewise is present in all uses of English and in fact, rather than interfering with meaning, is necessary to its production, as listeners/readers translate and negotiate possible meanings from specific utterances, which are then renegotiated as the discourse continues.[15] It is a testament to the power of monolingualist ideology that the gap between language as practiced, on the one hand, and, on the other, that ideology's representations of language, remains largely invisible, its manifestations evaded by being dismissed as aberrations, special problem cases, deviations, or threats to be eliminated or quarantined.

Translinguality and Labor in Composition

Language understood as the ongoing, always-emergent outcome of practices troubles the issue of labor in composition partly by calling into question claims to what it is that labor is meant to produce. We can see one manifestation of that troubling in ongoing disputes in the field of second language acquisition over who is best qualified to teach second languages, disputes that provide a telling parallel to debates on qualifications for those hired to teach composition and their working conditions. Disputes over who is qualified to teach second languages hinge precisely on whether or not the aim of such instruction is to enable students to achieve "native-like" fluency in producing a "standard" version of the "target" language, or whether these conceptions of language and fluency are inadequate and inaccurate to the circumstances in which language users find themselves. In ESL, there is a longstanding tradition of hiring those deemed to be native English speakers in preference to "nonnative" speakers of English on the presumption that the former are better equipped to teach English language learners insofar as they can model that norm (Jenkins 172). That tradition treats English as a "native" language as the "target" norm to which all speakers of English must aspire to conform, and toward which English-language teaching should be aimed.

However, in light of the presence of competing versions of world Englishes, their fluctuating character, and the fact that the majority of uses of English occur among those for whom English is not a "native" language, scholars of ELF (among others) have argued against this practice. As they note, not only do nonnative-English-speaking teachers have the benefit of better understanding the difficulties students face in learning English, and hence may be better able to explain the challenges English poses to ESL students; it is also no longer clear which version of English, if any, is to be preferred as the "target" language to be taught. For example, many English language learners will be using English to speak not to native English speakers but to nonnative speakers of English, and hence idiomatic "native" English, even if difficulties identifying it were to be overcome, would not be more communicatively effective for their purposes. And finally, many of the features of standardized Anglo-American spoken English, while difficult to learn, have nil or a negligible effect on intelligibility, especially though not exclusively in communications between ESL speakers (see McKay, "EIL"; Seidlhofer).

In short, treating "Native-Speaker English" as a norm for all speakers of English to be taught and to use is problematic on the one hand insofar as it overlooks the existence of competing norms for English represented by the various world Englishes—Australian English, Chinese English, Singaporean English, Nigerian English, and so on—and, on the other, insofar as it is inefficient and ineffective both pedagogically and communicatively. In light of such arguments, continued efforts to privilege Native English speakers in the selection of instructors and in the design and selection of teaching materials for ESL students is increasingly being rejected as a means of using language as a proxy for cultural imperialism and even racism.[16] All these arguments work against privileging what is deemed "Native-Speaker English" as the global norm, and thus presumably against English Only arguments for making it the norm of global communication. Indeed, it is no longer clear, if it ever was, who counts as a native speaker of English nor what constitutes standard English (Coupland; Leung et al.), hence no valid reason for giving preference in hiring English-language teachers to individuals who might have formerly been understood to "own" a single, uniform version of "standard English" which they could model, and thereby transmit, to students (Widdowson; Horner and Lu, "Resisting").

Common practices in hiring and training English composition instructors follow assumptions parallel to those governing the hiring and training of English-language instructors. These include the assumption that there is a uniform stable entity known as Standard Written English, and that any native English speaker with demonstrated mastery in using SWE is capable of transmitting its characteristics—the "target"—to those unfortunates who have not yet mastered its use.

We see the invocation of such a stance in one of the four overlapping accounts Richard Miller and Michael Cripps offer of the Rutgers University composition program's approach to staffing its courses.[17] Briefly, that program shifted from relying primarily on adjuncts and English department graduate students to staff its courses to drawing not only on a larger pool of adjuncts but on an expanded pool of graduate students from a wide range of disciplines other than English (Miller and Cripps 124–31). In one account Miller and Cripps offer, this change is justified in terms of the equivalency, and indeed uniformity as well as stability, of the skill to be transmitted. As they put it,

> a first-time English TA [teaching assistant], drawn to Rutgers by its outstanding graduate program in literatures in English, is not, a priori, better prepared than an advanced graduate student in art history or political science or physics and astronomy to begin the hard work of teaching first-year students how to read with care, how to draft a thoughtful response, or how to use revision to produce a supple argument. (136)

Or, as they put it elsewhere, by expanding the labor pool on which to draw, their program succeeded in "put[ting] qualified instructors in front of students" (127), a success all the more impressive in light of Rutgers' failure to increase the number of faculty lines at a time of significant growth in its student enrollment and a reduction in its TA teaching loads (124–27).

At least in this version Miller and Cripps offer of what transpired at Rutgers, what constitutes a careful reading, a thoughtful response, or a supple argument is not questioned. Instead, these, or the skills to produce them, are treated as commodities whose value remains the same across contexts. Quality control over the teachers was assured by a barrage of administrative procedures of teacher training and review. As Miller and Cripps observe, this gave the program administrators confidence that

> [they] could provide the TAs from the other disciplines with the training they needed to succeed in the classroom . . . because [Miller and Cripps] had years of experience training creative writers, journalists, and screenwriters to work within [their] system. (129)

That training ensures a uniform product. As they further explain, the program requires

> a practical adherence to its pedagogy during the term of employment. Consistency in the number and type of writing assignments across all sections of the program's writing courses, consistency in pedagogical approach, and consistency in the application of the shared evaluative criteria are all that is required. These three consistencies make it possible to provide over ten thousand students each year with a common learning experience in their writing classes. (137)

In this model, it would appear that, as Miller and Cripps partially acknowledge, "anyone can teach freshman composition" (137), for, as they attest, in their experience, "over 90 percent of TAs from outside English are capable of meeting these criteria" (138). And if anyone can, then it is not surprising that it would be difficult to make a "market" argument for improving the working conditions for teachers of freshman composition: the labor supply would, in fact, appear to be enormous and growing.

However, there is an alternative perspective that emerges in Version Three of their account (titled "On Unintended Consequences"). In that account, they report that while the move to include TAs from other disciplines was prompted initially by a simple desire to put a sufficient number of instructors in front of a burgeoning number of sections of first-year composition, bringing TAs from these other disciplines to the program had the unintended consequence of "transform[ing] how the Writing Program defines its mission to itself, to the English Department, and to the university at large" (130). Specifically, TAs from outside the English department called into question the universality of the approach to reading and writing the program had hitherto taught, that is, "close textual analysis of cultural studies texts" (131). From the perspective of these other TAs, that approach was not universal but a "discipline-specific" approach that "did not readily transfer to writing for history, philosophy, or political science" (131). In short, these other TAs introduced competing notions of what might constitute careful reading, thoughtful responses, and supple arguments, just as the emergence of world Englishes has introduced competing notions of what constitutes "standard English" that challenge the assumption of a single standard English to be taught to all "English-language learners."

Of course, one possible response to the emergence of such competing notions of language, reading, and writing would be to accept a plurality of "standards" for language each of which is held, and taught as, discrete from others. Such an archipelago response effectively pluralizes monolingualism: in place of English Only applied universally, it offers a plurality of discrete monolinguistic utopias: Indian English for the Indians, Australian English for the Australians, and so on. The equivalent in composition appears in some arguments to replace the first-year composition course with a writing in the disciplines (WID) program offering a plurality of discrete types of writing: chemistry writing for the chemists, business writing for business, history writing in the history department, and so on (see, for example, Petraglia).

While such a response grants legitimacy to different varieties of language practices, it simultaneously reinforces, by understating, the role of power relations in determining what may or may not show "competence" in using language "appropriate" to a given situation, and according to what and whose interests a particular practice is deemed "appropriate" (see Dubin; Fairclough; Leung, "Convivial" 131–32; McKay, "Toward"). There is an acknowledged but also assigned place for every language, or form of writing, but it is also expected that every language and form of writing is set and will be kept in its place, with the politics of how what is and is not appropriate to that site or occasion sidestepped through invocations of "appropriateness."

This is not, however, what transpired at Rutgers. Instead, as Miller and Cripps explain, in response to the introduction of competing notions of writing and reading by TAs from across the disciplines, it was decided that because "the first-year course could never prepare students to write in every discipline, the best pedagogical response might well lie with challenging students to build connections across disciplinary boundaries to generate responses to pressing contemporary problems," problems that could not be claimed by any one discipline (131). In so doing, it may be said that rather than attempting to convert its instructional staff and their students to production of a uniform, consistent, "standard" set of reading and writing practices, or sets of these, the Rutgers program availed itself of (1) the resource represented by the different language practices of its teaching staff (and, presumably, students) and also (2) the inadequacy of any one set of reified language and disciplinary practices to address the intellectual challenges faced by the students, their teachers, and the community at large.

Miller and Cripps themselves do not make this particular claim, and the unintended consequence of altering the focus of the course is only one of four accounts they offer to the question posed in the title of their story, "Who Should Teach First-Year Writing?" Instead, within their account of unintended consequences, they present the consequence as representing a shift from asking the question "Who Should Teach First-Year Writing" to asking "Who is the course for," to which they answer, all students regardless of major (131). In other words, they shift to an argument for the course as service to the students.

This is a tempting and therefore not uncommon move in arguments about labor in composition, deployed both to justify improved working conditions for teachers and to insist on strong management of those teachers: in the interest of students, one can insist on well-resourced laborers (teachers) and the best management of their labor. In other words, one can argue for improved conditions for teachers (better job security, benefits, professional development opportunities, more favorable teaching loads) not simply as a matter of social justice but as necessary to ensure better teaching. I'll have more to say about the discourse of such debates in chapter 4. Here I recall that such arguments position students as the recipients of rather than participants in labor. To return to Miller and Cripps's program, from the perspective I am advancing in this chapter, the more pressing question to pose is neither who is qualified to teach its courses, nor whom the courses are for, but instead what the courses are meant to do, albeit for and by both students and teachers (and, ultimately, others). The English-only variant of monolingualist ideology charges courses like freshman composition at Rutgers with transmitting the code of SWE from teachers to students to ensure a population that is homogeneous in linguistic and civic identity and (hence) to provide conditions conducive to the smooth global exchange of goods, services, and information: the ability to produce what presumably will be recognized universally as a careful reading, thoughtful response, and supple argument. I have argued above that this aim is based on flawed assumptions about language and contradicted by evidence of language practices globally (including, of course, within the United States). The practice of hiring presumably monolingual, native-English speakers with a commitment to "English" in the singular to transmit the "code" of SWE is complicit with that ideology. If the code is imagined to be set and in the possession of those with training in it—documented by, say, possession of a BA or MA in English, or being an "advanced graduate student," and/or having experience writing (in English, of course)—then the labor pool on which to draw is large and often largely unemployed, and the task for those hired is the simple one of transmission, as attested to by the rhetoric of a million handbooks. The alternative of offering a plurality of discrete writing courses teaching discrete forms of writing—business writing, chemistry writing, etc.—is a simple multiplication of that approach, a pluralization of monolingualism, rendering students the equivalent of monolingualism's myth of bilinguals as "two monolinguals in one person."

The converse to adopting either a uniform English-only approach or a pluralization of that approach in the form of an archipelago of WID courses addresses intersecting forms of what various scholars of language spread have identified as "traffic" (Kramsch, "Traffic"; Pennycook, "English"). First, there is the traffic of humans from site to site, community to community; second, there is the traffic in meanings among these; and finally, there is the traffic in linguistic forms used. Applied to the situation of the academy, individual students take courses in many different disciplines, people in disciplines talk to one another, and their disciplinary practices and identities intermingle and change, with the result that students and their professors commonly engage in a plethora of heterogeneous and changing practices across as well as within languages and disciplines.

Programs that accepted this traffic as the norm would abandon the effort to transmit codifications of particular practices in language, including writing practices, for any such codifications transmitted would be at best misleading, and their transmission would fail to address the challenges of traffic. In lieu of viewing language pedagogy in terms of code transmission, these programs would instead put their curricula to work as sites for investigating, with students, ways and strategies by which English is and might be rewritten, to what effects and under what circumstances, and to training in the development of the attitudes that would sustain development of such investigations and strategies. Adopting such a view of language education would take linguistic heterogeneity and fluctuation as the norm rather than deviation. The question its teachers and students would then face, and face together, would be how best to engage that norm. Such engagements would necessarily involve "translation" in the sense of accepting as normal, and working with, the semiodiversity as well as glossodiversity of language, including English (see Pennycook, "English"). And they would recognize the translation and semiodiversity accomplished even in what might seem, within the tenets of monolingualism, to be iterations of "the same." For rewriting includes decisions to engage in such iterations, for particular purposes. Differences in meaning, inevitable as a consequence of the unique location of all utterances in time and space, would remain. But whether a seeming "repetition" or "deviation," every utterance would be subject to questioning for what it might be accomplishing, and whether such an accomplishment is worthwhile, for whom, how, and why.[18]

At the very least, a writing program that accepted linguistic heterogeneity and fluctuation and traffic in language practices as the norm would face the need to radically alter traditional criteria for hiring teachers of writing, whether writing English or any other language. First, given the plurality and fluctuation of Englishes, a person's status as a "native" speaker of English would not only be suspect. Even if it could be established, it would be of no consequence: speakers of some variety dubbed "native" would have no greater claim to authority over the "English" students were to be taught to write than speakers of other languages and varieties of language. Likewise, individuals' credentials as established writers "in," and readers of, English, as represented either by possession of a degree in English or experience writing English, would in itself count for little. For from the perspective of English as necessarily and always reworked, an individual's insular mastery of a specific set of conventions would not in itself demonstrate his or her ability to work with, on, and across language differences.

Conversely, those individuals with experience and other forms of knowledge in working with and across multiple languages might well be preferred for positions teaching writing. Monolingualism, rather than being seen as the norm, would instead be recognized for the limitation it is, and multilingualism for the advantages it might bring. Those individuals who abjured status as "native" English speakers would, from this perspective, have potentially more to offer in teaching the writing of English insofar as they were (1) more representative of the majority of users of English worldwide, (2) more familiar with working across and between English and other languages, and (3) less willing to claim a spurious authority on what does and doesn't constitute SWE.

But this would not, in itself, preclude hiring those with assigned status as Native English Speakers, nor would it mean giving preference to any and all those individuals assigned Non-Native-English-speaker status. After all, dispositions toward language difference are not determined by nor specific to assigned language status, and those claiming status as multilinguals might well subscribe to monolingualist tenets in their approach to English and other languages, just as those claiming to be monolinguals need not subscribe to monolingualist tenets in their approach. Instead, the "mastery" required of teachers would not be a mastery of reifications of any language or languages, but rather possession of and willingness to work to maintain dispositions toward language differences helpful in developing strategies for interacting with these—a willingness to understand "mastery," or, better, language learning, as an ongoing project for all, in which students can be enlisted as collaborators.[19]

Nor is this to argue that we substitute the teaching of specific interactional strategies for the teaching of the ostensible "code" of SWE (or the "codes" of discrete disciplines and professions). For, just as studies of ELF have observed that even the pragmatic strategies of ELF are situationally specific (Canagarajah, "Lingua Franca" 926), so interactional strategies across languages and language varieties vary. Instead, teachers would work with their students to investigate and experiment with ways of working across languages, of "translating" across languages and language varieties and across ways and genres of writing English (and would be hired on the promise of their ability to do such work). While, in the process, both students and teachers might develop a broader range of repertoires for interacting with and across languages, the broadening of that repertoire, if it obtained, would be a byproduct rather than driving aim of the course. For in place of a transmission model for writing and its teaching, writing courses would be sites for collaborative investigations into writing languages, with any writing "solutions" arrived at by definition contingent.

This renders the work of writing courses difficult: not difficult in the sense of overcoming students' cognitive or affective recalcitrance to learning a fixed code, but in the sense of working together on challenges for which there are no fixed or sure solutions. Just as Miller and Cripps end up reimagining Rutgers' first-year writing course as a site for engaging questions of pressing concern that are the province of no single discipline, so shifting writing courses away from English Only assumptions reorients them toward writing that is the province of neither a single discipline, a single language, nor a single set of language practices but that is translingual, moving across the defining boundaries of these.[20] Thus the course is no longer remedial in function, aiming to give students what it is presumed they ought already to know, with all the low status and poor working conditions attending such a function (as catch-up "service"), but intellectually substantive, engaging in cutting-edge, vital investigations of writing differences. The absence of remedial function would not in itself justify eliminating the requirement that students take the course, just as the absence of a remedial function to science does not render it purely optional for undergraduate education. Instead, it would be a requirement for graduation (but not necessarily a prerequisite to other courses) insofar as it constitutes a fundamental area of inquiry comparable to study of natural and social sciences and humanities, say, or world history, required for graduation at many schools.[21]

And here is where the imaginative thought experiment I have just been engaged in would encounter several difficulties of a different kind. First, redefining first-year writing in this way would likely encounter opposition insofar as it would work against the interests served by monolingualist ideology. For writing programs, these include the interests of those hoping to retain the privileges afforded native-speaker status; those whose authority to teach writing in U.S. schools depends on their claims to ostensible mastery of an ostensible "standard written English"; those whose authority, and even job security, appear to be threatened by movements to make multilingualism rather than monolingualism the cultural "norm"; and those responsible for keeping the costs of writing instruction low, no matter the effects on the nature and quality of that instruction.

More broadly, there would be resistance to granting the fact and contribution of the concrete labor of all to language through their practices with it (and, here, specifically the contribution of students to the ongoing [re]constitution of "academic" writing). For the value of labor is more easily appropriated when it is not recognized as labor at all. Just as proposals for a universal or citizenship income in light of the contribution of all to social relations as a productive force have met with strong opposition from those committed to terms of negotiation set by conventional wage relations of pay in exchange only for contracted labor, so any suggestion that the ordinary practices of ordinary (or "subordinate") members of the academic community might merit support for the contributions they inevitably make through writing language would likely be met with powerful opposition. At most, only some such contributions would be granted recognition, likely those emerging from the practices of those already granted authority to make such contributions in the first place: tenure-line faculty, with contributions by students and contingent faculty dismissed as insubstantial because of either their form as reiterations (defined as "nothing new") or their identification as student or (worse) contingent faculty contributions and hence by definition suspect as at best having only ephemeral consequence, and therefore of no merit. Class relations, after all, remain deeply sedimented.

But to acknowledge these difficulties is not to resign ourselves to their sway. It is to prepare counterarguments in policies for hiring (and rehiring), and for changes in our graduate as well as undergraduate teaching. Those arguments would be necessary, for example, when justifying a WPA's refusal to hire, or rehire, those teachers who define their work as SWE transmission, or who uncritically invoke monolithic notions of "good writing" (careful reading, thoughtful response, and supple argument) and "good English" (and claim to be masters of these). Likewise, they would be necessary when justifying a WPA's refusals to accommodate administrators' demands to draw on the large unemployed (and therefore cheap) pool of such teachers professing such pretensions to staff every first-year writing course every fall, and when justifying refusals to credit courses in transmitting SWE at other institutions as equivalent to courses in translingual writing. They would be necessary in redefining the mission and design of our courses for our students and our colleagues.[22]

They would also require at least exploring the possibility of greater collaboration with colleagues in other language departments (as well as ESL programs where those are institutionally distinct). While there is every reason to believe that there are as many of these colleagues who are monolingualist in their dispositions as there are in English departments, the reverse is also true, and such dispositions themselves are subject to fraying in the face of the facts of linguistic heterogeneity and fluctuation.[23] Making visible the linguistically heterogeneous and fluctuating character of college and university scholar-writers, and their writing, may be helpful in shifting colleagues' language orientations and expectations for writing courses. As Paul Kei Matsuda has observed, "Since the English language has become the dominant language of international communication, the audience of scholarly communication is no longer limited to native speakers of dominant varieties of English," and, hence, "the nature of rhetorical situations in academia [is changing]" ("Alternative" 193–94): even were all students to be English monolinguals, they may well be writing to faculty who know English as an additional language and whose English language practices, expectations, and demands vary from those of their colleagues and their students. In making these counterarguments, compositionists might well invoke the trumpeting of "internationalization" and trade on schools' desperate claims of trying to prepare students for a "globalized" future. But this will require arguing against claims that "standard" English already is the global lingua franca, and against a commodified version of multilingualism that overlooks the difficulties of translation across languages.[24]

The dominant political economy of language(s) in composition depends on the commodification of a set of language practices which is offered as the effective currency of thought: one communicates one's thinking using that currency, and none other, as a matter of both surety and efficiency in transmission. Put simply, if it's recognized as SWE, it has legitimacy as the currency of the academic realm. Those deemed to possess mastery of SWE thus are authorized to communicate thought, and deemed able to think. Against that view of the economy of languages I have been arguing for an economy highlighting the labor of readers and writers in making meaning through the difficult and confusing process of translating across languages—whether between English and other languages or between various practices with English. If in the former, the friction composition students and teachers encounter in their work with language is deemed a detriment to be overcome, in the latter, it is the normal stuff of reading and writing, the making of meaning that is necessary to the vitality and movement of English as a living language rather than code (see Lu, "Living"). Highlighting that friction as part of the necessary labor of composition in working with English as a language "always in translation" can shift the value of composition away from mere "service" as skills conduit to an occasion not merely for writing "in" English but for rewriting English, again and again, in concert and negotiation with others, to better us all. It is to take on, in collaboration with our students, a different understanding of the work we have always already been doing all the while: the continuous and necessary labor of writing language.

* * *

I began this chapter by identifying language as what brings trouble to the common distinction between work and labor, a distinction that precludes recognition of the labor of writing language in which composition engages. To recognize writing language as the labor of composition is necessary but not sufficient to ending composition's "labor troubles." For recognition takes shape in language—what I argue in chapter 2 is the ongoing product of practices. Chapter 3 has defined the labor of composition as that practice: writing language—a definition at odds with the dominant's refusal to recognize that practice as labor at all. In chapter 4, I take up the ways composition has, and might, broker that recognition: the language practices by which it has and might represent the value of the labor of composition to itself and its others.

4. *Value/Evaluation*

To designate an activity or set of activities "work" is to assign it a particular value, distinct from the value of other kinds of activities—not work, not real work, labor, and, of course, play. That is, as I discuss in chapter 3, "work" serves to hierarchize forms of labor ("labor" as "manual" and "low" unlike mental/intellectual "work," say), as well as to mark some forms of activity as work and others not at all.

As this practice illustrates, value is not something inherent to particular entities or activities but, rather, produced through language. It should but cannot go without saying that value is thus the product, not the object, of acts of evaluation: the application of particular criteria produces a sense of the value of a particular object or act. Brokers participate in such acts of evaluation, working to achieve consensus on value—to persuade to "recognition" of the claimed value of a particular object or act. Thus, so long as language continues (that is, for all practical purposes, forever), the contingent character of the value assigned an entity or action—what is identified as its value—continues. This is true of both "exchange" and "use" value. Use value is realized only in use and is therefore contingent on use, on practice. Exchange value is likewise "realized" only in the act of exchange and is likewise, if more obviously, contingent, as fluctuations in the stock market demonstrate. Language contributes to the evaluation/value for use and/or exchange of labor and entities, thereby troubling not only what counts as labor—that is, what is given the value of being recognized as labor by being called "labor"—but (thereby) also its value (or lack thereof) in relation to other phenomena also designated "labor."

The value of the work of composition, like the value of any other work, is thus contingent on language—or, to be more precise, language practices. At least some of the efforts discussed in chapter 1 to rename or add other terms to "composition" as a "field" or discipline (*rhetoric*, *multimodality*, *American studies*, *cultural rhetoric*, etc.) evince language practices aimed at changing the recognized value of the work being named. Such practices, I have argued, in attempting to affiliate composition with these other fields, accept dominant valuations of these and, therefore, implicitly accept dominant valuations of composition itself as lacking, in need of these others. (Note that none of the other fields attempt to add "composition" to their names to increase their perceived value.) That is to say that such moves evince an acceptance of dominant frameworks even in their efforts to change the valuation of composition, thereby reinforcing, rather than escaping from, the terms set by the dominant responsible for its devaluation in the first place.

Chapter 1 focused on efforts to rename, add to, or leave composition. Here, focusing on dominant WPA discourse and what I will call here the discourse of unionism, I examine similar moves in efforts to change the valuation of specific kinds of work within the purview of Composition: the work of WPAs, teachers, and (by implication) students. My argument is that in the claims they make for the value of this work, dominant WPA discourse and a discourse of unionism[1] contribute to the debasement of their work by effectively acceding to dominant terms of valuation by which that work must be judged negatively. In so doing they (unsurprisingly) contribute to its continuing denigration: the seemingly inevitable angst of the WPA and the poor working conditions of composition teachers so prevalent in colleges and universities across North America.

I begin by examining confusions in the kinds of value accorded work in composition and the role of commodification in the valuation of that work. I then show the operation of these confusions in specific arguments for the value of work in composition: the Council of Writing Program Administrators' position statement "Evaluating the Intellectual Work of Writing Administration," and recent exchanges in composition forums about labor relations in composition. The discourses in these, I argue, participate in commodifications of the work of composition that operate to the detriment of its value in the economies in which those commodities circulate. They do so by occluding the labor involved in the realization of the value of that work, distorting and undercutting its demands and its potential as work both within and on the social.

I then turn to consideration of WPAs' brokering of the value of that work in the current context of the free-market fundamentalism of so-called "fast" capitalism manifested in the privatization and commodification of education as part of the move to a "knowledge" or "information" economy, and in demands for efficiency in the global communication of goods, services, and knowledge, efficiency often attributed to reliance on a standardized English as the "lingua franca" for communication. Arguments to broker a superior "brand" (to) composition as an alternative to commodification of work in composition, I argue, conflate commodification with a specific, fordist, mode of production, thereby acceding to post-fordist, fast-capitalist valuations of composition work complicit with its denigration. As an alternative, I argue for attending to the local points of "friction" necessary to global movement to pose terms for exchange in which the constitutive role of labor is recognized.

Work, Labor, and Value

Arguments for the value of the work of WPAs, composition teachers, and students are frequently marred by confusing the various forms of exchange and use values to be realized from that work, and neglecting the contingent nature of any potential value itself. The relationship between the value of each type of work is also confused by how the relationship between types of work itself is defined: how the work of the WPA is understood to be related to the work of teaching composition (and vice versa), how the work of teaching composition is understood to be related to the work of students (and vice versa), and how the value of each form of work is understood to be related to the value of the other. Central to any discussion of the value of work is the concept of commodification. Labor is commodified when the value of the product of that labor is identified as an objective property of the product itself (Marx, *Capital, I* 153–54). In this identification, the concrete labor involved in producing the value is largely occluded. Ordinarily, this is understood to mean that the labor of those who appear to be most directly involved in the making of a product—the labor of steel mill workers, say, in making steel, or coal miners in mining coal—is not given its due; instead, the difference between the value of these workers' labor and the price at which the product is sold is "realized"—that is, taken—by the capitalist as profit. Hence the workers are said to be exploited by the capitalist.

Without discounting the real exploitation of workers in this manner, such exploitation is not all there is to commodification. While such exploitation occludes some of the value of the labor of those involved in producing the commodity—again, say, steel or coal—the use value of that commodity itself is realized through a host of concrete labor practices. The "value" of a computer, for example, at least according to most of those seeking one, can be realized only under particular conditions: reliable electrical and telecommunication infrastructure, a mass of individuals with training in computers, a demand for the kinds of information that computers are "equipped" to store and produce, and so on. While it's certain that the workers involved in making computer hardware and software are exploited, the labor occluded through commodification of the computer includes not only their labor but the labor of all those involved in the practices responsible for the value of computers: for the infrastructure, the training, a society that believes it needs the kind of information that can be stored and generated only by computers, and so on. Through commodification, the entire material social process by which particular values are realized is occluded.[2] It is in this sense that commodification denies the full social materiality of work. And it is in this sense that dominant WPA discourse and dominant discourse on unionism participate in the commodification of the work of composition.

The participation of dominant WPA discourse in this commodification takes two forms distinguished by the particular economy of value in which the discourse is exercised. Within the economy of academic positions of hiring, tenure, and promotion, in which scholarly work carries greater exchange value than forms of work deemed "service" or "teaching," WPA work is defined as valuable insofar as it is "intellectual." Within the larger social economies of tuition revenue and marketable skills, the value of WPA work and, along with it the value of the work of teaching composition, is defined in terms of the tuition earned through writing programs and the marketable skills that writing programs ostensibly produce. Student work is valued only in what circulates in the economy of credits and grades. What links these despite their differences is their occlusion of the social materiality of the work: the location of that work in and the dependence of its value on specific concrete labor practices and material social conditions. And insofar as WPA work, like the work of teaching composition generally and the work of student composition, is located more undeniably in such practices and conditions, discourses that claim value for that work in terms of its distance from these inevitably put those involved in that work at a disadvantage in comparison to those who can more credibly deny the materiality of their work.

The Value of Composition Work as "Intellectual"

We can see examples of this first form of valuation in the document "Evaluating the Intellectual Work of Writing Administration," a position statement (hereafter "Evaluating") of the Council of Writing Program Administrators. "Evaluating" is not aimed at countering the ways in which the academic work of writing program administrators is commonly evaluated. Instead, as its title suggests, it accepts that only forms of work that can in some fashion be identified as "intellectual" ought to be rewarded. The question it addresses, therefore, is how to make the work of WPAs more readily recognizable as "intellectual" so that those evaluating WPA work can better determine its worth within the academic economy, what the document tellingly identifies as "the system of academic judgments and rewards we are all familiar with." As it states,

> Our concern in this document is to present a framework by which writing administration can be seen as scholarly work and therefore subject to the same kinds of evaluation as other forms of disciplinary production, such as books, articles, and reviews. (n.p.)

What is needed, it is thought, is not a change in the dominant terms of valuation but a better translation of WPA work into those terms.

The problem WPAs face, according to the authors of "Evaluating," is that WPA work does not appear in the forms that most academics recognize as evidence of scholarship: university press books, refereed journal articles. Instead, it resembles too closely forms of work that have come to be recognized as "service," which has little to no exchange value within the academic institution's economy of faculty status and rewards. To illustrate this problem, they present several hypothetical cases of junior tenure-line English faculty.

In their hypothetical example of Assistant Professor Mary C., literary scholar and poet, Mary's work—"refereed articles, poems in magazines with good literary reputations, and a book with a major university press"—is understood to be "the production of specific commodities—albeit scholarly commodities—with a clear exchange value, perhaps not on the general market but certainly in academic institutions" ("Evaluating" n.p.). By contrast, in their hypothetical example case of Cheryl W., overworked assistant professor and writing program administrator, many of Cheryl's department colleagues

> are not sure that she has been doing "real work." Others, who think her efforts have been valuable to the department, have difficulty specifying her accomplishments other than stating that "she has done an excellent job running the writing program." ("Evaluating" n.p.)

What Cheryl must do, the authors of "Evaluating" state, is demonstrate the intellectual value of her work to distinguish it from service, which is assumed to be evidence not of intellectual value but of professional citizenship, "doing good"—that is to say, the labor of maintaining and shaping social relations, seen as not labor at all insofar as the productive force of social relations is denied. To help Cheryl and others facing similar predicaments, the authors of "Evaluating," drawing largely on the 1996 report of the MLA Commission on Professional Service document "Making Faculty Work Visible" and Ernest Boyer's *Scholarship Reconsidered: Priorities of the Professoriate*, suggest that work ordinarily recognized as mere "service" can nonetheless be recognized "as part of scholarship if it derives from and is reinforced by scholarly knowledge and disciplinary understanding" ("Evaluating" n.p.). Thus, rather than attempting to challenge the current terms of the academic economy that understands scholarship, teaching, and service as distinct, "Evaluating," like "Making Faculty Work Visible" and Boyer's argument, retains dominant terms of evaluation but argues that scholarship can be recognized in forms other than the traditional ones of the book or research article. It does so by applying the criteria by which the traditional forms of scholarship are evaluated to forms that WPA work typically takes. Such work is deemed intellectual, the authors of "Evaluating" explain, "when it meets two tests. First, it needs to advance knowledge—its production, clarification, connection, reinterpretation, or application. Second, it results in products or activities that can be evaluated by others."

Thus "Evaluating" participates in treating the work of both Mary and Cheryl (and, as well, Mary and Cheryl themselves) as commodities.

It does so by removing "their" work from the full material social process of which it is a part and renaming it, or attempting to rename it, as "theirs": products they produce by themselves, and whose value is inherent in the products, with "intellectual" used to distinguish these as work—or, rather, "works"—from its/their location in the material social process. In the hypothetical case of Mary, for example, it ignores Mary's possible course releases and grants, access to libraries and research assistance, and the entire industry of literary scholarship—journals, institutional subscriptions, English departments—within which Mary's work is possible and takes on meaning and particular value. If we were to view Mary's curriculum vitae, it would be apparent that Mary understandably (like all her colleagues) claims as her own accomplishments work that in fact she alone could not accomplish or even conceive of attempting.

The difficulty Cheryl faces in making similar claims about the work in which she engages is that its location in the material social process—like most work identified as "service" work in the academy—is far more difficult to elide. The authors of "Evaluating" identify five categories of characteristic WPA work—program creation, curricular design, faculty development, program assessment and evaluation, and program-related textual production—and they recommend that the WPA "create a portfolio that reflects her or his scholarly and intellectual accomplishments as an administrator." But this presumes that such accomplishments can be identifiable as the administrator's own—as commodities that the WPA herself has produced. In practice, however, WPA work is virtually impossible to claim as a set of individual accomplishments. The authors of "Evaluating" invoke what they term the "intellectual character" of this work to mark it as commodifiable. Such work, they argue, "can be considered as part of scholarship if it derives from and is reinforced by scholarly knowledge and disciplinary understanding" ("Evaluating" n.p.). It is scholarly, that is, insofar as it is derives from scholarship as ordinarily recognized, already understood as the sort of commodity "produced" by the likes of Mary C.

It is difficult, however, to argue that WPA work has an "intellectual" character that can distinguish it in this way from the work of academic "professional citizenship." In saying this, I am not adopting the anti-intellectual position of claiming that scholarship has nothing to contribute to the work of WPAs. It does, and all writing programs can benefit from such scholarship (I discuss the relation of scholarship to such work in chapter 5). Instead, I am saying that such scholarship is only one of several factors that shape the "accomplishments" that WPAs might otherwise wish to claim as their own, as "products." This is, of course, true of all scholarship. However, (1) it is more readily recognizable as true of WPA work, and (2) most academics have a vested interest in recognizing the "social" character of WPA work and refusing to recognize its "intellectual" character. WPA work, like "women's" work, appears to be more "shared" (and therefore somehow less real) than other work, when, indeed, it is recognized as work at all.

For example, the work of faculty development and program creation by definition requires contributions from multiple individuals and institutional units. As the authors of "Evaluating" acknowledge, "Staff development cannot be accomplished by fiat. Instructors cannot simply be ordered and coerced, no matter how subordinate their position within the university." The authors argue that the success of staff development depends primarily on "the degree to which those being administered value and respect the writing administrator," which they take to result from the ability of the WPA to "incorporate current research and theory into the training" and to "demonstrate that knowledge through both word and deed." But there is no reason to believe that staff value and respect WPAs strictly as a result of their assessment of the WPA's knowledge of current research and theory. Typically, staff members are not in a position to recognize, let alone evaluate, the WPA's command of this knowledge. Like the "periphery" scholars described by Canagarajah, they commonly lack access to the resources necessary to make such evaluations, most obviously time. What they might recognize as "new research and theory" may well be anything but (Canagarajah, "Nondiscursive"). Further, as typically overworked staff, they may have a vested interest in rejecting a WPA's attempts to introduce programmatic changes informed by such research and theory when it means significant disruptions to their practices, even if they were in a position to recognize or even value them as "new." But in any event, as "staff" they lack by definition the institutional status of being experts whose recognition would confer value on the WPA's knowledge. Whatever knowledge staff may possess as practitioners of teaching composition is likely to count for little in the economy of academic work—typically not as knowledge at all—because it does not take forms recognized *as* knowledge within that economy.

Moreover, much of the work of staff and faculty development that the authors of "Evaluating" identify has little to do with "knowledge of current research and theory." For example, providing "financial support for staff activities in course design, pedagogical development, and research" is typically not within the WPA's control alone, nor does it require particular scholarly knowledge (certainly not as ordinarily conceived). It requires, instead, at the very least a supportive dean or provost. Thus, whether or not a WPA succeeds in providing such support is difficult to identify as either the WPA's own responsibility or an intellectual accomplishment. Similarly, "maintain[ing] an atmosphere of openness and support for the development and sharing of effective teaching ideas and curricular emphases . . . [and] open lines of communication among administrators, support staff, and faculty; etc.," which the authors of "Evaluating" identify as necessary to staff development, may require particular skills, but not any reified scholarly knowledge of composition. And insofar as communication is, by definition, two way, whether or not the "lines" are "open" is not something for which the WPA alone can be held responsible, for praise or blame.

The authors of "Evaluating" themselves allude to this in some of their comments. For example, while stressing that "program creation" ought to be informed by "significant disciplinary knowledge, a national perspective that takes into account the successes and failures of other composition programs, and a combined practical and theoretical understanding of learning theory, the composing process, the philosophy of composition, rhetorical theory, etc.," they also acknowledge that often writing programs fail simply "on the basis of budget and ideology." While the authors claim as well that programs fail because of a lack of "scholarly foundation," there is no reason to believe that this is the case. Writing programs that defy the disciplinary knowledge of composition can be highly "successful" (and vice versa): it depends on how failure and success are measured (and by whom), which returns us to issues of "budget and ideology" (see Scott, "Politics").

More significantly, in their attempt to claim the intellectual character of WPA work, the authors of "Evaluating" inevitably reveal both the (often unrecognized) intellectual character of all work and its social materiality. We can see hints of this in their nervousness about distinguishing some textual production from others as somehow more "intellectual." "Clearly," they insist, "boundaries must be set; not every memo, descriptive comment, or teaching evaluation embodies the concept of intellectual work." But as work in literacy studies and everyday cognition has shown, it's not at all clear how to determine the degree to which a text might or might not embody intellectual work. Moreover, as literacy scholarship has also demonstrated, if "the concept of intellectual work" includes the concept of individual authorship, then no writing can fully embody that concept insofar as all literacy is a "social" rather than "individual" achievement (see Scribner). And the kinds of documents identified in "Evaluating" as typical of WPAs—course syllabi, funding proposals, statements of teaching philosophy, resource materials for staff—are notoriously collaborative in authorship, texts of the program rather than the WPA him- or herself.

The authors' nervousness about setting boundaries is understandable, since such boundaries are necessary for maintaining the ideological division between physical and intellectual labor serving class and gender interests by designating some labor as more intellectual, and hence "higher" in worth, than others, and therefore more deserving of status and rewards.[3] The authors' concern for how WPAs can claim as commodities all those activities which are demonstrably not the product of the individual WPA alone is understandable in light of the requirement for individual WPAs to make such claims in order to continue their employment: the authors want to help create a more "level" playing field for the real-life counterparts to their hypothetical cases of junior tenure-line faculty. They acknowledge that "activities other than research and teaching . . . have little exchange value, no matter how highly they might be valued on an individual basis by fellow faculty, by administrators, or society"; hence they attempt to show ways by which exchange value might nonetheless be conferred on these activities by redefining them from being "service" to being "scholarship" in light of their "intellectual" character. In doing so, however, they overlook the threat that their claims for the intellectuality of what is ordinarily deemed "service" work pose to the interests responsible for the designation of such work as service to begin with and that such designations continue to serve. By inadvertently calling attention to the productive force of social relations generally in academic work, the authors of "Evaluating" reveal the limitations in the rules of the game being played on the field of tenure and promotion. In short, the fact that colleagues have difficulty recognizing WPA work as "real," (that is) "intellectual," and therefore "worthy of recognition and reward" is not simply a matter of unintended ignorance to be addressed through communication but the manifestation of an ideological perspective serving particular interests—here, the colleagues' interest in denying the location of all academic work, including the colleagues' "own" work, in the material social realm and thus dependent on material social conditions that WPA work, like the composition programs they administer, makes possible. Like dominant culture's pairing of its praise for wives and mothers with a refusal to recognize what they do as work or as contributions to the work ascribed to others (for example, husbands), faculty's inevitable coupling of their inevitable expressions of gratitude to WPAs with a firm denial of the intellectual value of WPA work is ideological, an interested withholding of recognition and value, a textbook case of Bourdieuian misrecognition.

The Value of Composition Work as Skills Production

There are two alternative strategies by which the value of the work of composition—both the work of the WPA and the work of teaching composition—is sometimes pursued. First, instead of calling on terms of evaluation operating among faculty, in which faculty are judged according to their production of (abstract) knowledge, the work of composition is claimed to have value insofar as it produces not only tuition dollars for the institution (as a "cash cow") but also skills (in students) for society. WPAs in particular are often tempted to justify their programs in these terms. For example, both composition teachers and WPAs might argue that composition teachers deserve higher pay in light of the crucial importance (to the university and society at large) of the writing skills they impart. As John Trimbur has noted, composition studies was in one sense one of the few beneficiaries of the 1975 national hue and cry about a putative "literacy crisis" heralded by "Why Johnny Can't Write" (Trimbur, "Literacy"; see also Faigley, *Fragments*). Like those lined up, following Sputnik, with hands open for funding to fight communism by teaching French, compositionists could argue that the usefulness of their work to the nation merited better funding.

However, as shown by feminist critiques of composition (and mothering and housework), the current salaries of many CEOs, and truck drivers' wages, as well as the current poor working conditions and status of composition teachers, there is no one-to-one correspondence between recognized "usefulness," social status, and pay (see Holbrook, S. Miller, Schell, Tuell). To argue that composition teachers somehow deserve better pay in light of the importance of their work is to assume that, in general, such a correspondence exists—to assume that CEO salaries are the mathematical expression of the vital character of their particular contributions to society, for example—and that there has simply been a miscalculation that has resulted in composition teachers' abysmal working conditions. In other words, such arguments are based on two confusions regarding value. First, they confuse exchange value—the value accorded a commodity on the "market"—with use value. This ignores the fact that exchange value is conferred through and contingent on recognition, and hence is ideological. Second, such arguments participate in the commodification of the use value of an activity (here, teaching composition) that by definition occludes the role of labor and the material social process in the realization of that value. They do so by claiming that composition teaching does in fact impart objective "skills" that will have the same use wherever they are employed. However, as scholarship has shown, it is difficult to identify, let alone teach, general writing skills (see Petraglia, and discussion in chapter 1), and thus common for students who appear to do well in learning to write in particular ways for composition courses to have trouble, at least initially, when faced with novel writing tasks (for example, writing in an unfamiliar genre or about an unfamiliar topic or for an unfamiliar audience). Writing skills—like "language" skills, are an ongoing social accomplishment rather than a stable, transferable possession (see chapter 2). Those claiming that composition instruction, properly funded, will produce student-citizens armed with the necessary writing skills are thus asking instructors to be judged according to their ability to produce something that, in fact, they are not in a position to produce. The cycles of complaints about a writing crisis (usually accompanied by strident complaints about the poor quality of writing instruction), followed by pleas for greater funding, followed by complaints about the futility of "throwing money at problems," followed by a writing crisis, evince this problem. Such arguments and the cycle of crises/pleas/complaints are also likely to spawn calls for more efficient means of producing these putative writing skills—through use of online outsourcing of grading, for example, or "MOOCs" (massive open online courses) (see, for example, Banocy-Payne, Pearson, Smarthinking). Within institutions, moreover, such claims contribute to the low status of composition as mere preparatory "service" work supposedly more properly the task of high schools or, at best, two-year colleges. For according to the terms of the academy's economy of status and rewards, composition's ostensible economic exchange value of writing skills undermines its cultural exchange value—again, as the ongoing, and long, history of low status and poor pay for writing instruction attests.

Ethics and the Value of Composition Work

A second strategy for arguing for the value of composition work alternative to either its intellectual character or the usefulness on the job market of the commodities it is supposed to produce is the argument of justice. Arguments adopting this strategy are found in both a discourse of unionism and WPA discourse. At their worst, such arguments sacrifice historical accuracy and effectivity for a patina of moral righteousness and outrage, as in some of the rhetoric of "abolition" and its characterizations of WPAs as "boss" compositionist overseers of an enslaved labor force (see, for example, Sledd), and in arguments that herald teacher unions as the end solution to, rather than a strategy for addressing, the problem of poor working conditions (cf. Rhoades, "Afterword"), along with other social injustices—hence a discourse not so much about, for, and of unions but simply of unionism. While at their best, some of the arguments for justice engage in the kind of crucial utopian thinking that forwards the struggle for that justice, typically, in making the case for what should be, these arguments neglect details of the concrete reality that is. Invoking the discourse of ethics, in short, denies the operation of material history and concrete labor in the pursuit of ethical achievement.

To highlight these problems, let me focus on three exchanges: the exchange over (and including) Marc Bousquet's essay "Composition as Management Science"; the collection (edited by Bousquet and others) *Tenured Bosses and Disposable Teachers: Writing Instruction in the Managed University*; and a series of summer 2005 postings on the WPA-L listserv about "Work load, vacation time, and course release." Bousquet's essay, which appeared in somewhat different forms in *JAC*, the *Minnesota Review*, and as the lead chapter of *Tenured Bosses and Disposable Teachers*, prompted a variety of responses both in a subsequent issue of *JAC* and on the WPA-Listserv, as well as elsewhere (see Grabill et al.; Harris, "Behind"; Horner, Review; O'Neill). For the purpose of my argument here, what is most salient about the exchange surrounding Bousquet's essay is the disjunction between the appeal to justice in light of a utopian vision of what should be and a concern with immediate and historical specificity. Briefly, I read Bousquet to be arguing against a "managerial" discourse in composition because of its paternalistic treatment of composition teachers, and to be arguing for an organization of composition programs in which a collective of composition teachers with the right to collective bargaining and tenure would determine collaboratively the composition curriculum.

On its face, it is difficult to argue against such positions: paternalistic treatment is at best ethically suspect, the right of all workers to collective bargaining should be honored, and collaborative decision-making about matters such as curriculum sounds ideal. And to my knowledge, none of the critics of Bousquet's essay argue for paternalism as an ethically sound arrangement nor against collective bargaining or collaborative decision-making. Instead, they fault Bousquet for drawing inaccurate comparisons between past labor history and current labor conditions for composition teachers (Harris, "Behind Blue" 892), for ignoring the role of English departments, and especially literature faculty, in contributing to those conditions (O'Neill 908–11), and for being naïve about how a collective comprised of current composition instructors might work in practice (O'Neill 912). In short, they fault Bousquet for failing to ground his argument fully in the past and ongoing history of composition. While Bousquet's argument identifies what, ideally, a writing program might be like, it is idealist*ic* in imagining how to get "Toward a University without a WPA" by failing to recognize the point(s) from which those who work in composition, in whatever capacity, might be coming (see Harris, "Behind Blue" 895). For example, while a collective of teachers determining the composition curriculum in collaborative fashion might sound good in theory, it's difficult to see how to get there from here very fast in a way that would not lead to a seriously problematic curriculum (on this possibility, see Lipson and Voorheis 123–25). And while Bousquet's argument deplores the paternalism of WPAs toward composition teachers, paternalism toward students—to the extent that students are acknowledged at all—goes unchallenged, and their labor unrecognized.

The very poverty of the conditions in which most adjunct composition teachers work that is lamented by both Bousquet and his critics means that those teachers do not have the resources of time, space, leisure, or access to scholarship to make decisions responsibly about composition curricula. For example, in "Teaching Writing in a Managed Environment," Eric Marshall reports that despite being a wholly unprepared and inexperienced graduate student, he was assigned to teach two basic writing courses for subliving wages, no health care, and no office space in which to conduct mandatory office hours (Marshall; see also McConnel). A collective comprised of instructors similarly situated would be ill equipped to design or revise curricula. In light of the fact that at least some WPAs are equally ill equipped to undertake such work (see, for example, William Vaughn's "I Was an Adjunct Administrator" and Roskelly), the presence of tenure-line WPAs with at least some training and knowledge in composition and provided with some material support to enable them to undertake such work is an encouraging sign rather than a step to be lamented, evidence of some recognition of the fact that teaching requires knowledge that can result only with sufficient resources of time, training, access.

Katie Malcolm's recent account of the success she and her colleague Holly Gilman had redesigning the composition program at a community college in the Pacific Northwest is illustrative in this regard. Both Malcolm and Gilman were part-time instructors. However, thanks to a Title III grant, their own graduate education in composition, and the decision of their college dean to assign these two instructors to somehow improve the retention and pass rates of the college's "remedial" students, the two were able to eliminate the college's existing noncredit composition courses and thereby improve the students' retention and pass rates and (not coincidentally) the curriculum from a "skills" curriculum to one focused on reading and writing as material social practices (Malcolm). But it's clear that "their" success was possible only as a result of having adequate time, funding, and training to undertake such work. Arguments that otherwise show great awareness of the limitations ordinarily imposed by current working conditions on composition teachers which then advocate assigning tasks like curriculum design to those working under such conditions deny, ironically, the conditions necessary to carry out such tasks.

Such arguments operate in concert with more common arguments about collective bargaining that focus almost exclusively on questions of hourly wages and job security. These arguments, rehearsing dominant trends in U.S. labor, end up ceding much of the control over concrete work activities by foregrounding only some aspects of the materiality of their work (see Luke 309–10). By focusing almost exclusively on questions of hours and pay, they leave unquestioned, and contribute to, the commodification of work: all work, no matter by whom, comes to be viewed as having equivalent value: an hour's work for an hour's pay, no matter the worker or the material social specificities of that hour's activities. In so doing, such arguments leave open the possibility of an enormous and growing population of competitors, as illustrated by the recent devaluation of public school teachers, and public schools, and the competition for more "efficient" private schools.[4]

A comparable neglect of the specificities of material social history is evident in some of the unionist discourse invoked in some of the chapters of the collection *Tenured Bosses* (as well as elsewhere). That neglect appears to have prompted Gary Rhoades, in his afterword to that collection, to warn that in many of the chapters unionization is posed as the answer to the current challenges faced by those who work in composition, rather than as a strategy, "the contested beginning of an exploration, and a means to an end, not an ending, or an end in itself" (Rhoades, "Afterword" 264). Such discourse elides the long and ongoing history of labor relations and collective bargaining in the United States as well as elsewhere, most remarkably the history of unionizing K-12 teachers, invoking such histories if at all in general and consequently unhelpful or misleading ways. (For notable exceptions, see Godley and Trainor; Hendricks; Luke; Rhoades, *Managed*). That history (and those histories) would surely prompt legitimate questions, not simply about what is morally right, but what might be effective (or ineffective) strategically, for workers in composition to attempt, and effective at what: a discourse on unions, rather than a discourse of unionism. After all, the history of unions in the United States is replete with false starts, missteps, cooptation, divisiveness, and corruption as well as radical successes in democratizing workplaces and society, improving the lives and working conditions of workers, and educating the public. It may well be, as Bill Hendricks argues, that unions are "the single most important instrument that composition teachers and other workers have to effect social justice" (84). But as Hendricks also observes, even "when they are working right, faculty unions are a pain in the ass" (91). Unionizing of the academic workplace is in itself not the solution but rather the name given to a set of strategies that must themselves be continuously, laboriously, even painfully (re)worked in pursuing social justice.

Hendricks's salutary acknowledgment of the concrete work of unions is lost in the discourse of unionism, which settles for the language of the political rally: statements of personal belief; statements of utopian vision couched as demands; rhetorical questions. We learn, for instance, at the end of Christopher Carter's chapter of *Tenured Bosses* that "in [his] view, the dignity of composition work . . . depends on the collective organization and mutual support of labor, not management" (191). Paul Lauter concludes "From Adelphi to Enron—and Back" with the stirring call, "What is necessary now . . . is a thorough-going critique of the damaging influence of corporate culture on higher education in America" (79). Ruth Kiefson ends her chapter with a series of demands aimed at building "a movement that can ultimately transform society" (149). However inspiring, such rhetoric necessarily begs all manner of questions about movement building, the use of critique, and how to engineer and recognize collective organization and the mutual support of labor. Instead, "collective organization," "labor," "mutual support," "critique," and "movement" are invoked as fetishes: "autonomous figures endowed with a life of their own, which enter into relations both with each other and with the human race" (Marx, *Capital, I* 164–65). The labor of creating (and revising, and recreating, and revising) a movement, forms of mutual support, and critiques is thus elided, as is the need for the material conditions supporting engagement in such labor (for exceptions, see Jacobsohn, Tingle and Kirscht). And insofar as that labor is elided, its value is rendered nil, replaced by the exchange value of the commodity in the economy of more and less ethical statements. In place of critique, a movement, collective organization, and mutual support, or useful studies of what these might involve, we get "critique," "movement," "collective organization," "mutual support."

And finally, in such discourse, dominant definitions of labor in composition, and dominant distinctions between labor and the students on whom that labor is directed, remain firmly in place. Students are at best presented as the clients of the labor of those whose interests are to be advanced (or, more often, vessels for the products of that labor), rather than participants in and contributors to that labor. Ironically, this cuts off a significant population of those with as strong a stake in the working conditions of composition teachers as the teachers themselves—those who also do its work, but whose work goes unrecognized—here, by "labor."

A series of posts on the WPA-Listserv on the subject "Work load, vacation time, and course release" (originally "news alert"), and related postings on the same listserv on the subject "hours per week," demonstrates the pervasiveness of many of these confusions about how to value the work of composition. While the series began as an alert about a PBS documentary on working conditions in colleges (*Declining by Degrees*), it quickly shifted to discussions of the average number of hours per week academics spend working in comparison to the rewards they receive (and don't) for that work, the forms of support for that work (such as summers "off" and course releases), and the "fairness" of these arrangements. While the postings included a number of useful references to studies on faculty workloads and thoughtful commentary on the nature, rewards, and problems of academic work, the terms of debate operating in the postings largely reiterated valuations of work in terms of hours spent and the "difficulty" of the work performed. Complaints about the injustice of inadequate compensation and unreal expectations for academic work (of being a WPA, an academic, a composition teacher) were met with admonishments about the injustice of inadequate compensation and working conditions for others and with acknowledgments that the reward that the pleasure of engaging in work that these writers find intellectually stimulating and ethically important compensates, to some extent, for the lack of financial rewards and status that this same work earns.

Some of the writers point to limitations in the arguments being made. For example, Deb Morton expresses concern that her acknowledgment that having a life where "thinking, intellectual conversation, learning, and service are valued" works as "a trade off" of sorts could be used "to justify why academics SHOULD work more hours than others." Marcy Bauman, after questioning the number of hours academics might realistically be working or expected to work, warns that this focus on hours worked is itself deleterious. As she explains,

> We've got to be *realistic* about what we do. I think there's a mythology floating around that says that we have to justify our jobs by saying that we put in really long hours—partly to counter the prevailing winds in our culture that say that teachers have it easy. But if we keep saying, "No we don't; we work really long hours and produce produce produce!" we contribute to *another* myth—the

> one that says that pre-tenure people can be *expected* to work long hours, be incredibly prolific researchers, and excellent teachers to boot. We are participating in, and perpetuating, the very conditions that make our lives crazy. (Bauman)

Bauman here suggests the entrapment of much of the discourse on the valuation of labor in terms that, in her words, "make our lives crazy." In dominant discourse of work and value, work is valued because it is "hard"—somehow requiring extra effort (in the form of training, genius, hours, effort)—or because it produces greater goods, or more goods more efficiently. It is within and according to that discourse—the discourse of meritocracy and free-market ideology—that CEOs are said to "earn" (that is, merit) more than their employees, "hard" workers more than slackers, celebrities more than unknown amateurs. While what is recognized as "difficult" and "good" is largely, if not wholly, contingent on dominant interests, appeals for recognizing the goodness and difficulty of work that does not conform to those interests allows the ideological character of any such recognitions to go unchallenged. Thus, complaints about the culture's failure to recognize the goodness and difficulty of composition work ultimately appear closer to laments about the nature of things than challenges to what just seems natural.

I have been arguing that discourse within composition studies about the value of work in composition has colluded in the debasement of both WPA work and the work of teaching composition in the terms by which that work is claimed to have value. Invocations of the "intellectual" character of WPA work (or, for that matter, the work of teaching composition), its production of "skills," its difficulty (by whatever measure), or the injustices endured by its workers treat the work of composition as a commodity even in the attention it gives to the "workers." It does so by accepting a linear model of production that begins with the workers and proceeds to the consumption of the product of their work: here, the students, the schools, and society. That model occludes the full material social process of production. In that process, social relations constitute a productive force, and consumption of the "product" of the work of composition, rather than occurring after its production, is present in the production process from the "start."

While negotiations for the improvement of working conditions for composition may make small gains within the terms of such discourse, they are equally likely to lead to further debasements of that work: for example, as we've seen in discourse on K-12 education, demands for greater efficiencies (through outsourcing), more accountability, evidence of more "satisfied" student "consumers," competition for even cheaper labor ("what the market will bear"). This is not to deny the concrete use values to be realized in particular circumstances from heralding the exchange value within certain economies (in terms of institutional efficiencies, student satisfaction, and the like) of particular changes to working conditions (for example, lower class sizes, better pay and job security for adjuncts, course releases for curriculum development) for the production of particular commodities (writing skills, tuition revenue). Good things can and often do happen when small groups of students led by trained, dedicated, and well-paid instructors are afforded sufficient time and other resources to engage seriously in projects of writing, reading, reflection, and rewriting, often despite the claims made about the value of such work. I am arguing, however, that different projects can be pursued, and different values can be accorded those projects, that are more in keeping with what we know about writing and reading as material social practices, and thus ultimately are more integral to our identities as teacherscholars of composition and more justifiable to the students with whom we work, than the terms in which the value of work in composition is so often defined. Redefining the work of composition in a way that acknowledged that work as an activity that involves all its participants—students as well as teachers, WPAs, and untold others working both within and on the social through what and how they write, reflect on their writing, and revise—would be a step toward a more accurate, just, and intellectually honest assessment of its real and potential value.

Brokering the Value of Composition

Thus far in this chapter, my references to "the social"—as in the statement just preceding this—do not locate the social in space or time except in the most general sense. That is, I've invoked the social as a theoretical concept to elucidate its role as a productive force generally. But from the cultural materialist perspective I am attempting to advance, theoretical concepts must also always be understood in terms of their material instantiations, in other words, *as* material. And this requires locating concepts such as "the social" in time and space. It follows that understanding contemporary valuations of the work of composition requires locating those valuations in the larger context of free-market fundamentalism and so-called "fast" capitalism, manifested in the privatization and commodification of education as part of the move to a "knowledge" or "information" economy, and in demands for efficiency in the global communication of goods, services, and knowledge, efficiency often attributed to reliance on a standardized English as the "lingua franca" for communication.

In the United States, negotiating the valuation of the work of composition falls most directly, though not exclusively, on WPAs in their positioning as brokers of the value of that work. Not only are WPAs the ones, at large and medium-sized U.S. research universities, public and private, responsible for the design and management of the programs of first-year undergraduate composition, and all those who teach and all those students who take courses in the programs—in most schools, virtually the entire undergraduate student population. Because of the size of composition programs at research universities and the dominant role those types of institutions play in the popular imaginary of U.S. higher education, it is WPAs who have led those managing such programs to take center stage in discussions of composition writ large: what any one such WPA decides, and what happens to any one WPA, not only can and does have effects on significant numbers of composition teachers, courses, and students in one fell swoop at a particular institution but also has repercussions felt beyond the WPA's specific institution, as stories of these events circulate over listservs, at conferences, and in the scholarly literature. It is thus that scholarship on, by, and for these WPAs dominates the field of composition studies in its representations of and for the work of those teaching and taking composition courses despite the fact that the majority of actual composition teaching in the U.S. takes place not at large research universities but, instead, at other types of institutions (two-year "community" colleges and small and mid-sized colleges and universities) (see Gladstein and Regaignon). While WPAs are monolithic in neither their thinking nor their practices, and represent at best a dominant, not total, force in composition, as a dominant group their work has significance beyond the institutions where individual

WPAs work (hence Dobrin's devotion of an entire chapter to WPAs in *Postcomposition*). That said, from a broader perspective, WPAs are best understood as what Bourdieu has identified as the dominated of the dominant—in subordinate position to larger material social forces. The work WPAs do is, in other words, shaped by and responds to changes to the larger economic and cultural landscape, changes that increasingly pressure higher education to be "transparent," "efficient," and "accountable" and to compete not just nationally but internationally. While much of the work of WPAs has always consisted of "brokering" writing and its learning and teaching, increases in the speed and scope of the flow of capital and labor associated with current globalizing of communication technologies, the market economy, and its concomitant privatization and commodification of all aspects of education, including knowledge work in English, mandates that WPAs take into account the global context in which their brokering is conducted in order to resist those effects of globalizing that further threaten the value of the work of writing and its learning and teaching.

WPAs work as "brokers" in the sense of being "intermediaries" or "middlemen," mediating between the work conducted in the programs they direct and the demands made on that work. As Geoffrey Chase warns in an essay appearing in a popular collection intended as a sourcebook for new as well as experienced WPAs,

> WPAs have the unenviable task of serving many constituents [faculty and instructors within the writing program, department colleagues, colleagues from other departments, department chairs, other university administrators, students, and parents], all of whom have different perceptions, and often contradictory expectations, about the aims and goals of composition. Meeting [their] expectations and demands . . . and serving as a mediator between these many stakeholders are both critical and stressful. (243)

In a model he proposes for analyzing how best to address this task, Chase warns that WPAs must understand "local [institutional] conditions," achieve "internal coherence" within the program being directed, and insure that the program also has "external relevance," advising that WPAs "must become spokespersons for writing who are able both to listen carefully to external expectations and to articulate clearly how those expectations might better line up with internal program goals" (246). In this sense, WPAs' brokering also includes the work of interpretation, as they explain the relationship, or "line up," between what might seem to be competing, even contradictory, expectations. In Joyce Kinkead and Jeanne Simpson's contribution to the same collection, they advise WPAs to prepare for this work of interpretation by learning how to "'talk the talk'" of "admin-speak" by mastering the acronyms it uses to name the currency of school administrative budgeting (such as FTEs [full-time equivalents] and SCHs [student credit hours]) as well as administrators' preferred genres of proposals and bulleted memoranda and the intricacies of institutional governance (68 and passim; see also Schwalm, "Writing" 16–22). Similarly, in his contribution to the same collection, Doug Hesse provides WPAs with a guide to organizations and publications that are likely to be contributing to these administrators' thinking so that WPAs' own ideas for their programs can appear more likely to be "fitting" to the worlds in which these administrators move (311 and passim).

Such discourse locates WPA brokering at three sites: (1) within the program directed by the WPA, as WPAs mediate courses and course sections within their programs; (2) within the local academic institutional site, as WPAs broker the relationship between their program and the various other administrative units comprising their home institutions (for example, in struggles for funding and program control); and (3) within the network of other postsecondary institutions with which the WPA's home institution has relationships, including other colleges and universities with which the WPA's school has articulation agreements. However, brokering also occurs, and increasingly so, within a fourth, much larger spectrum of private and public schools and testing services. As David Schwalm warns new WPAs in his essay for the same collection,

> You must recognize that your institution is not totally independent. Students constantly move back and forth among institutions. . . . Your campus will be involved with other universities, colleges, and community colleges in statewide (if not national) "articulation agreements" that govern the transfer of courses from one campus to another. . . . Because first-year composition is the course most frequently transferred from one institution to another you will need to become very familiar with the transfer processes and the procedures whereby

> course equivalences are established. You must be willing to work collegially with faculty from other institutions (and other kinds of institutions) to conduct the business of articulation. . . . Similarly, you will be involved in determining how your institution handles credit earned through advanced placement, international baccalaureate, CLEP, or other test-based sources of credit. ("Writing" 15)

Though Schwalm identifies this network as extending only nationally, the privatization and commodification of all aspects of education affiliated with the current globalizing of the market economy mandates that this brokering network now be understood as extending globally—at the very least, for example, involving the traffic and exchange of academic credit and students globally as postsecondary schools compete for international status, students, and funding (see Ziguras, Raduntz).

In a study of the work of "literacy brokers" in the production of English-medium scholarly texts by central and eastern European scholars—such as the scholars' peers, copy editors and translators, and nonprofessionals offering informal support to the scholars—Theresa Lillis and Mary Curry note that such literacy brokering is constrained by particular power relations not only at the individual and institutional but also geohistorical levels (29–30), including those power relations "privileging English-center literacy and rhetorical practices and the differential power relations between center-periphery relations regarding knowledge production" (30). For example, in the process of brokering the production and publication of these central and eastern European scholars' texts in English-medium international journals, brokers were in a position to make significant changes to the knowledge claims made by the scholars, even to the point of redefining claims as constituting confirmation of existing knowledge rather than new contributions to knowledge (Lillis and Curry 30).

While WPAs do not work as literacy brokers in quite the same way, their brokering of the work of the writing and learning and teaching of writing conducted in their programs is likewise constrained by such power relations. Perhaps most obviously, the globalizing of the market economy has increased the demand for a standardizing of English—Lillis and Curry's "privileging of English-center literacy and rhetorical practices"—but also the commodification of the "skill" in producing this standardized written English as the new "lingua franca" of global commerce, and for the commodification of the skill of instructing students in this skill (see Lu, "Essay"). Insofar as universities are now charged with producing knowledge workers with this skill, and with insuring the standardization of English as a means to efficient communication of information as well as goods and services, then WPAs broker these as well.

WPA brokering thus involves them as not just mediators and interpreters but also retailers of commodities. They have to broker commodifications of both writing and the teaching of writing at the local institutional level and oversee the exchange of these in the marketplace of academic courses and credits in the negotiation of articulation agreements with other schools regarding course and credit transfer, arguing for specific terms for the exchange of these as "equivalent" commodities. Recalling that in commodity fetishism "the commodity reflects the social characteristics of men's own labour as objective characteristics of the products of labour themselves" (Marx *Capital, I* 164–65), WPAs engage in commodity fetishism insofar as they occlude the concrete labor involved in producing particular values in writing—the concrete labor of readers and writers and the social relations necessary to the production of such values—and instead treat writing abstractly as having in itself particular values irrespective of the work of readers, writers, or the social relations in which the writing is produced. Likewise, the work of teaching and learning writing is fetishized insofar as the value of such work is treated as independent of the social characteristics of the concrete labor of those involved. With the "marketization" of education, as Helen Raduntz observes, "the knowledge of educators is commodified and packaged," "because capitalist forms of exchange cannot deal with quality education nor with social, ethical, or equity concerns . . . [but] only with quantifiable 'things' as commodities" (242). In the case of the teaching and learning of writing this fetishizing manifests in the transformation of the concrete labor practices of a particular writing course involving specific students and instructors into units of abstract labor, or academic credit, with exchange value within the economy of academic credits and graduation requirements within and outside the WPA's institution, and, simultaneously, into the production of units of abstract skills of writing (say, for example, the skill of "effective" argumentation, treated as universally applicable) for exchange in the globalized job market.

Eliding the "social characteristics" of the concrete labor involved in the work of both writing and the teaching of writing through commodification of these as abstract skills exchangeable on the marketplace occludes the arbitrary and contingent character of the valuations of those commodities. More problematically, it occludes the demands of fast capitalism in the production of such valuations: the demand for writing that is clear (to all) and (thus) efficient in its communication of knowledge globally. This occlusion takes place even in efforts to intervene in market valuations of compositional work.

For example, Keith Rhodes has proposed "branding" composition as a way to redefine the value of that work from dominant valuations of composition as, say, mere error correction (Rhodes, "You Are"; see also Rhodes, "Marketing"). In light of the achievement of such brands as Nike and Starbucks (to which we can all add other examples), Rhodes argues that the Council of Writing Program Administrators (CWPA) should develop a CWPA brand for composition that, like Nike and Starbucks, establishes a benchmark for composition generally. Asserting that "we know that we have a good 'product'" and that "our brand 'sells' once people understand it" (71), he argues that establishing a CWPA brand for the "product" of composition would improve composition generally. Claiming that "Starbucks has raised the average level of coffee quality by raising the competitive bar on coffee quality and increasing the desire for better coffee," he concludes that "[a] good writing brand should do the same for composition" (72).

Rhodes wants to avoid claiming commodity status for composition, cautioning that "CWPA writing instruction would never be a stable thing like 'grammar' or 'process'" (75). Instead, it would seem that the CWPA brand would function something like the *Good Housekeeping* seal of approval—just as, to use Rhodes's example, the Nike brand stands not so much for "shoes or equipment but instead . . . a constantly evolving focus on performance" (75). In line with this, the "CWPA" brand would ideally, for Rhodes,

> say more about a commitment to ethics, evidence, and a faith in the largeness of writing, properly conceived, than about, say, rhetorical analysis and grammar in context. The details might change; the promise that it is the best available version of something vital would not. (75)

As suggested by Rhodes's advocacy of "branding" and, in his earlier essay "Marketing Composition for the 21st Century," Total Quality Management (TQM), he ends up heralding as an alternative to commodification of writing and its teaching a fast-capitalist mode of production—an "alternative," in other words, fully aligned with dominant neoliberal ideology directed at maintaining loyalty not to a generic product (for example, coffee) but a brand and all it represents (Starbucks). The confusion arises in part through his conflation of commodification with fordist production, against which post-fordist modes of production seem to offer an escape. We can see this confusion in Rhodes's claim, for example, that the brand version represents a demonstrably "better" product than the generic version (in other words, Starbucks coffee is somehow "better" than, well, just coffee, just as Dove soap is somehow better than plain soap, or Kleenex better than other brands of facial tissue). This overlooks the ways in which branding, and brand consumption, are now linked far more with lifestyle and social identity than with the ostensible use value of the product itself (coffee, soap, facial tissue). Starbucks, after all, represents not simply a brew of coffee but an experience, an attitude, a lifestyle, and above all a set of values (cleanliness, speed, emotionally cool taste, individual choice, blending of work and leisure) infusing every sip.

Such arguments overlook, most obviously, the ideological production of definitions of "better" to distinguish coffee, sporting goods, cars, or writing instruction. So, for example, the TQM that Rhodes advocates for its "empowerment of those actually doing the work, and a focus on processes, not error correction, as the key to better products" ("Marketing" 51) takes as a given what the products made by "those actually doing the work" might be better *for*—what values, beliefs, interests, social relations, and material conditions they might both require and advance (cf. Gee et al.). And when Rhodes argues that composition can offer the "sleek, powerful, versatile, high-tech higher education" that "the Boyer Commission and its local counterparts are looking for" ("Marketing" 58), he fails to question the values, beliefs, interests, social relations and material conditions that might account for why that commission and its counterparts are looking for just such a form of higher education as opposed to some other form of higher education advancing other values, beliefs, interests, social relations, and material conditions. This is not to deny arguments that—according to some set of beliefs, values, and material social conditions—any one form of these might be "better" at doing something for some people. Rather, it is to insist on the contingent character of such valuations: the restriction of their currency to being "local" in the sense of being located in material social history. Branding is meant to deny that local character (Starbucks is always everywhere). Rhodes's argument that "when we do good work locally, we should not just do it; we should market it" ("You Are" 73) is aligned with such a denial.

Such valuations overlook what Anna Lowenhaupt Tsing, in her critique of dominant, fast-capitalist models of global exchange, calls the necessity of "friction" in any exchange. For any kind of movement, she explains, friction is in fact necessary, yet it is neglected in fast-capitalist ideology's accounts of the "fluidity" of capital. In the case of writing, we can identify this friction in the concrete labor readers and writers necessarily engage in of "translating" any material instantiations of writing, in English or any other language, into various meanings (see Pennycook "English"; my discussion of Tsing, chapter 3). Against representations of reading and writing as neutral and friction-free conduits of fixed meanings, writing (and reading) are social practices in which the friction of difference and resistance are crucial contributors to the production of meaning. Likewise, teaching (and learning), far from representing the neutral and friction-free transmission of fixed skills—whether deemed "mechanical" or more "advanced," "rhetorical" skills—constitutes a site of necessary friction as meanings and skills are continually reworked through the concrete labor of teachers and students.[5]

In brokering exchanges of commodified skills of writing English and its teaching, WPAs neglect the role of such friction in the production of writing and reading and thereby risk earning the more unsavory meanings that have attached to "brokers" as being not just "middlemen" and "retailers" but procurers, pimps, and panders: those who prey on weakness by pretending to offer, or treat, what they know are not commodities as if they were (see *OED*). After all, WPAs have known for some time now that, as Susan Miller put it back in 1991, "good" writing

> is the result of established cultural privileging mechanisms, not of pure "taste,". . . . that a mixture of ideas, timing, entitlements, and luck have designated some rather than others as "important" writers/thinkers. . . . [that] [t]he field's most productive methods of

> evaluation also judge writing by situational rather than by universal standards. (*Textual* 187)

WPAs bring their knowledge of what Miller refers to as "the arbitrariness of evaluations [of writing] and their relativity to particular power structures" (*Textual* 187) to their brokering of the value of writing and its learning and teaching. However, brokering the value of writing and its learning and teaching as commodities belies the contingent character of the value of what is offered (and the necessity of the concrete labor of "translation" in any act of reading and writing and the "translation" of specific practices of reading and writing that teaching and learning involve). Such brokering allows the operation of such power relations in conferring value on writing and its teaching to go unopposed, with deleterious effects to both the achievement of internal program coherence and the working conditions for composition instructors.

The pervasive reliance on exploited labor for composition instruction is illustrative in this regard. A number of critics, of course, have articulated the ways that dominant gender, class, and race ideologies have contributed to the continuation of composition's exploitative labor practices (see, for example, S. Miller, "Feminization"; Schell; Strickland; Tuell; Horner, *Terms* 1–18, 146–47). But the privatization of postsecondary education and the development of communication technologies for "delivery" of such education in keeping with the globalizing market economy add to the pressure on institutions, and by implication WPAs, to accommodate such ideologies (see Raduntz, Ziguras). Schooling is no longer seen as a "public" but a "private" good, with the consequence that less and less public funding is made available for schooling. Schools faced with less and less public funding are forced to look for ways to cut costs. Institutions' efforts to cut costs work in concert with ideologies that have long denigrated the teaching of composition as "women's work" undeserving of pay to demand more and more of composition teachers in exchange for less and less. (The privatization of the costs of teachers' health care and retirement, of course, furthers this deterioration of working conditions.) The privatization of postsecondary education has also led to an increase in the number of "for-profit" schools and the development of "distance learning" schools.[6] As Schwalm warns WPAs further, "You will also be among the first who will have to address the transfer of a whole range of courses delivered via technology by a range of mysterious providers" ("Writing" 15). Most traditional colleges and universities must now compete with these "mysterious providers" for not only students but their tuition dollars as well as other funding, increasing pressure on them to pay less to composition instructors (who for ideological reasons have less cultural and social capital with which to resist such treatment) and to search for ways to "outsource" this work elsewhere to achieve even greater cost savings (see Dingo et al., Jaschik, Rai). In short, globalizing of the market economy encourages institutions to view composition instructors as so much "flexible" labor, as indicated by the various terms used to name those now responsible for the majority of postsecondary composition instruction—"adjunct," "temporary," "part-time," "contingent."

I am arguing that both the treatment of composition instructors as "flexible" and the treatment of the work of composition courses as the production of commodities constitute responses to the same pressures of a globalized market economy for efficiency in the production of English writing skills understood as a commodity for information communication. To the extent that composition courses at any university are treated as readily exchangeable for composition courses at any other, then those teaching these courses can be drawn from anywhere, and are thus in competition with their peers anywhere (again, see Dingo et al., Jaschik, Rai), so long as they are imagined to have the equivalent skills. It is inconsequential from this perspective whether the commodity in question is a generic skill—as in "general writing skills" with ostensibly universal transferability—or a "brand." Here Rhodes's blindness to the profit interests underlying TQM and fast-capitalist marketing of brands rather than products is illustrative: post-fordist modes of production have introduced and exacerbated, rather than resisted, the casualization of labor, as the contracts of those working at franchises under such brands as Starbucks, McDonalds, Nike, etc. illustrate.[7]

I am suggesting that globalization of the market economy encourages both the degeneration of courses in the first-year composition curriculum into efforts at the ostensible production of skills easily exchangeable in the marketplace of academic credits and general education requirements and, concomitantly, the denigration of those involved in its teaching as just as easily exchangeable in the buyer's market for composition instructors. The valuation of each is contingent on the valuation of the other; neoliberal free-market fundamentalism's demand for efficiency (often couched in terms of accountability) works to ensure the devaluation of both. Of course, while this is justified in terms of "flexibility," as Zygmunt Bauman explains, the "flexibility" on the demand side requires a different kind of flexibility from the supply side of the labor market:

> Flexibility on the demand side, rebounds on all those cast on the supply side as hard, cruel, impregnable and unassailable fate: jobs come and go, they vanish as soon as they appeared, they are cut in pieces and withdrawn without notice while the rules of the hiring/firing game change without warning and there is little the job-holders and job-seekers may do to stop the see-saw. (*Globalization* 104–5)

The interdependence of curriculum and labor practices in composition programs is mediated within dominant WPA discourse through various forms of professional development to achieve what is identified as program "coherence." Program coherence is often defined in terms of consistency in instruction, assessment procedures, and goals. Instructors are expected to teach all sections of each course in the same way, pursue the same goals, and assess student writing similarly, and different courses within the program are expected to work in concert toward similar goals. Three of the components Chase identifies as necessary to achieving internal program coherence are "common goals specific and detailed enough to be meaningful and useful," "common assignments," and "standard methods for evaluation and assessment across multiple sections" (245). Miller and Cripps's account of Rutgers' writing program (discussed in chapter 3) is illustrative. The concern of their program, they state,

> is not to convert any of its teachers to its method; it does demand, though, a practical adherence to its pedagogy during the term of employment. Consistency in the number and type of writing assignments across all sections of the program's writing courses, consistency in pedagogical approach, and consistency in the application of the shared evaluative criteria are all that is required. These three consistencies make it possible to provide over ten thousand students each year with a common learning experience in their writing classes. (137)

Those failing to demonstrate such practical adherence are judged to be inflexible but, fortunately, easily replaced. A similar consistency to achieve program coherence was pursued at the institution where I once served as writing program director. At that time and under my "direction," teachers of first-year composition (consisting by default strictly of TAs and contingent instructors) were warned that they must "Follow the curriculum and syllabus approved for the course" and "Use texts approved for the course" ("Responsibilities"). Such consistency was achieved through various forms of instructor mentoring and assessment. For example, at that institution, course coordinators and I oversaw a barrage of institutionalized procedures to ensure that only the approved curricula and texts were used, and that they were used in consistent ways. These procedures included extensive orientation meetings, mentoring, portfolio assessment, teaching observations, and teaching evaluation instruments. Similarly, Miller and Cripps report that the Rutgers program employs a "highly elaborated program" of orientation, mentoring, midterm and end-of-term folder review sessions to ensure "oversight and quality control" (139).

Frequently, however, such internal program coherence is seen as both vital and yet in competition with the need to claim "external relevance" to the department and university communities within which the composition programs are housed and the public at large. Goals that might be "meaningful and useful" to students, teachers, and WPAs might not be perceived as such by others, nor might the "standard methods for evaluation"—hence the need Chase identifies for WPAs to become "spokespersons for writing" (246). But in light of the pressures to commodify writing and writing instruction as uniform skills for exchange in a globalized market, it is not surprising that WPAs feel pressured to redefine the common goals for their programs in terms of teaching such skills, valued in such terms. Unfortunately, however, as I have been suggesting, to do so achieves a false coherence through commodification of the work of teaching composition that contributes to its denigration, undermining WPAs' own efforts and contributing to the denigration of composition instructors. WPAs yielding to such pressure end up defending claims about their courses that they know belie the complexity of writing and the contingent character of any writing's value, and that in fact undermine their efforts to improve the working conditions of instructors in their programs. Brokering that implicitly accepts a commodified notion of teaching and writing skills puts composition instructors in global competition with one another for jobs "producing" a commodity: writing skills. The poor working conditions resulting from the ensuing race to the bottom then reinforce the difficulty of achieving the program coherence that is sought. For insofar as exploited labor tends to be unreliable—those exploited tending, not surprisingly, either to resist efforts to control their labor or to be unable, as a consequence of their exploited condition, to meet demands made of them—creating or maintaining "coherence" in a writing program staffed with exploited labor eminently "flexible" in light of their ostensible ability to produce the commodity of skilled writing is largely an ongoing exercise in futility—hence the "feeling of disappointment" among WPAs that has become a phenomenon worthy of scholarly investigation (see Micciche). WPAs find themselves in the position of having to broker what they know to be degraded and degrading: the production of ostensible "skills" in what is termed "human capital" by those working under degrading working conditions. The treatment of instructors as embodiments of the commodities of abstract teaching skills belies the need for professional development—why, after all, should instructors in possession of these skills need to reacquire them? Consequently, WPAs are hard pressed to justify the expense involved in providing the orientation and mentoring that they know the concrete labor of teaching writing in fact requires.

Of course, there is now a raft of scholarship documenting and posing ways to combat the practice of relying heavily on adjunct instructors and GTAs to staff composition courses at cut-rate pay and few or no benefits, including calls to abolish the first-year composition requirement, unionize composition teachers, and enforce standards for instructor pay and benefits set forth by such professional organizations as MLA and CCCC (see, for example, Bousquet et al., Crowley, Schell and Stock). But while in much of this literature the effects of the globalizing of the market economy on postsecondary education generally are acknowledged (see, for example, Bousquet et al., Downing et al., Ohmann, Introduction xxxvii ff.), accounts of WPAs' responses to what I have been identifying as effects of the globalizing of market economies are typically couched in terms of "local" institutional solutions, understood not in dialectical relation to those globalizing forces or as contingent but rather in ranked relation—a discrete set of phenomena and conditions to which WPAs must perforce adapt. In other words, despite the pervasiveness of similar conditions at a multitude of institutional settings, which suggests the operation of forces beyond the local institutional site and the interaction between these other forces and local conditions, WPAs describe their responses as developing "local" solutions that address what are defined as purely "local" rather than "globalizing" conditions, and they warn against imagining solutions that would respond to these conditions in ways that define them as, in fact, anything other than "local."

For example, in a model Chase offers for "examining the complex relationships that determine the day-to-day practices in our composition programs . . . for writing throughout our colleges and universities," Chase emphasizes the need to "think about the *local conditions* at our institutions" (244, emphasis in original). He defines these as "those features of our colleges and universities that make our institutions *distinct* from each other. Budgets, teaching loads, requirements, building design, pay scales, computer availability, and the students themselves" (244–45, emphasis added). While he acknowledges that "at times, it may seem that because there are general statements we can make about higher education, all our campuses are essentially the same," he asserts that, in fact, "this is, obviously, not the case and we would be wise as we pursue changes in our program to focus on these *differences* [between campuses] and how *local conditions* shape the programs and opportunities at our schools" (245, emphasis added). Regarding his own program's solutions to the problem it faced when it was clear "additional resources were not going to be pumped into the [writing] program to alleviate pressures caused by increasing enrollment," he warns, "It is unrealistic and unwise to assume that what works effectively on one campus is well suited to another campus without local adaptation" (251). Miller and Cripps go further. While the conditions they contended with at Rutgers closely mirror those Chase describes at his institution and those at countless others—increased enrollments, no improved budgetary climate and thus no increase in faculty lines and virtually complete reliance on TAs and part-timers to teach burgeoning numbers of sections of first-year composition—on the question of who teaches first-year writing courses, they conclude, "We think that this question can only be answered locally" (138), arguing that the answer to that question

> is determined not only by the local WPA's philosophical, pedagogical, and political commitments, but also by a host of [local] variables entirely beyond the local WPA's control; the pool of possible applicants in the region; the home institution's history with writing instruction; the financial well-being of the home institution; and

who happens to be department chair, area dean, and provost at any given moment. (123)

There is, of course, a genuine, practical logic to such a focus on the "local"—understood as one's own institutional conditions. For, to be sure, there are, after all, significant differences as well as similarities in the local conditions obtaining at different institutions, including those at Chase's school and Miller and Cripps's school. Moreover, WPAs need to know the "local" institutional landscape of people, procedures, and policies in order to do their work. Knowing a dean's quirks, or a local institutional funding possibility, or loopholes in hiring procedures, as well as the specific instructors and the students at that institution can be crucial in enabling a WPA to maintain and improve the strength of the program he or she is "administering." At the same time, such a "practical" response is also susceptible to defining the local in limited ways and thus limiting the scope of actions to solutions that work only within rather than also against those economic forces producing or exacerbating the problems in the first place with which the WPA, here significantly imagined as working solo, contends.

In short, the practical logic that dictates attending strictly to the specific institutional conditions obtaining at one's particular location—conditions WPAs would of course be foolish to ignore—can also encourage a kind of fatalism that allows the widespread prevalence of those conditions to continue: here, to accede to "globalism's" insistence that There Is No Alternative to the global hegemony of neoliberal market fundamentalism (see Beck 9, Ramonet). As Raymond Williams, writing on the term "realistic," observes, "'Let's be realistic' probably more often means 'let us accept the limits of this situation' (*limits* meaning *hard facts*, often of power or money in their existing and established forms)" (*Keywords* 217–18, emphasis in original). Chase and Miller and Cripps, for example, all seem to accept as givens that enrollments are up, budgets for public schooling are down, only TAs and adjuncts can be persuaded to teach composition, and no collective resistance to these current practices is possible. Why enrollments are up, funding is down, and WPAs are being expected to hire instructors only from "the pool of possible applicants in the region" remains unchallenged. In attempting to understand and explain what is to be done, at least at their institutions, here and now, WPAs' attention is diverted from both why it is that these conditions currently seem to prevail generally as well as immediately at their individual institutions, and how they might be improved. And while WPAs' immediate concern is understandably likely to be with what is to be done, well, immediately (and locally) within their institutional setting, that focus can mute not only questions, but also answers, addressing the larger forces producing these questions.

Alternatively, WPAs, composition instructors, and their students can examine the relationship between the institutional conditions in which they find themselves locally and the pressures globally to acquire the skill of producing "standard written English" as quickly and cheaply as possible, for example, with the results of burgeoning enrollments, exploited teaching labor, heavy student debt, and so on, and they can develop responses, if not solutions, to those problems that resist these pressures in meaningful ways that do more than simply adapt to them. We can see a move toward finding goals that are meaningful in terms other than skills exchange or branding and that potentially address the relationship between local institutional conditions and the global in the fourth component Chase identifies as crucial to achieving internal program coherence: "a commitment to examining and discussing these shared features [of common goals, assignments, and methods for evaluation and assessment] openly," as in the decision at his institution to focus the first-year writing course on the themes of environmental sustainability (Chase 246, 249). Such a decision would make it possible for students and teachers to identify and pursue writing practices, needs, and interests routinely devalued by, and potentially resisting, effects of global capitalism.

WPAs might then argue for the need to hire only those instructors who have a sensitivity to and thus can contribute to such practices. Those instructors would be hired not because they possessed the "minimum qualifications" for teaching commodified writing skills or allegiance to serving a brand ethos but because the concerns they would bring to their teaching might have the potential to advance the understanding of writing and what writers might accomplish in addressing effects of fast capitalism unrecognized—unrecognizable, even—within its ideology. In other words, if, as David Harvey observes, "it is important for capital that new skills emerge . . . which allow for flexibility and adaptability and, above all, for *substitutability*—that are non-monopolizable" (109), then WPAs can interfere with capital by insisting that their programs require teachers with skills that are in fact not substitutable and *are* monopolizable.

These examples suggest that WPAs' articulations of the value of composition courses in their brokering need not simply "line up with" the commodification of knowledge work and its workers and the privatization of education, imagined now as necessary only to individuals' private portfolios of marketable skills, to meet with what the likes of Boyer commissions currently demand, in the private and public sectors. Instead, in their brokering, WPAs might articulate the value of the courses in their programs in terms that resist tendencies toward the commodification of writing and the learning and teaching of writing while being responsive both to WPAs' own understanding of that work and to effects of globalization—for example, environmental destruction—unacknowledged within the ideology of global capitalism. It does not follow from the literature challenging the legitimacy of the teaching of "general writing skills" either that required first-year composition courses should be abolished or that some other set of "skills" or branding should be offered in their place. It does, however, mean that some other value for them must be articulated (see Bazerman, "Response"; Horner, *Terms* 54–57, 127–33).

In chapter 3, I've suggested one alternative that responds to challenges to the standardizing of English and linguistic imperialism which are themselves brought on by globalizing of the market economy and which might better enable WPAs to achieve program coherence without colluding with exploitative labor practices in their hiring of instructors. Globalizing of the market economy has led not only to demands for a standardized English "lingua franca" but also to challenges to the monolithic view of standard written English by the burgeoning number of Englishes and the increasing awareness of the complex power relations involved in the negotiation of differences among Englishes and between English and other languages in writing. WPAs might use such challenges in conjunction with the knowledge they have of the contingencies of the value of any writing with any language to argue for a universal first-year composition requirement, not on the basis that these courses will give students (and certify them as possessing) some general and readily exchangeable writing skills on the global job market (for example, the ability to produce "Standard Written English"), but by arguing that the complexity of writing and the role of power relations in judgments about it, the shifting nature and burgeoning multiplicity of written forms of English(es), the growing need for translation between Englishes as well as between Englishes and other languages, and the pervasiveness of literacy in a globalized world merit some of the attention of all undergraduate students for sixteen or thirty-two weeks—something like arguments for why students should learn world history, or the arts.

In other words, composition courses might be the site for explicitly negotiating conflicts between definitions of writing and its value by specific language users, on one hand, and global market fundamentalists, on the other, both thematically and practically, in the writing produced, activating students' and teachers' sense of the importance of writing practices and interests devalued by global capitalism. (For accounts of related pedagogies, see Canagarajah, "Place"; Horner and Lu, "Resisting"; T. Scott, *Dangerous*). And, of course, WPAs might design their programs and train instructors in ways that are in accord with such a conceptualization of the value of their programs. By the same token, WPAs directing such programs, faced with the task of evaluating whether or not courses from elsewhere might "transfer" as equivalent to composition courses at their home institutions, could legitimately reject, say, the equivalence of courses that do not seem to address writing in ways that honor that complexity. For such courses, however valuable in many respects, would conceive of the value of writing, and thus a writing course, differently, and not at all equivalent to the value of the writing courses offered in the WPA's program. Thus, rather than attempting a kind of universally applicable brand of composition, whether "CWPA" or otherwise, as Rhodes suggests (which private-sector entities no doubt are already competing in avidly marketing), or settling for offering a false, fordist equivalent of generic writing skills, as composition programs are commonly charged with producing, we might highlight the specific, local values produced through compositional work by specific teachers and students.

How might articulating the value of writing program courses in terms other than writing skills affect the valuation accorded those teaching them? First, insofar as the writing program is not valued simply as one site among and in competition with many others for the production of abstracted "general writing skills," then those teaching in the program would not so easily be exchanged for, and in competition with, others teaching at those other sites. Even within the terms of capitalist "free-market" logic/ideology, greater job security and pay would thus be merited for these teachers. Secondly, insofar as composition programs were not assigned the dubious task of "skills instruction" but of teaching about a subject—writing—whose nature is complex, whose valuation is politically and socially contingent, and consequently whose study is even more complex, the teaching of writing would be less susceptible to ideologies that denigrate such work—which is to say, echoing my discussion in chapter 3, that WPAs who make such different claims about the value of their program would face strong opposition from others, including some within their ranks, who insist on making more traditional ascriptions of the value of their programs, just as they would face opposition from those within and outside their institutions claiming "equivalency" between very different types of composition courses. The "collegiality" that Schwalm calls for between WPAs at different institutions might thus be strained.

Thirdly, in a program that imagined its subject in more complex ways than in a program offering to do no more than teach "general writing skills," usually denigrated as "the basics," or to carry a brand of its commitment to "quality" writing, there would be a more likely recognition of the need for initial and ongoing professional development and training for those teaching the program's courses, not at developing skills understood as abstract units that individuals either do or don't "possess" but at exploring the specific issues pursued.[8] For example, qualifications for teachers to be sensitive and able to contribute to the study of differences in writing and the negotiation of global as well as local language relations in confronting these differences, and to engage their students in such study and negotiation, would justify a demand for greater support for initiating instructors to the program and keeping them, unlike what most "freeway flyers" report experiencing in moving from school to school. There would be greater reliance on veterans to the program because of their knowledge of and experience in teaching its particular focus, and greater need for giving instructors continued opportunities for professional development in the form of course reductions, travel to conferences, and the like to further instructors' own study of differences in writing. Thus a program defining itself in such ways would be able to justify demanding not only such qualifications from its instructors but the improved working conditions of job security and opportunities for professional development that would further instructors' ability to do the work demanded of them in their teaching.

In making hiring decisions, such a program would not exclude instructors from around the world nor seek them out as cheap competition for local labor. Instead, it would value their input differently. For example, while a more traditional composition program might question the qualifications of an instructor for whom English is a second language to teach standardized English writing skills, a program that recognizes and takes as its charge addressing the complexity of English(es) globally would view such an instructor as at least potentially bringing valuable insights on what it might mean to write "in English" to the program, let alone that instructor's potential insights into the challenges of translating between languages and the power relations involved in all of these issues. WPAs might argue for the need to hire only those instructors, or a pool of instructors, who have a sensitivity to and thus can contribute to the study of differences and changes in writing, and in writing in English, and to give those instructors working conditions of pay, teaching load, benefits, and opportunities for professional development making it possible for them to study and teach such matters—in other words, on the basis of curriculum.

* * *

I have argued that much of the normal "brokering" work WPAs are called upon to do is at odds with WPAs' own understanding of the nature of writing and its teaching and assessment, and that normal practice works in collusion with the globalizing of the market economy that tends to the denigration of composition courses and those who teach them by participating in the commodification and privatization of the work of composition—writing, English, and its learning and teaching. At the same time, I am suggesting that WPAs might heed other effects of the globalizing of the market economy, such as recognition of writing differences and power relations operating in the mediation of those differences, in their design of composition courses and in their brokering—in hiring, training, supervising, and pleading on behalf of those involved in the teaching of these courses. The challenges of being a WPA are often treated as a balancing act: WPAs attempt to address different audiences with different demands, and to speak the language appropriate to each, all under unpromising conditions, and hoping all the while that no one will notice the difference and subterfuge (see George). While it would be foolhardy, in light of the extreme circumstances prevailing at some institutions, to deny the need for such balancing, and even subterfuge, I'm suggesting that WPAs can achieve a more coherent balance and redeem their reputation as brokers and simultaneously the work they broker by mediating the work of writing and the learning and teaching of writing on terms that address more directly the contradictions of globalization and the necessary friction of the labor of reading and writing as meaning production rather than communication commodity. WPAs can in their brokering resist the forces of privatization and commodification of writing and its learning and teaching while drawing on the challenges posed by differences with and within writing English that global capitalism has itself unleashed.

WPAs, the teachers and programs they "administer," and the students in the courses they "direct" are all engaged inevitably in the struggle over and for (re)production of the value of writing and its teaching and learning. Language is the terrain on which that struggle takes place. Dominant approaches attempt to occlude the concrete labor of that ongoing struggle through reification of writing and its value—abstracting from that labor a skill or set of skills and abilities, and a value to these. That occlusion contributes to the ongoing denigration of all involved in that labor through elision of their contributions to writing and its value and to the elision of the contingent character of that value. Efforts to substitute alternative reifications of these further rather than break with that process, accepting dominant frameworks for understanding both writing and its valuation.

There remains, of course, a different framework of valuation dominant within the academic realm, if increasingly residual in the larger culture: the value of what is termed (academic) disciplinary knowledge. That is, there exists within the academic economy a set of terms of valuation different than, and often at odds with, the terms of valuation circulating outside the academy (which inevitably infringe on, shape, and respond to academic terms of valuation). Within that academic framework, work is assigned value in terms of its contribution to the "discipline" through production of "disciplinary" or "subject" knowledge. One way of accounting (*sic*) for the low academic institutional standing of composition is in terms of its lack of disciplinary status, or (alternatively) its status as a strictly "applied" (hence "impure") discipline (like education), hence its failure to produce the kind of knowledge carrying value within that economy. Against such a valuation stands a large and growing body of scholarship on composition and, more broadly, writing and literacy generally. In chapter 1, I have taken up some of the limitations of moves to improve the status of composition through extending the reach of its disciplinary definition by renaming it "writing studies" or adding to it terms such as *rhetoric*, *multimodal*, etc., focusing especially on the location of work in composition within the terrain of competing disciplinary fields. In chapter 5, I return to a consideration of such efforts, but now from the perspective of the conditions of production, reception, and circulation of that knowledge within the global economy of knowledge production, and the very different terms of value and exchange those conditions do and might make it possible to negotiate.

5. *Discipline*

Knowledge exists only in the instance of its knowing. This is true even in the case of knowledge embedded in objects, in Marx's sense of "General Intellect," for objects in themselves know nothing. It is only through engagement in specific, learned practices with those objects that the knowledge thought to inhere in them is activated or "released."[1] Thus the value of knowledge is preeminently use value, to be realized only in use, and use, of course, requires labor. Attempts to commodify knowledge must therefore gloss over the contradiction between claims to the inherent, stable, portable value of knowledge as commodity and the location of the realization of knowledge in time and space as practice—in other words, the dependence for the realization of knowledge on the labor of knowing. While this contradiction is an attribute of all commodification, it is more undeniably evident in knowledge (a seemingly immaterial entity) as a consequence of its social character and its inevitable transformation through its articulation—what "I know" is only realized, and simultaneously transformed, as I articulate it to you and is also always necessarily transformed in the act of your (re)articulation and realization—in every act of "our knowing," by translating, what it is (we say) "we know." The mediation of knowledge through its rearticulation in language in the labor of reading and writing, speaking and listening, participates centrally in that transformation.[2]

As a "teaching subject" focused on language, composition is ideally situated to bring out the contradictions in knowledge commodification. Composition gets into trouble, as it does, not when it brings out such contradictions but, rather, when, in pursuit of professional academic disciplinary status, it accedes to commodifications of the knowledge of composition itself through claims to that knowledge as a discrete entity (in the form of skills and subject knowledge) that it produces, possesses (owns), maintains, and distributes through research on and training in writing and its teaching.

In what follows, I first review ways by which pursuit of academic disciplinary status accedes to such commodification before considering the alternative: a return to and insistence on the always-emergent character of composition knowledge. In line with arguments presented in previous chapters of this book, I will argue here that pursuit of academic disciplinarity all too often accedes to terms of exchange set by dominant culture—both dominant academic institutional culture for granting the status of academic disciplinarity and the broader culture of professionalism—terms by which the exchange value of composition knowledge is necessarily low. Composition's alignment with the language ideology of monolingualism exacerbates this consequence not only, and not merely, by excluding from consideration writing in languages other than English but by adhering to an impoverished conception of the work of writing English that guarantees the low status of composition within the terms set in the academic institutional economy for defining professional academic disciplinarity. Against such efforts I will pose an aim for disciplinary work in composition simultaneously more "ordinary" and more radical in its openness to and engagement with knowledge in composition as the ongoing product of labor.

Academic Disciplinarity and the Professionalization of Composition

Contemporary academic disciplinarity represents a form of professionalization that attempts to trade on the exchange value of commodifications of knowledge. In keeping with this, arguments for the value of composition knowledge are typically couched as arguments for the professionalization of composition—for composition as a professional academic disciplinary field of knowledge with all the rights and privileges that members of such a field expect to enjoy. As James Slevin has put it,

> Composition wants to become a discipline; those of us who study writers and how they learn want to be recognized as a distinct discipline of research. And we want the teaching of our discipline, because it is a recognized discipline and so among the ranks of

the privileged, to be taken seriously and rewarded appropriately. ("Disciplining" 155)

Academic disciplinarity, however, has a complicated relationship to professionalization.[3] On the one hand, academic disciplines can be understood as professions insofar as, like (other) professions, they have succeeded in establishing themselves as the keepers and owners of bodies of esoteric knowledge whose benefits members bestow on the public in a disinterested fashion, with claims to expertise in that knowledge and a commitment to its deployment for the public good, and with, therefore, the assigned exclusive right to control training in that knowledge and its deployment (see Slevin, "Disciplining" 155). What distinguishes academic disciplines as *academic* professions is the professed commitment of their members not only to the deployment of esoteric knowledge, but also to the field of knowledge itself—to preserving, testing, and, when necessary, revising that knowledge for "the good of the field." Teaching is among the primary points at which academic disciplinary professions' commitment to the field of knowledge intersects with their commitment to disseminating the benefits of that knowledge to the public, with the twist that the benefits to be disseminated are understood to be the knowledge itself. As Slevin further observes, "The activity of passing on important knowledge and nurturing in a new generation the powers that enable such knowledge may in and of itself reasonably constitute what the term 'discipline' means" ("Disciplining" 156).

Insofar as the professional commitment of members of an academic discipline to the field of knowledge itself is recognized as necessary to the general public good (however tenuous and uncertain the relationship of that knowledge to the public good may seem to be), academic disciplinary professionals are paid not fees for specific services to specific clients—as are physicians, lawyers, engineers, and accountants—but through salaries, tenure, academic freedom.[4] In exchange for caring for and improving the knowledge of their fields, members of academic disciplinary professions are granted monopoly rights over their knowledge and access to membership, relative freedom in their concrete labor practices, and the material means to carry out those practices.

From a traditional labor standpoint, professionalization is also, of course, a strategy by which to improve working conditions by gaining control over who does what kind of work how and at what cost. Workers establish and maintain professional status (think the medical and legal professions and the "skilled" trades) by claiming a stable, esoteric subject knowledge for which there appears to be a public need; a "professional" commitment by members to distributing that knowledge in the service of the public; and the right to regulate who is licensed as members of the profession—control exercised through an elaborated system of training and testing (think "board certified" physicians, law boards, skilled trade apprenticeships).

Some compositionists have in fact argued for attempting to follow this logic to improve working conditions for composition. Having a stable subject knowledge about which we might claim disciplinary expertise (authority, ownership) would itself seem to promise to bring some stability to work in composition, a welcome change from the common experience of program "churn"—a constantly fluctuating workforce by definition always in need of training in that program's curriculum (see, for example, T. Scott, "Politics"). Recall that Wardle and Downs's argument for turning the first-year composition course into a course on "Writing about Writing," discussed in chapter 1, includes the hope that giving the course a disciplinary subject (writing) to be taught only by those with certified disciplinary expertise in that subject might itself serve to sharply limit the pool of labor on which to draw and thereby (following market logic) drive up the price to be paid for that labor. Guild disciplinarity might thus shelter composition from the vagaries of competing in the global (free) marketplace of skills production by laying claim to expertise about such work. In short, by producing and laying exclusive claim to a body of knowledge about composition as a disciplinary subject, it is hoped that composition might win the right to control the training and certification of those in possession of that body of knowledge, and hence persuade colleges and universities to pay them for their services as teachers of that subject insofar as they are recognized as the true experts in composition.

But these and other efforts at pursuing and claiming professional academic disciplinarity mistake official claims about professional academic disciplinarity for the full range of actual material social practices constituting such disciplinarity and its knowledge. More damagingly, they ignore professional academic disciplinarity's elision of the labor necessary to the (re)production of knowledge (an elision accomplished through its commodification of knowledge) as well as to recognition of that knowledge, the very labor on which work in (and on) composition is centrally focused. As Slevin notes, even the identification of teaching as a central part of the constitution of academic disciplinarity typically elides the transformation of knowledge through teaching by refusing to recognize the central role played by students as well as teachers in disciplinary work ("Disciplining" 156–57). That is, arguments to improve the labor situation of composition through achievement of professional academic disciplinarity accede to commodification's elision of the necessity of labor to the realization of knowledge (its "production" and also its "reproduction"), and hence they accept terms of exchange that exclude questions of labor altogether. Insofar as the knowledge commodified is "English," over which compositionists have difficulty claiming either exclusive ownership or esoteric knowledge, such tactics are even more unpromising.

In short, the professional academic disciplinarity composition seeks, as traditionally measured, is based on a chimera that composition is particularly ill-positioned to have pretensions to. Composition is assigned a low academic status not because as a field it is somehow lacking what true academic disciplinary fields possess. Rather, it is because by virtue of its irredeemably undeniable location in the material social realm, composition manifests more powerfully and undeniably than other academic disciplinary fields the dependence of all knowledge (re)production on concrete labor practices, and (hence) the ineluctable social materiality of knowledge denied through academic disciplinary professions' commodification of that knowledge—commodifications on which the professions are based. Composition's difficulty in its relation to more established academic disciplinary professions and in its efforts to achieve comparable academic disciplinary professional status is not so much a sign that it is unlike these other fields but, rather, that these other fields have more in common with composition than they dare acknowledge—all the more reason to keep composition at arm's length as the uninvited, unwelcome relative trying to crash the family gathering.

The Problematics of Composition as a Professional Academic Discipline

Arguments for improving the quality of both scholarship and teaching in composition (including "teacher education") demonstrate efforts to elide the necessity of labor to work in composition and its removal of that work from the material social realm. What unites such arguments despite their differences is their acceptance of mystifications of knowledge as commodity in their treatment of such knowledge as existing outside the material social realm as a discrete entity with an inherent value transferable across time and space. Such treatments elide the problematics of what has come to be known as knowledge mobilization—the overdetermined character of compositional knowledge. Alternatively, composition, in its identity as not only what Joseph Harris has termed a "teaching subject" but also and more specifically, a learning discipline, is well positioned to address precisely these problematics.[5]

To illustrate these elisions, I begin by considering two different attempts to assess the status of composition as a professional academic discipline: Richard Haswell's "NCTE/CCCC's Recent War on Scholarship" and Richard Fulkerson's "Composition at the Turn of the Twenty-First Century," both published in 2005. Haswell focuses on composition scholarship, Fulkerson on its teaching, but both measure composition's professional academic disciplinary status in terms of the stability of its subject knowledge, understood as an objectified, transferable, transmittable entity. Not all readers will agree, or have agreed, with these writers' specific representations of work in composition, nor with their arguments or recommendations. Nonetheless, to the extent that their arguments resonate with comparable laments about composition's inability to define itself and its lacks, discussed in chapter 1, and with strategies to address such lacks, they manifest the ways in which the tendency in composition to accede to dominant terms of exchange and evaluation plays out in questions of composition's professional academic disciplinary status.[6] I then consider their arguments in light of Richard Ohmann's location of composition in the broader ongoing history and difficulties of academic professions to show how the apocalyptic rhetoric deployed by all three Richards—Haswell, Fulkerson, and Ohmann—manifests, albeit from quite different perspectives, an alignment with hegemonic representations of knowledge and its commodification in the ideology of professional academic disciplinarity.

Composition Scholarship and Professional Academic Disciplinarity

In "NCTE/CCCC's Recent War on Scholarship," Haswell argues that NCTE/CCCC—the flagship national professional organizations for composition—have waged a war on the most vital forms of scholarship. He bases this argument on an analysis of changes in the publication venues and rates of appearance of studies he characterizes as "RAD"—"replicable, aggregable, and data-supported" (201)—and on the history of efforts to produce a bibliography of rhetoric and composition scholarship. His analysis, he claims, shows that while RAD studies are commonly produced in other disciplines, they have declined sharply in the flagship NCTE/CCCC journals (*College English*, *College Composition and Communication*, *Research in the Teaching of English*). And efforts to produce comprehensive bibliographies of scholarship in composition have flagged and failed. These phenomena lead Haswell to conclude that NCTE/CCCC is hostile to RAD research. More ominously, though he accepts the legitimacy of non-RAD research, he argues that given what he sees as the dominant position of RAD research in other academic disciplines, composition as a legitimate academic disciplinary field is headed for destruction. In his words,

> The kind of scholarship [NCTE and CCCC] are killing off happens to be essential to the rest they nurture. Define scholarship as broadly or diversely as they want, when essential nutrients are cut off, eventually the whole system will die. As when a body undermines its own immune system, when college composition as a whole treats the data-gathering, data-validating, and data-aggregating part of itself as alien, then the whole may be doomed. Even now, the profession's immune system—its ability to deflect outside criticism with solid and ever-strengthening data—is on shaky pins. (219)

One might criticize many features of Haswell's argument: his methodology in determining what count as "RAD" studies, his rhetoric (the "war" and organism metaphors), the vagueness of the ecumenism in types of research he pleads for. By the terms of his own argument, Haswell himself would presumably welcome at least some of these criticisms as a means of advancing scholarly knowledge (for example, by someone conducting a study using a more rigorous means of determining the RAD-ness of studies). More substantially, some will no doubt dispute his valorization of RAD studies themselves, challenging the legitimacy and the politics of claims that studies of writing or its teaching *can* be replicable, aggregable, or data-supported in the way studies of, say, reactions of chemical compounds may be (see Lingard et al. 217).

For the purposes of this chapter, however, I will focus primarily on two other interrelated features of Haswell's argument: (1) his removal of the production of scholarship from the material social realm as practices engaging labor whose effects are contingent, a removal that signals (2) his accession to dominant institutional terms for assigning professional academic disciplinary status. That accession is marked from the start of Haswell's essay in the epitaph "No profession can exist without a body of systematically produced knowledge" (198), a statement he subsequently reiterates (219).[7] Haswell identifies RAD with scholarship and, more pointedly, the kind of scholarship that "does not need defending" insofar as it is "currently healthy and supported by every other academic discipline in the world [than composition]" (200). While he accepts the legitimacy of other forms of scholarship that composition studies engages in as well—pleading for methodological ecumenism (200)—he sees RAD research as both the norm of professional academic disciplinary work and, therefore, as the most vital to the field's health, as illustrated by his deployment of organic metaphors of immune systems in the quotation above. The assumption appears to be that such research has rightly always been the vital core of professional academic disciplinary work: while he demurs from asserting absolutely what will be the outcome of NCTE/CCCC's putative "war" on scholarship, exercised through its ostensible refusal to publish "systematically produced knowledge," he does so because, he claims, "nothing like these events has [yet] happened in the history of academic disciplines" (220).

There is then in Haswell an embrace of a form of scholarship ostensibly dominant in disciplines outside composition *because* of its (apparent) dominance elsewhere. So, for example, he laments the decline in studies of the research paper and of peer critique in NCTE/CCCC-sponsored venues in light of a growth in studies of these in non-NCTE/CCCC-sponsored venues, rather than treating the growth of these studies elsewhere as a phenomenon worthy of investigation in light of the failure of these other fields to comport with the benchmark set by NCTE/CCCC's practice. That is, Haswell assumes that the continued publication of studies of these topics in other fields is *prima facie* evidence of the merit of the studies, rather than the reverse (for example, that these merely duplicate extant, and hence now unnecessary, scholarship in composition). With RAD, more is always better.

In comparing NCTE/CCCC's practice with the research of other disciplines, Haswell thus ascribes a normative functionality to these other disciplines (and to RAD research). In so doing, he removes disciplinary work from the material social realm. This is perhaps best illustrated by his assumption that RAD research develops through the steady accretion of findings, an accretion made possible only through systematic review of past research on which current researchers may build. As he puts it, "In the postsecondary teaching of written communication, as in every professional field, the value of RAD scholarship is its capacity for growth—its comparability, replicability, and accruability" (201–2). That view leads him to lament the lack of possibility of reviewing past studies of peer review (as well as other topics) consequent on the failure of NCTE/CCCC to produce a reliable bibliography of research.

But a review of research on actual disciplinary work would suggest that such work, far from functioning systematically in the way Haswell imagines, is in fact far messier than either its advocates or detractors believe.[8] As Charles Bazerman has observed, critics of disciplinary writing often believe "too readily . . . that the disciplines are simply what they represent themselves to be to neophyte students," ignoring the messy, nonlinear, and conflictual character of disciplinary practices ("From Cultural Criticism" 63). As Bazerman observes further, "The notion that the rhetoric of a discipline is a uniform, synchronic system hides both the historical struggle of heterogeneous forces that lies behind the apparent regularity and the contemporary contention and complexity of discourse that is played out against the school-taught formulas of current convention," leading to a blindness to disciplines as, in fact, "the locales of heteroglossic contention" ("From" 63). Further, as suggested by, for example, scholarship in the history and practice of the sciences, support for and the production of RAD-style research, as well as its reception, is profoundly shaped by ideologies (see for example Keller, Kuhn, and below).

Haswell need not have looked beyond work in composition for evidence of this. For, closer to home, Patrick Hartwell's 1985 review of studies of grammar instruction ("Grammar, Grammars, and the Teaching of Grammar"), published twenty years prior to Haswell's complaint and frequently reprinted in collections intended for graduate courses in composition, demonstrates that it is ideology rather than lack of research of whatever stripe that has kept the "grammar" debate alive in composition. A normative functionalist representation of disciplinary work elides such factors, treating research instead as operating on material social history from a privileged location outside that history. Most obviously, Haswell's representation of normative disciplinary work ignores the need for the material support necessary to conduct RAD research (including funding for that research and for producing bibliographies of such research).[9] Less obviously, it ignores the shaping of research production, distribution, and reception by material social conditions. In place of such terms, Haswell substitutes others—systematicity, data-supported, etc.—by which composition work is doomed to be found wanting, likely insofar as it lacks the unstated material conditions for producing work meeting these criteria—like "failing" public schools punished for lacking the resources to do work that such resources might make it possible to accomplish.

Curiously, Haswell depicts college composition as being (at least at the time of his writing) a "legitimate field of study. . . . a professional discipline with professional privileges and professional clout"—even one higher in status than "surrounding disciplines . . . in discourse and communication studies, technical communication, second-language writing, social sciences, professional schools, and schools of education"—albeit one that is in danger of disappearing (217–18). It is pleasant to imagine workers in composition occupying such a position in relation to these other disciplines and schools and enjoying such status, privileges, and clout. But such a representation is clearly at odds with the facts: NCTE/CCCC struggles to gain any notice at all in the public sphere, and composition continues to be perceived in most schools as the handmaid to literary study and creative writing, a service program with all the lack of privilege, clout, and funding attending such programs.

At times, Haswell seems to be aware of some of these facts, but the contradiction they pose to his notion that good RAD research will be recognized and rewarded prevents him from responding to these facts by revising his conclusions. Instead, he sees these as the result, not the cause, of its "failings." So, for example, he notes that

> right now, rhetoric and composition is not a category in the National Research Council classification of disciplines used by accrediting agencies, nor a numerical code in its Annual Survey of Earned Doctorates, nor a category in the *Chronicle of Higher Education* for new

> academic books, nor a field used by the National Endowment for the Humanities for grants. (219)

This would seem to suggest that composition has yet to enjoy status as a legitimate academic discipline and the privileges and clout that ostensibly come with such status. In order to avoid this inference, Haswell reverts to his organism metaphor, asserting that these facts, rather than explaining the kind of research undertaken (and not), are instead

> just symptoms of a deeper malaise. . . . [,] the field's inability, as yet, to convince scholars outside the field that it is serious about facts, perhaps its inability to convince them that it is not afraid of what those facts might uncover about its favorite practices . . . , perhaps the inability of its members—teachers and researchers alike—to rid themselves entirely of the suspicion that their scholarship, however defined, is maybe no more than a private epideictic. (219)

In other words, rather than using these facts to explain the kind of research composition does and does not undertake, Haswell sees them as a consequence of the failure of composition to undertake such research—research, however, that requires very different conditions than those currently obtaining. According to Haswell, composition could "deflect outside criticism" with "solid and ever-strengthening data," if only it would produce such data. Its inability to do so is the result of its lack of a "systematically produced knowledge" (219, quoting Carr and Kemmis 8; but see footnote 7). It cannot produce such knowledge because it does not have it, and it does not have it because NCTE/CCCC does not valorize it or have the apparatus to support it—which takes us back to the material social conditions Haswell rules out of consideration.

Haswell recognizes that all research is imperfect, necessarily limited, and its findings therefore meriting scrutiny and being subject to revision by subsequent researchers (203). So far so good. But by locating research outside the material social realm, he precludes the possibility of accounting for its subjection to the contingencies of that realm in its production, distribution, and reception. Conversely, for example, were Haswell to locate the apparent turn in composition studies to classroom ethnography—a form of research by definition nonreplicable and unaggregable—in the material social realm, he could account for it in terms of the immediate availability of the classroom to those whose work is directed (*sic*) primarily toward teaching and by the tradition of the "lone ethnographer," just as teachers well versed in reading student writing and trained in "close reading" have tended to produce scholarship offering close readings of student writing.[10] There would be no need to invoke a personified NCTE/CCCC waging "war" on scholarship to account for such turns.

Likewise, understanding the effects of composition scholarship (of whatever stripe) in material social terms would enable recognition of the problematics of what has come to be known as knowledge mobilization, complicating the perception that the profession is weakened simply by its failure to produce appropriate forms of scholarship. For contrary to the dominant ideology of professional academic disciplinarity and the commodification of knowledge on which it depends, knowledge production is not a one-time event but, rather, ongoing, dependent on reproduction in and through, and for, "its" circulation and reception in the material social realm. So, for example, contrary to the implication of conservative pleas for basing educational policy on "scientific" research, what counts as such research—that is, what is encouraged and taken up as legitimate—is shaped by particular ideologies and interests, not simply through disinterested review of available studies (as, again, Hartwell's review of grammar studies also shows).[11]

Even knowledge produced under the most desirable of circumstances is subject to change as it is "mobilized." As Levin and Cooper observe in their study of the mobilization of research knowledge in education,

> The simple idea that research would have direct effects on policy and practice has long been abandoned by those who study these issues, even though it may still be held by some researchers, who seem surprised or even dismayed that their work is not immediately adopted into policy or practice. (20)

In other words, knowledge is not simply a "portable" entity produced in one place for consumption elsewhere that remains unchanged by its travels. Rather, it is subject and inevitably subjected to transformation by a wide range of factors. As Levin and Cooper caution,

> Real policy choices are almost always the result of some combination of education knowledge, personal experience, political considerations and the interpersonal dynamics of the organization, all of which

> change over time. So the task of observing or distinguishing in this mélange the influence of empirical research is daunting if it is even possible. (Cooper and Levin 24; see also Ungerleider; Edwards 54)

More subtly but equally profoundly, there is an inevitable "translation" of "data-based knowledge" that, as Jenny Ozga observes, "reveal[s] the gap between the fluid dream of data-based governance and the sticky reality" (74). Practitioners attempting such translations must negotiate between local knowledge and "distinctive practices and experiences," on the one hand, and, on the other, the "idea of data as independent, objective and intelligent information that guides and shapes action" (Ozga 78–79). Educational research—the kind that Haswell appears to be most concerned with—involves, as Lingard and colleagues observe, "the application of social science theories and methodologies . . . with a commitment to improvement to both policy and practice" (211). However, as Lingard and coauthors warn, while "implicit in this definition is the researcher's desire for what approximates universal knowledge," insofar as this knowledge is applied to specific, contingent circumstances, it is necessarily subjected to "rearticulation through teacher professional knowledge and reading of specific situations" (211).[12]

The role of ideology in shaping the production and reception of scholarship is illustrated by the absence of consideration of Hartwell's argument in Haswell's development of his own. Hartwell's article has been widely circulated, and its topic—grammar instruction—is notorious in the public imaginary. But because Hartwell's argument does not accord with a view of disciplinarity as the disinterested ("professional") and systematic accretion of stable knowledge, it disappears ("systematically") from consideration. This is not to condemn Haswell for failing to live up to the RAD ideal he heralds or to chastise him for this omission. As Haswell cautions, all research is necessarily imperfect and limited. Rather, it is to point out the inevitable role of ideology in the shaping of research. Nor is it to reject the potential use value of conducting research of whatever stripe, nor the importance of doing so in a disciplined way (in the best sense of that term), because of the ideological character of its production, circulation, and reception—a conclusion that would betray a pre-postmodern nostalgia for escape from ideology (see Bizzell, "Marxist" 55). Rather it is to insist on the contingent (use and exchange) value of such research in light of its character as material social practice. So, for example, studies by Chris Thaiss and Terry Zawacki, and by Mary Lea and Brian Street, (among others) have demonstrated the invalidity of claims to a single, uniform academic writing standard. David Bartholomae has demonstrated what appears to be student writers' production of an "interlanguage" set of rules that results in patterns of errors in their writing ("Study"). Building on Bartholomae's study, Haswell himself has demonstrated the value of "minimal marking" in responding to perceived errors in students' writing ("Minimal"). And Elaine Lees has demonstrated a lack of agreement among professional writing teachers about what constitutes erroneous writing ("'Exceptable'"; see also J. Williams). Such work (some of it arguably fitting Haswell's definition of RAD research), while certainly meriting disciplined scrutiny, is also to be applauded (as is Haswell et al.'s ongoing work in producing the *CompPile* bibliography and attendant resources, work which may better explain why other attempts at producing research bibliographies in composition have fallen by the wayside: they can't—and need not—compete). Nonetheless, at the same time, those engaging in such work, in their scholarship and teaching, as well as those admiring it, need also to come to terms with the contingent relationship of that work to practices, policies, and "learning." Dominant perspectives on and treatments of "error" in student writing remain frustratingly oblivious to the findings of the research I have just cited, and belief in a single, uniform, autonomous academic literacy remains dominant despite the best efforts of Thaiss and Zawacki, Lea and Street, and their colleagues. Haswell's own admirable skewering of Richard Arum and colleagues' *Academically Adrift*, to cite just one of a myriad of examples, has had no effect on the popularity of that study or the widespread practice of citing it in support of various policy initiatives, at my own institution and, no doubt, elsewhere (Haswell, "Methodologically Adrift"; see also Gunner, "Everything That Rises" and, for more sympathetic reviews, Calhoon-Dillahunt, Redd). Further, even deliberate efforts to revise teaching practices in light of the findings of such research must inevitably rework those findings, and hence the knowledge they ostensibly represent, in the light of specific conditions: this student, that draft, this course, that week, by this teacher in that place (see Levin and Cooper 21).

I point out these inconvenient, seemingly depressing facts not to bemoan the fallen, corrupt nature of contemporary society but, rather, to return us to the necessity of locating knowledge in the material social realm as always emerging rather than as a commodifiable entity. As Levin and Cooper observe,

> Significant barriers to better KM [knowledge mobilization] exist in both the context of research and the context of practice or policy. Barriers include skill issues (such as the ability to convey findings in plain language, or the ability to read quantitative data results), resource issues (lack of time, access to materials) and reward systems (not much push in the university to provide research relevant to educators, and not much push in the schools to read research. . . . Another way to read these barriers . . . is that they indicate the lack of priority given to knowledge mobilization both in research-producing and research-consuming organizations. (21)

While Levin and Cooper would seem in some ways simply to be calling for more material resources (of time, training, materials, all of which require funding)—and while I believe that is a legitimate argument (not coincidentally aligned with my own)—more pertinent to this chapter is the illustration their observation provides of the power of an ideology of professional academic disciplinarity to preclude attention to the need for such material resources.[13] Against the claim of that ideology that the discovery of knowledge through professional academic disciplinary work will in itself be rewarded and affect practice and policy, Levin and Cooper and the decidedly mixed history of the "uptake" of knowledge "discovered"—let alone the history of its production—suggest that knowledge is a material social historical project, not a commodity whose inherent benefits insure that it will, by itself, inevitably win the day in the free marketplace of ideas. Engaging ourselves and our students in that project, understood in these other terms, can enable more productive engagement with—in place of ongoing denials of or lamentations about—the location of knowledge in the material social realm.

Composition Teaching and Professional Academic Disciplinarity

If Haswell's article focuses on scholarship, albeit scholarship primarily devoted to the study of teaching postsecondary writing, Fulkerson's "Composition at the Turn of the Twenty-First Century" focuses instead on what appear to be dominant teaching practices in composition and changes to these, irrespective of the scholarly support for those practices, practices that he categorizes in terms of their axiology, view of process (writing production), view of pedagogy, and epistemology (658; see also his earlier "Composition in the Eighties").[14] Prompted, he avers, by recurring frustration in his efforts to make sense of composition studies and, more immediately, by having to select texts and devise a syllabus for a writing program he was directing, he has sought to discover "who we are, what we wish to achieve with students, and how we ought to go about it" (654). To that end, he compares two collections of essays presenting different approaches to teaching composition, one from 1980 (Donovan and McClelland) and one from 2001 (Tate et al.), to glean what the available and dominant approaches to teaching composition are, have been, and will be, supplementing his analysis of the two collections with a review of scholarship, position statements, and composition textbooks and their publication histories.

As with Haswell and, indeed, any study, readers may criticize his methodology as well as his analysis and the specific conclusions drawn from that analysis. For example, having identified specific accounts of teaching as representing specific categories of pedagogy, evidence that the teaching does not conform to those categories leads Fulkerson to conclude not that his categorizations are flawed but that the pedagogies themselves are flawed. For example, the pedagogy presented in Russel Durst's *Collision Course*, identified by Fulkerson as an instance of "critical/cultural studies" ("CCS") pedagogy (663–65), appears on closer inspection to be concerned with producing ostensibly more rhetorically effective arguments (Fulkerson 672–73) and is, in any event, presented by Durst himself as deeply problematic: a "collision course." However, rather than concluding from this and other features of the course studied (on more of which, see below) that it is unsuitable as a representative of CCS pedagogy in comparison to, say, an account of a course explicitly presented by its author as an example of CCS pedagogy at its best, or concluding that he needs to develop alternative categories, Fulkerson retains the example as an illustration of what he perceives to be the flaws of that pedagogy. And in treating CCS approaches as distinct from and in conflict with approaches focusing on the rhetoric of genres and discourse forms, he ignores how the latter engage just as much in the study (and practice) of culture (which, after all, genres and discourse forms studied are in co-constitutive relation to), and how cultural studies approaches engage the study (and practice) of the rhetoric of genres and discourse forms.

In short, by the criterion of disciplinary rigor, Fulkerson's article falls short. And of course, inevitably, it is limited: as Fulkerson himself acknowledges, though he is attempting to describe dominant trends in composition teaching practices, he has no direct way of ascertaining them, and hence has had to rely on indirect, and therefore by definition suspect, evidence suggested by collections of descriptions of teaching approaches, organization statements, scholarly publications, textbooks and their publication histories, and "personal discussions" (682, note 3).

Without discounting the significance of these features of Fulkerson's article, for the purposes of the present argument I will focus on two other features of Fulkerson's essay: (1) his driving assumption that preparing (future) teachers of composition requires a stable and uniform knowledge of "who we are, what we wish to achieve with students, and how we ought to go about it" (654; see also 681), and (2) his failure to recognize the necessity and inevitability of the (re)working of any and all such knowledge in its teaching and learning. On the first point, having reached the conclusion that there is no (longer) consensus in composition about either axiology, epistemology, pedagogy, methodology, or process, he warns, in an eerie echo of Haswell, that we are in a "dangerous situation" (681). The only strategies he can imagine for preparing composition teachers, given this lack of consensus, are forms of uneasy accommodation: either throwing in one's graduate program's lot with one of the currently trendy approaches, hoping that the market for graduates carrying that brand will continue, or attempt to "prepare students as utility players able to fit into several positions" (680)—the flexible portfolio people of the new capitalism (see Gee, "New People").

On the second point, Fulkerson appears to assume a direct, immediate transmission of knowledge from teacher to student in which that knowledge remains intact and unchanged. It is that assumption that produces his anxiety about which knowledge to transmit—"critical cultural studies" or "expressivism" or some version of the "rhetorical approach" to prepare students for the job market. The model of graduate education here—at least insofar as teacher education goes—is a model of transmitting a commodification of teaching knowledge (and commodifying the teachers themselves as passive carriers of that knowledge). The same assumption accounts for Fulkerson's anxiety that critical and cultural studies approaches lead to "indoctrination" (665–66) All evidence to the contrary notwithstanding—including evidence he references in the

Durst course he sees as illustrating such a pedagogy—even the most vigorous efforts at transmitting a particular set of beliefs face the challenge of intransigent minds. Students might learn to produce writing they believe will earn them a better grade from teachers attempting such indoctrination, but that hardly constitutes evidence that indoctrination has occurred. Instead, any knowledge presented by teachers to students is inevitably and necessarily subjected to mediation by the students, even when the latter aim earnestly to access and reproduce that knowledge intact. Difference, recall, is the norm of language practice, in iteration as well as recognizable deviation, hence the significance of the "mobilization" of knowledge as it is rearticulated/reproduced in and through language in learning and teaching. Mobility, as Tsing reminds us, requires friction, the heat of which charges and changes what is moved.

Fulkerson is not alone in imagining graduate composition education as the transmission of a commodified knowledge. As Sidney Dobrin observes of the "practicum"—the one universally required course in graduate composition education (typically required of all graduate students teaching composition, whatever their planned area of study), that course "more often than not serves as an introduction to composition theory, to research methodologies, to pedagogical theory, to histories of composition studies as a discipline, and to larger disciplinary questions about writing, not just to teaching writing per se" (Introduction 1–2). As indicated by the insertion of the qualifier "just" to "teaching writing," "teaching writing per se" is commonly understood as fairly elementary rather than something meriting or even requiring recurring attention, hence the need to beef up practica with the rest.[15] More to the point, because it is often the only course focusing on (just?) teaching writing, and one typically taken at the beginning of teachers' careers, the practicum all too often comes to be treated not as an occasion for reflecting on and reworking knowledge about the teaching of composition but as an occasion for introducing captive students to a commodification of composition as disembodied knowledge—as Dobrin puts it, for "the propagation of composition studies' cultural capital" (1). Most commonly, this takes the form of loading students up, or down, with a pile of readings on everything from the history of composition to theories of the writing process to tips on classroom management to research methodologies to classical and contemporary rhetorical theory (Dobrin, Introduction 19–20).

Such practices treat knowledge about teaching composition as a commodified entity that, by definition, once received, is in no need of being reworked. It follows that, likewise, any such reworking is not a material practice in itself and so not in need of the time, space, collaboration, and other forms of support that other courses devoted to study of that practice would provide. Like the assumption that there exists a universal and autonomous academic literacy for transmission to students that, once transmitted via FYC, will equip students to meet all future writing challenges, the assumption of such practica is that once knowledge of teaching composition has been transmitted, the student/teachers will be equipped to meet all future challenges of composition teaching. Any reworking of that knowledge is understood as remedial, and relegated to staff meetings—occasions that might be required of teachers but that, typically, they earn no credit, status, or pay for participating in. Thus, the labor of reworking teaching knowledge—in the form of, say, reading, rereading, writing, or rewriting responses to representations of it—is occluded: denied or effectively prevented. Instead, the knowledge is treated as a commodity, as literally and figuratively disembodied.

Alternatively, rather than accepting either of the choices Fulkerson offers of deciding which commodified knowledge(s) to transmit to teachers (or how many), we might instead use "practica" as well as other graduate composition courses as occasions to engage, in concert with our student/teachers, with the challenges of that mediation of such knowledge: both how it might be (re)mobilized, and how in turn to bring to conscious awareness, exploration, and experimentation the mediation by students of that knowledge, most obviously in and through their writing. And, in parallel fashion, the courses taught by such teachers can likewise be occasions for exploring and experimenting with the reworking of such knowledge—specifically, as I have argued in previous chapters, the (inevitable) rewriting of English through writing.

This gives a different cast to the flawed character of the pedagogy Durst describes, identified by Fulkerson as illustrating the flaws of a critical/cultural studies approach. The graduate student teaching the course on whom Durst and Fulkerson focus (Sherry Cook Stanforth) is inevitably engaged in reworking the design of an imposed curriculum, just as her students are faced with the challenge of reworking her reworkings of it—knowledge is, after all, always "on the move" and, in the process, transforming (see Stanforth 169). But Fulkerson assumes that the curriculum, or more properly the knowledge of composition it represents, can exist absent such mobilization and hence either—by itself—works or doesn't, for teachers and/or their students. The talk among teachers that Durst describes and that Fulkerson relates can be read as teachers' effort to engage in such reworking, albeit apparently without much guidance (see Stanforth 160–61; Fulkerson 664). Practica as well as other courses, alternatively, could be designed to focus precisely on such reworking.

In saying this, I am iterating (anew) something close to a view William Coles articulated way back in 1978 at a point when, in Coles's words, "we [teachers of writing] have begun again to have a discipline, a profession to refer to," "a renewed sense of purpose, a revitalized feeling of professional legitimacy and worth," marked by the assumption of all the substantive knowledge about writing and its teaching that teachers (then) began to feel that they knew, signaled, paradoxically, by the conventionalized talk of the time about "how much there is we do not know yet" ("New Presbyters" 4, 3). Coles warns:

> The other side of placing the premium we do on the substantive knowledge we are all so busily in pursuit of, is to seem to suggest that the mastery of substantive knowledge *itself* will be enough to produce teachers of writing and enable such teachers to produce writers. It is to seem to suggest that when we *do* come to know enough, that *that* will be enough; that mastery of some body of substantive knowledge will do *for* prospective teachers of writing what in fact such people, if they are ever to become effective teachers of writing, will have to be left to do for themselves. Nor will the mechanical solution of requiring courses in methodology or teaching techniques be other than to offer as a solution what is but another form of the problem. (6, emphasis in original)

That "problem," it bears emphasizing, is not one that will go away or be solved through finally knowing all that we can, or knowing more. Rather, it is the problem of having always to make whatever (substantive) "knowledge" one has ostensibly "mastered" or "learned" "one's own,"—a perennial, ongoing labor rather than a one-time hurdle, but—fortunately—a labor shared with one's colleagues and students.[16]

Composition's Disciplinary Status and the Regime of Flexible Accumulation

Both Haswell and Fulkerson accede to dominant notions of academic disciplinary professionalism in positing a commodified body of knowledge neither changed by nor in need of concrete labor: the movement of knowledge remains untheorized. But it might also be argued that what unites their arguments more significantly is their alignment with, and plea for maintaining or achieving, a model of academic disciplinary professionalism that is already disappearing—that Haswell and Fulkerson are belatedly attempting to escort composition to a professional academic disciplinary party that has long been winding down. Richard Ohmann suggests just such a possibility. Composition, Ohmann says, "seems a late arrival in that intermediate state" of academic disciplinary professional status. Ohmann acknowledges that composition now possesses such accoutrements of an academic disciplinary profession as "a moderately cohesive though also variable and contested base of knowledge, or at least a disciplinary conversation with recognizable topoi"; conferences, learned journals, professional publications and organizations; and even "substantial control over content, method, and working conditions" at least for "some well-paying jobs" (*Politics* 80).

But in Ohmann's telling of the history of composition's professionalization, that process has been marked by some anomalies. On the one hand, as he observes, there is the traditional demand of its organization (the Conference on College Composition and Communication) for "better pay and lower teaching loads," respect, credentialing of expertise in composition, and so on (81–82). But, he says, "Unless I've missed something, composition never did agree upon a single 'informing discipline' or theory but has made do with a shifting assortment of issues and texts that frame the professional discourse and give it continuity" (82). More significantly, unlike other candidates for professional academic disciplinary status, composition has never eschewed politics. Instead,

> the conventions of authority and dignity a nascent profession would ordinarily call upon to set practitioner apart from client were all interrogated, and in the core venues of the discipline. Likewise, questions of political derivation were allowed to subvert academic conventions of writing in the journal: the passionate appeal, the

> free-form essay, the collage, gained admittance to *CCC [College Composition and Communication]*, as if to forgo the exclusions and reassurances implicit in a shared, specialized, and emotionally restrained style of address. Composition was airing unseemly questions about neutrality, detachment, and partisanship, and even about whether to act like a profession. (83)

In short, in contradiction to the normal course of a field's professionalization, Ohmann sees "conflict and politics as durable presences through the time of composition's professionalizing movement," leading him to ask, "Why did it happen this way? And with what consequences for current work and future prospects in composition?" (84).

Ohmann ends the chapter on "Politics and Commitment in Writing Instruction, as It Became a Profession," from which this quotation is taken, with those questions unanswered (*Politics* 77–84). One answer—perhaps the answer Haswell and Fulkerson might offer—is that the consequences have been disastrous.[17] But Ohmann himself elsewhere suggests a different outcome, not of composition's doing, but resulting from the changes from an industrial mode of production to the regime of flexible accumulation, which, he argues, is bringing a swift end to the need for academic professional disciplinarity of any kind. Indeed, he goes so far as to state that "English has, it would almost seem, served as a small laboratory for innovative uses of flexible, highly skilled labor power. Within universities, we stand as a microcosm of the shrinking labor market core and the expanding periphery" (*Politics* 34).

There is plenty of evidence to support this picture of composition work—the casualization and outsourcing of its labor, the demands for "accountability" and efficiency in writing instruction, the increasing identification of writing instruction strictly with production of employable "skills." Jeanne Gunner goes further, seeing market forces leading to a "purification" of composition from disciplinarity altogether. As she puts it,

> As market forces demand and reward institutions of higher education for the commodification of learning and the increased "portability" of administration and writing instruction, a *de-disciplinizing* effect ensues, resulting in an increasing enclosure of research and an accelerated weakening in the connection of programs and disciplinary work. ("Disciplinary" 618, emphasis added)

And, as Gunner warns, while "managerial discourse is one mechanism" for alienating writing instruction from disciplinary work, "the de-disciplinizing effects . . . also derive from our own accommodations with market forces and from the often unexpected alignment of disciplinary practices, theories, and affects with quite different, even antithetical, institutional agendas" ("Disciplinary" 619). Both managerial discourse—exemplified for Gunner by Stanley Fish's detachment of administration from disciplinarity and reduction of writing to forms—and moves to disciplinary purity—exemplified for Gunner by Sidney Dobrin's detachment of writing from rhetoric and composition, administration, and teaching (in his *Postcomposition*)—"align well with the established managerial regime" (Gunner 626). For both discourses "afford and accelerate the critical operations of commodification and portability, two processes that effectuate de-disciplinizing brand evolution" (626). On the one hand, the transmission of empty forms requires no disciplinary grounding—indeed, it abjures such grounding. On the other hand, Dobrin's disciplinarity purified of material social practice is all the more easily commodifiable as boutique brand, window-dressing for institutions pursuing more elite market status (see Gunner 626).

Ohmann's dominant representation of composition and its ostensible place under the new regime of flexible accumulation as a successful transmitter of skills—in contradistinction to literary study, with its lack of "product" other than cultural capital—aligns with this outcome for work "purified" of disciplinarity. As Ohmann argues,

> Higher education as a whole has reconfigured itself on the model of literacy work, having learned from English 101 how to give the customer decent service while keeping costs down and the labor force contingent. The professionalization of composition, while installing the usual apparatus (journals, conferences, a professional society, graduate programs and degrees), bringing a great advance in theoretical sophistication, and winning job security and good compensation for advanced practitioners, has made little if any difference in who does the front line work, under what regimen, for what pay, and so on. Meanwhile English, the old professional home of literacy work, has itself fallen on hard times, along with most academic professions, losing much of its ability to maintain a market haven

> for its members. So the adjuncts and graduate students who teach composition instantiate well the floating, peripheral labor force of contemporary capitalism. (*Politics* 133)

The consequence, Ohmann predicts, is that "composition will go on being taught chiefly at the university, in a kind of sweatshop operation. . . . [A] dispossessed intellectual works at survival wages transmitting skills to people hoping they can trade these for more-than-survival wages" (133), with the credentials of that dispossessed intellectual (MA, BA, PhD, ABD) irrelevant: all must endure "low pay, low status, and job insecurity" (133). While Ohmann imagines the possibility of a hopeful outcome if WPAs join forces with the teaching proletariat by "downplay[ing] the economic justification for composition, stressing instead historical, social, and critical thinking," he assumes that regardless, "we're in for tough times" (135).

"Doomed," "a dangerous situation," "tough times"—the apocalyptic rhetoric invoked in Haswell, Fulkerson, and Ohmann is striking in emanating from three scholarly reviews of composition from three quite different perspectives. One might conclude that in light of this consensus from three such eminent scholars of such different political persuasions, we are in fact doomed or at the very least in for tough times in a dangerous situation. Such rhetoric is also striking in echoing the kind of apocalyptic rhetoric found in Smit and Dobrin, discussed in chapter 1. But such rhetoric leaves little hope precisely because it accedes to the dominant's representation of itself as, in fact, total in its hegemony. Alternatively, and, again, without denying the challenges faced by those working in composition, rather than operating within the terms of exchange set by the dominant for understanding the dominant and its others, it is instead possible, following Gibson-Graham, to cut the dominant theoretically—as well as practically—down to size.

As I've already suggested, professional academic disciplinarity is based on a commodification of knowledge as reified, portable entity that denies the necessity of labor for its ongoing (re)production. What unites Ohmann's argument with Fulkerson's and Haswell's is, perversely, its faith in the erasure of labor claimed in the commodification of knowledge. Haswell values commodification of scholarly knowledge, represented for him by the results of RAD research, just as Fulkerson values commodification of knowledge of teaching to be transmitted to future teachers and writing program administrators. For his part, Ohmann presumes the successful commodification of skills knowledge. Ignoring scholarship putting into radical challenge the portability—in other words, the "transferability"—of writing skills and highlighting the situated character of writing (and, more broadly, critiques of the inadequacy of demarcations of literacy, workplace, and other "skills"—see, for example, Darrah), Ohmann appears to accept the legitimacy of claims that composition does, in fact, succeed in transmitting portable writing skills—that it knows "how to give the customer decent service while keeping costs down and the labor force contingent" (133). While Ohmann laments what Fulkerson and Hartwell treat as good and necessary, Ohmann's argument overlooks the contradiction in commodification. That is to say, Ohmann accepts, if with downcast eye, the story the regime of flexible accumulation tells (of) itself, rather than recognizing the contradictions in that story's claims. This is the error of functionalism, by which capitalism is granted a privileged status outside history to operate on it—beneficently or maleficently. Thus Ohmann's argument aligns with Haswell's and Fulkerson's despite what appear to be significant differences in their political alignments in accepting, if not the legitimacy, then the functionality of the current regime. Haswell and Fulkerson appear to wish to better align composition's work with that regime, whereas Ohmann hopes for some form of resistance to it—suggesting that academic professionals can "obey the market or fight back—and you can do a little of both" (148). But such a suggestion assumes that obedience to the market is, in fact, a possibility—that one can, in fact, offer what's on demand. As Ohmann claims, obedience

> entails seeking to give students the kinds of practical learning they might otherwise purchase in bits from proprietary schools or be offered within the corporations where they work. For people in English, this strategy will obviously mean an emphasis on writing, not just the basic composition courses, but training in more specialized and saleable skills. (148)

This assumes that such training, and skills, are in fact portable commodities, all evidence (and scholarship) to the contrary notwithstanding. This leaves "fighting back" the only alternative. For Ohmann, fighting back means forming "working alliances of writing instructors with students as well as with other campus workers," a possibility he predicts will "become more plausible in the present situation, since all these groups occupy similar, vulnerable positions in the regime of flexible accumulation" (149). Without discounting either the vulnerability of these groups or the potential value in their forming such alliances, Ohmann's strategy appears to be based on the assumption that the regime will be so successful that the immiseration of the masses it accomplishes will unite them in opposition to the regime itself—a possibility pleasant to contemplate only for those of us who might escape such immiseration. The apparent choices, then, are not good.

But in place of this agonistic framework of fighting hegemony with the strength of masses united in their misery, one might instead cut hegemony down to size by attending to the many failures of whatever one identifies as the current regime—its *non*functionality—and locating in these failures more likely prospects for hope. Instead of Ohmann's narrative of the loss of professional academic disciplinary autonomy, for example, or of the failures of composition itself to achieve the kind of autonomy that others putatively have, we might refuse claims to the historical achievement of such an ideal in light of the contradictions at its base. So, for example, whereas Ohmann claims that "the reorganization and extension of capital's work [under the regime of flexible accumulation] challenges the professions," and that the "commodification of knowledge and the marketization of professional services are in direct conflict with professional [academic disciplinary] autonomy," one might instead see that claims to such autonomy have always been spurious, based as they are on a commodification of knowledge that is neither new nor in conflict with, but rather the established mythical basis of, professional autonomy. (It is not for nothing that movements for patients' rights, for example, have arisen challenging such autonomy and the portability of expert medical professionals' knowledge.) And rather than seeing composition as complicit with the current regime in offering deliverables—writing skills—on the knowledge market, we can instead see hope precisely in composition's actual failure—its inability—to "deliver" writing skills, and in its focus, instead, on the fictionality of "delivery" and the generative role of friction in the ongoing production of knowledge as practice, as labor.

Recent accounts of efforts to export a commodification of composition's knowledge to locations outside the United States illustrate both the fictional character of such commodifications and the inevitability, and necessity, of such friction. For example, the essays gathered in David Martins's collection on transnational writing program administration demonstrate above all not the easy export of models of writing programs or curricula—the tendency Christiane Donahue cautions against of seeing writing study elsewhere through the lens of composition's own "claims to unique knowledge, expertise, and ownership of writing instruction, and writing research in higher education" ("'Internationalization'" 213)—but, instead, the necessity to constantly rework any such (working) models in light of differences—in students, languages, institutions, locations, cultures, material resources, time zones, schedules, traditions, etc. Collectively, the essays demonstrate that the very effort to export models of writing instruction brings to light both the necessity of reworking those models and the ongoing character of such reworking. For example, faced with anxieties among some faculty and administrators at Saudi Arabia's Dar Al-Hekma ["DAH"] College about use of textbooks investigating homosexuality and representing women engaging in activities taboo in Saudi Arabia, Chris Anson and Christiane Donahue report that its program was reworked to accommodate this cultural difference: a textbook was selected with more culturally "appropriate" content (32–33). However, as Anson and Donahue report, the cultural blandness of the preferred textbook content led to the need to rework *this* decision in light of student complaints about feeling a lack of purpose for their writing, to students being "*disengaged* from their writing" (33, emphasis added). Thus the ostensibly (officially) "different" needs of the students to be protected from culturally objectionable content—content that led the original textbook selections to be deemed "unusable"—were contradicted by students' expressed needs (perhaps desires) for the opportunity to engage with such objectionable content.

As Anson and Donahue explain, the necessity of such ongoing reworking is at odds with an import/export model based on the assumption that "'learning to write' is independent of complex cultural practices, ideologies, and activity systems" (28). The hope, they explain, at least among officials of DAH, was to get "ideologically neutral structures into which [the officials could] fill culturally relevant (or entirely neutral) content" (32). This is the neoliberal fantasy of a friction-free transmission of knowledge, services, and goods as commodities, a fantasy that the liberal stance of tolerance for and accommodation of difference aims to accomplish—what Michael Byram identities as a "touristic" stance toward difference (1–2). But as Byram warns, the experience of travel in fact requires more substantive engagement with difference and with change, both to those at the site traveled to and to the would-be tourists themselves—in a word, labor. Claims to the contrary notwithstanding, commodities do not travel well. For friction is in fact inevitable (and generative).[18]

Rewriting Disciplinarity in Composition

If the challenge composition faces is not its failure to achieve professional academic disciplinarity but, rather, the dominant terms in which we have been led to understand such disciplinarity, disciplinarity must be defined using better terms. Of course, any definition will carry with it an odor of reification and exclusion, of defining what counts as disciplinary and what doesn't, and disciplining workers accordingly. What would fend off such an odor is frequent "airing" by insistence on continual reworkings of those terms—a task that composition's history suggests it is particularly adept at carrying out.

That odor can tempt a rejection of disciplinarity altogether—to pursue, or claim the achievement of, a state of being "postdisciplinary" or even anti-disciplinary: in other words, to refuse what is presented as an offer that cannot be refused. And in light of the treatment of composition by other academic disciplines, composition understandably has ambivalence toward disciplinarity. But as Chris Gallagher observes, "however uneasy many compositionists seem to be about the prospect of academic disciplinarity, and however sanguine some of us might be about the prospect of postdisciplinarity . . . , we cannot deny the lure of disciplinarity" (*Radical* 108–9). Gallagher explains this in terms of the "trappings" that disciplinarity appears to offer—"the tenure-track lines, the journals and conferences, the book series, the endowed chairs, the undergraduate and graduate programs, the sense of belonging to an academic community." The question for Gallagher, then, is whether such trappings can be had without what seems to be disciplinarity's "trap": "the containment and normalization of intellectual work and knowledge" (Gallagher, *Radical* 109).

But as my analysis of Haswell, Fulkerson, and Ohmann suggests, the "trap" itself, as much as the trappings, are, if not (al)luring, still very much inscribed in our thinking: an ideology of professional academic disciplinarity is not so much something one chooses to subscribe to or not in return for the payoff of trappings but, rather, inculcated as dispositions, the commodification of knowledge such common sense as not to be readily available for consideration as a choice—witness Ohmann's acceptance of the commodification of writing skills. Moreover, as the examples discussed in chapter 1 suggest, efforts to escape from or abandon the dominant are likely to take up positions that the dominant has already prepared for us—the lesson Paul Willis drew long ago of the "lads" whose "opposition" led directly to their continued oppression (*Learning to Labor*). Efforts to escape from academic professional disciplinarity, that is, are likely to lead us even more fully into the embrace of the regime of flexible accumulation (or whatever regime currently is in ascendance), rather than offer an alternative to it. Those presuming to have escaped from the material social realm of disciplines find themselves in the position not of being free of that realm but, rather, in a worse position: nowadays, the freeway flyers who, lacking both the trappings of professional academic disciplinarity and discipline, experience free fall in the "free" market of neoliberalism.

This does not mean that the only choices are an embrace of conventional professional academic disciplinarity or abandonment to market forces. It does mean sorting through the kind of disciplinarity to which any alternative is posed, and the relation of that alternative to dominant forms of disciplinarity. So, for example, conflating disciplinarity with an officially dominant (say, "RAD") form of scholarship, understood as in opposition to teaching, and heralding the latter as the alternative to disciplinarity, merely flips the dominant research/teaching binary, leaving dominant definitions of both terms undisturbed. Scholarship is then seen as in opposition to and conducted at the expense of teaching (and teachers), just as, conversely, teaching is seen as an impediment to scholarship. In extreme versions of this, any complaint against any scholarship, or teaching, is seen as a complaint against all of one and a heralding of all of the other. Gallagher, for example, cites statements by Chris Ferry, Robert Yagelski, David Bartholomae, and myself concerned with teaching as arguments against scholarship (Gallagher, "We" 78–79), which then appear as instances of irony if not hypocrisy, given that these arguments are, after all, themselves instances of published scholarship.

But this is to accept dominant definitions of teaching and scholarship as uniform and interchangeable, when these practices are anything but.

As Gallagher himself points out, seeing teaching as in competition with research appears to accept dominant equations of teaching in terms of contact hours—the more one teaches, the greater one's commitment to teaching ("We" 79). But as he notes, "time spent in the classroom is an impoverished metric for either teaching commitment or teaching impact" ("We" 79), hence the reduced teaching loads of some compositionists is not in itself evidence of a lack of interest in or commitment to teaching, just as the high teaching loads cobbled together by adjuncts to make ends meet is evidence not of their strong commitment to teaching but of their exploitation. (It is in this sense that a commitment to teaching leads to a demand for lower, not higher, teaching loads, just as nurses' commitment to patient care has led to their demand for lower nurse/patient ratios). Such complaints accept dominant valuations of labor as abstract rather than concrete, measured in units of time seen as equivalent, in keeping with a still dominant industrial-capitalist model of labor and the terms by and in which labor is predominantly understood. Thus attempts to escape professional academic disciplinarity by heralding teaching in opposition to scholarship would leave teachers themselves in positions even further subordinated to those they already suffer from insofar as the work of teaching, and the accomplishment of teaching labor in re/producing knowledge (in concert with students) would be eviscerated. (So-called "teacher proof" curricular materials follow this logic.)

Haswell's treatment of RAD illustrates the complementary flip side: he heralds Janet Bean's study of gender differences in tutor talk purely insofar as it meets the definition of being RAD. According to Haswell, "It does not matter that Bean's (1999) data are scanty or that one of the participants was herself. Her study still functions as RAD inquiry" (Haswell 203). Setting aside the impossibility of replicating a study in which Bean herself was both a participant under study and the researcher,[19] this is a remarkable statement in rendering research methodology a guarantee of value no matter how exercised: the descriptor ("RAD") here serves simultaneously as valuation.[20] Such treatment leads to conflating any example of a particular form or method of scholarship with the qualities (good or bad) associated with all examples so categorized—"empirical," "ethnographic," "action," "qualitative," or "RAD." Fulkerson's framing of his argument in terms of which kind of pedagogy to advance—CCS, rhetorical, expressivist—suffers from a similar conflation that overlooks how any pedagogy falling into such a category is put to work (and, thence, reworked).

A related concern is to acknowledge even within commodifications of scholarly or teaching knowledge accomplished in traditional academic disciplinary work the continuing potential use value of that work.[21] Recall here that exchange value does not evacuate the potential use value of the commodity: paper money of all denominations, for example, can still be put to use as, say, cigarette paper, or kindling. In other words, rebuking work conducted under the aegis of traditional professional academic disciplinarity, or traditional teaching, participates in rather than undermining commodification's elision of labor. The extreme version of this would condemn scholarly publications simply insofar as these can be, are, and have been used as commodities beefing up the reputations of individuals, departments, and universities. But we need to recall that good work—work that does good—can be accomplished even if, under current social relations, commodifications of that work bring some form of capital—status, money, greater job security, institutional prestige—to those whom those social relations lead us to misrecognize as its sole producers. There is, then, no irony in writers publishing books and articles questioning the specific uses of publishing books and articles. The question, instead, is the use value to be made, and how, of such questioning.[22] To return to RAD scholarship, while it may be true that for purposes of categorization the scanty data in Bean's article and the fact that the researcher was also one of the participants may not matter—it still qualifies as "RAD" by Haswell's definition—these features of the research would matter very much for its use in understanding gender in tutor talk more broadly.

Further, paradoxically, we help to sustain commodifications of the work of composition when we condemn those forms of teaching and research that appear not to have a recognizable use. This would seem to be contradictory: shouldn't our teaching and scholarship, after all, be use-ful to have use value? But the contradiction is only apparent. For the use value of work is always potential and emergent, realized only in use. Alternatively, it is the commodity that, paradoxically, claims easy, recognizable, immediate use value (the dishwashers that wash dishes and the refrigerators that refrigerate, seemingly all by themselves, without human intervention). Demands for teaching and scholarship that appear to have immediate or obvious use value accept dominant constructions of what is and will be useful, and the social relations within which it is or will be (think, here, of the social relations within which iPads may and may not have use value, as designed). In other words, we cannot assume a fixed determination of what is or will be of "use": use value, instead, is a consequence of use by socially situated actors.

This is not to reject concerns that teaching and scholarship be somehow of use, only to include as part of the pursuit of such work the questioning of the material social relations advanced by such uses vs. others. The stalemate in the tired debate over whether to teach writing to help students get the credentials necessary to employment under current economic conditions or to help them see the problematic nature of those conditions arises from a neglect of just such questioning. Instead, "current economic conditions" and the skills necessary to success within it or to full critique of it are taken as fixed and knowable entities, all evidence to the contrary notwithstanding.[23]

As an alternative to attempting to produce scholarship and teaching with clear and immediate use value, we might instead treat use value not as a given but as a question, a project toward which any scholarship and teaching can be directed. For example, we might look to the potential use value of that work that appears to be entirely ordinary and (therefore) dismissable but which those of us in composition are quite familiar with: student writing that has its genesis within, and never circulates outside, the first-year composition course. The restrictions on its circulation and the seemingly artificial basis of its generation have led some compositionists to reject it as a kind of bastardized writing whose value is limited to a display of the student writers' skill, either at writing in general (a chimera) or at mimicking a particular subjectivity (for example, "earnestness").[24] The circumscribed location of such writing and its circulation to the first-year composition course likewise has been understood to drain it of any real legitimacy: where else but in FYC is FYC writing produced or read? In response, accompanying the longstanding tradition of complaint against such writing, there is an equally longstanding tradition of attempting to break with such restrictions either by introducing more "relevant" topics or forms of writing, or by circulating either the students or their writing (or both) outside the classroom (through, for example, service-learning projects, blogs, Wikipedia entries, and other recognizably "public" writing).[25]

Without discounting the potential use value of any of these strategies, underlying many arguments for them are the assumptions either that the official institutional charge for FYC evacuates any other possible work that might be accomplished in FYC, or that the material social conditions of such courses (including their official institutional charge) can only restrict, rather than make possible, work with potential use value, and that the exchange value that is recognized as circulating outside the course—represented as a contribution to the student's GPA, say, in official evaluations—represents the only real value of the work accomplished. Ohmann iterates the first and third of these. On the one hand, explicitly channeling Evan Watkins (see Watkins *Work Time* 83, 90–91), Ohmann argues that much of the work in English (broadly) is a "traffic in evaluations" and that, therefore,

> from the perspective of abstract labor and its uses to the economic system, it doesn't matter whether we spend our time commenting on themes or writing articles on Kate Chopin, whether our students write seminar papers on Milton or computer-scored tests on usage. (38)

On the other hand, he also argues (*pace* Smit) that English does meet "specific needs" in the form of producing writing skills (38). This leads him to the depressing conclusion that "some of the work we [in English] do is already, in effect, subcontracting for business, and it is altogether compatible with our work in [social] class reproduction" (38).

There is in such arguments a neglect of uses to be made on the ground through the concrete labor of students and teachers in their collective scholarship in light of what the dominant has claimed is the value of abstractions of such work (in GPAs, CVs, measures of faculty "productivity," abstract writing skills, etc.)—in short, another manifestation of assigning not just hegemonic status to the dominant but assuming its total hegemony, and assuming that its valuations exhaust the possible value of given work. Such arguments cede and contribute to the power of the dominant's own claims and, at the same time, diminish the possibility of recognizing, and thereby sustaining and strengthening, alternative uses and values for our work and for the material social conditions of that work.

Those conditions include, at least for the moment at many U.S. institutions (in contradiction to conditions obtaining by those working on academic literacies elsewhere), relatively small classes of students with a regular, reserved time and space for them and their instructor to meet for ten to fourteen weeks, the potential of collective and collaborative projects by these students and their teacher, the removal of these projects from significant public scrutiny and, therefore, the possibility of greater freedom in exploring, through drafts, approaches to these projects, and relative autonomy in terms of the design of such projects. It is worth emphasizing that such conditions are neither all nor always available to all in the same form, and that the high teaching loads (in terms of number of course sections being taught simultaneously, number of students per course section, and low pay per section), limited material resources (for example, of time, library and computing and Internet access, classroom facilities, office space), and limited institutional support (clerical, educational, administrative) significantly shape the design and execution of any course projects. Even those teachers enjoying a degree of autonomy in designing their courses may find that autonomy effectively meaningless as a consequence of experiencing some or all of the limitations I've just listed, which is all the more reason for insisting on improvements to such conditions. But common demands for just such improvements highlight what these conditions afford as valuable resources necessary to the work we do, rather than standing as an impediment to work that would matter more by escaping from such conditions. The restricted circulation of student work, for example, makes it possible for that work to take directions, and risks, that a less restricted circulation of that work would likely preclude, and for courses to sponsor work with such characteristics. Disdain for the "academic," conceived of in purely immaterial form, can lead us to neglect the potential use value of the material social conditions commonly reserved for conducting academic work, including conditions allowing for the possibility of the all-important work of revision. It is, ironically, a pejoratively "academic" view of what academic work entails: taking for granted what is in fact rare (and increasingly so).

Language and the Discipline of Rewriting Composition

In previous chapters I have defined composition as an ongoing historical project whose work engages and mediates differences in written language, and declared that the labor of composition is writing language. On their face, such definitions would seem to dictate a topic ("language" and "language differences" in writing) and a task ("writing language"), both for scholarship and teaching in composition, that could be used to designate a professional academic discipline as conventionally understood, though one perilously close to infringing on the disciplines of linguistics, literary study, and, possibly, the various modern languages.

But in defining its work as engaging and mediating differences in written language and as writing language, I mean to emphasize composition as not only studying but working on differences in written language, and as participating in the writing of language. It could be argued, of course, and rightly, that any and all writers participate in such work every time they write. This is the basis of James Slevin's claim that anyone and everyone who writes is a member of the discipline of composition (including seven-year-olds composing thank-you notes). All such writers participate in the intellectual work of composition. I would part from Slevin, however, in emphasizing the role that the material social location of that work plays in shaping it, and the advantages that the conditions of a separate curricular and institutional space for such work in colleges and universities (or the better working conditions some of us continue to enjoy at those institutions) bring to the conduct of that work as "intellectual."

This is to recall that "intellectual" work is, from a cultural materialist perspective, best understood as itself a material social practice therefore by definition contingent on material social conditions. This is not to deny the intellectual capacity of those not enjoying such conditions but to recognize the role such conditions play in the shape of engagement of that practice and in whether or not the intellectual character of one's work is recognized as such. From this perspective, "intellectual work" is work done by those designated to be intellectuals, whose designation is marked by specific material social conditions: not just training and credentials but also by institutional positioning with specific kinds of material social resources. Such designations are social historical and therefore contingent, variable, subject to contestation. And of course the valuation ascribed to work designated as intellectual is likewise contingent and variable, functioning sometimes as honorific, sometimes as pejorative.

The conditions of postsecondary academic institutions better enable particular ways of engaging the "task" of writing language, and the difference to be made through that task, including the treatment of that task as also simultaneously a "topic": in short, for action-reflection.[26] This is not to insist that composition courses should have "language difference in theory and practice" as either their explicit or nominal theme about which students write (though this of course would not be excluded). Rather, it is to remind ourselves that a continual focus of the work of composition, in teaching and in scholarship, will be the differences that are and might be made in and through and to the writing of language(s) ("about" anything, and with language understood broadly to include what, for lack of a better term, we might identify as the extralinguistic), and to what effect. Put thus broadly, the task is not defined by the topic but embodies and enacts it, and the task carries no defined end point. It is by definition ongoing and involving all those participating. And while all (forms of) writing might be in some fashion the topic and task, the project will be academic in its material social location: students and teachers working together *as* students and teachers on the writing of difference in language.

A corollary following this is that such work is intellectual in the sense of drawing on the resources academic institutions provide (identified above) but not simply to engage in the work of "technicians," in the sense of solving a (well-structured) problem, or even of producing knowledge recognizable as somehow "new." So, for example, from the (translingual) perspective I am arguing for, students who discover techniques and concepts that their instructors recognize as familiar are engaged in work as worthy of being deemed "intellectual" as students whose discoveries appear to their instructors and others as, in fact, new. For (again) from the perspective being advanced here, knowledge is located only in its continual (re)mobilization. Social reproduction, which for some has the status of all that is intellectually and politically repugnant, evidence of passivity and the absence of agency, purely mechanical action, is from this perspective both necessary and to be honored insofar as any iteration in fact is simultaneously "the same" as what is iterated but also, by virtue of its specific temporal-spatial location, new, contributing to further sedimenting (but with an inevitable difference) what is (re)produced, and raising inevitable questions for writers and their colleagues about whether, how, and why to engage or not in such further sedimentation.

I am suggesting that in the familiar forms of ordinary work in composition, represented in, for example, a composition course in which students produce writing that circulates only within the confines of that course, work of real, if always contingent, use value can take place, and that the material social conditions typical of the site of such a course makes possible academic intellectual work that cannot take place elsewhere, outside such conditions. Bartholomae points to this possibility in his explanation of why he teaches first-year composition. Rather than claiming a commitment to teaching in place of or opposition to research, he suggests, instead, that he teaches out of "a fundamental commitment to a certain kind of intellectual project—one that requires [him] to think out critical problems of language, knowledge, and culture through the work of 'ordinary' or 'novice' or student writers" ("What" 24). While he aligns this work with the project of criticism, it is a "practical criticism (or criticism-in-practice)" (21). He acknowledges that this kind of work is ordinary in the extreme, and that this is "professionally difficult. . . . It ends with revisions that are small, local, and difficult to value. It assumes the direct intervention in specific projects where (from a certain angle of vision) the gains are small" (21).

While Bartholomae phrases the project as his, we can inflect it to necessarily and inevitably involve students as well in thinking out "critical problems of language, knowledge, and culture": it is the students, after all, who will be making the revisions as they engage in "practical criticism." While those revisions may well appear, from dominant perspectives, to be "local, and difficult to value," with "gains [that] are small," we accept such perspectives at the peril of losing sight of the actual work accomplished through such "small," "local" gains. Even those gains that appear purely idiosyncratic, restricted to the individual student discovering what everyone around her seems to already know, are, from the perspective I've been advancing, real and the discovery new insofar as the writer is contributing to the sedimentation and mobilization of that knowledge, and (always) with a difference, however slight, in her writing of it, even if the writing appears highly conventional.

Moreover, and conversely, there is a use to the ordinariness and "smallness" of such gains. In his debate with Bartholomae, Peter Elbow called for preserving the writing course as a place to "cultivate . . . some tufts of what grows wild outside," protected from the academic ("Response" 90). But we can instead see the composition course as a preserve for what can grow "inside" the academic site as material social realm, somewhat, if not entirely, removed from the otherwise incessant pressure for commodification—recall Ohmann's observation (echoing Watkins) that it does not matter to the dominant economic realm what we do in our classes, a fact that he may lament but which points to some real potential. The fact that work in composition courses can appear useless, not relevant, not mattering, can allow for experimentation, thinking, and reflection of real use value, once we come to understand these as themselves material social practices more easily engaged in when there is an allotted space, meeting time, and the possibility of collaboration and a project: the briar patch we can, after all, find ourselves at home in.

For at least some of us, similar conditions make possible pursuit of seemingly useless, irrelevant research: reworking, by rewriting, the known, in myriad ways, to make it new. Earlier in this chapter, I've pointed to the significant barriers to knowledge mobilization, barriers that would seem to justify despair at engaging in research in light of the lack of impact it may have on policy and practice. But I am suggesting, too, that such despair is a consequence of allegiance to a mythical notion of academic professional disciplinarity and its claimed function in the first place: the lone scholar whose findings have universal application and are therefore universally applied, in unmediated fashion. Research, whether seemingly engaged or not, "action" or otherwise, may or may not affect policy and practice, and in unanticipated as well as expected ways. That is not a reason to stop researching nor to hearken back to a call for knowledge for knowledge's sake but, rather, to adopt a more humble perspective on such work: to take up (again and again) "basic" research, and to do so in a manner that embraces all the pejoratives associated with that term. It is to identify the disciplinary work of composition—in the sites of teaching and research—as learning, which (fortunately) is an inevitability but always with unanticipated consequences and results always contingent.

If knowledge, like language, is the always-emerging outcome of practices, discipline refers not to that knowledge, that outcome, but, rather, to the character of those practices. Representations of disciplines, as practices, shape subsequent practice and the outcomes of that practice: disciplinary knowledge and disciplinarity. Defining professional academic disciplinarity as practice (like languaging) whose always-emergent outcome is disciplinary knowledge defines such knowledge as always subject to and in need of being reworked through ongoing practice. Two intertwined features characterize disciplinary work responsive to that representation: the explicitly contingent character of its value, and its variability. Scholarship so understood would be disciplined, but not in the dominant sense of that term. Instead, it would be marked, like all learning, by its openness and even invitation to contest, by humility, and by its slow pace and (inevitably) uncertain direction, all understood as the marks of the labor of intellectual work.

The question of language in writing and written scholarship exemplifies this. In the last decade or so, those working in composition have come increasingly to recognize the field's containment by English-only monolingualism, and, simultaneously, its parochialism in treating as composition *tout court* what are in fact traditions of writing and its teaching characteristic at best of some in the United States, leaving unacknowledged and unexplored writing in other languages (in and outside the United States), and scholarship and teaching of writing beyond U.S. national borders. Of course, in some ways, this recognition has been forced on the field by the increasingly undeniable linguistic heterogeneity of students and teachers in U.S. composition programs and the growing traffic of peoples across national borders, as well as by the ever more urgent insistence for schools to "internationalize." But in any event, that recognition has forced a slowing down of the work of composition as teacherscholars attempt to translate, (and, inevitably, transform) both literally and figuratively, teaching and scholarship in academic literacies, *didactiques de l'écrit*, and so on to U.S. locations and vice versa. What had seemed transparent has grown almost opaque.[27] For example, recognition of the specificity of the local radically complicates any efforts to produce replicable, aggregable, data-driven research insofar as the research sites and researcher assumptions appear to be less and less easily, if at all, replicable.

These efforts at translation are inevitably humbling, as writers come to know (again), or, rather, relearn, the knowledge of languages, writing, and its teaching that they had thought they already possessed as well as the knowledge and, more significantly, the disciplinary practices giving rise to that knowledge, that they recognize as new to them. The necessity of labor to knowledge, or rather knowing, is made more difficult to elide. And such translation work is inevitably slow and its results contingent, open to contest and revision and, hence, humbling.[28] Often enough, those undertaking it do so without any clear sense of the direction to which it will lead or of the "gain" to be made, at least conventionally. In literal as well as figurative translation, it can often seem we are merely rediscovering, or laboriously rewording, the ordinary, or finding exotic what, to those claiming familiarity with the language and/or scholarly tradition, is the epitome of the mundane, when it is not simply off. My students, asked to do some (literal) cross-translation work (with French), have discovered, laboriously, that *education*, as éducation, can refer not simply to school, or acquisition of knowledge, but the social cultivation of manners and "training" in the sense of formation/*formation*, a sense of learning at odds with the ideology of innate individualism that has marked their own formation. Their work leads to an articulation, new at least for them, of knowledge not recognized by dominant culture as new, hence the gains, if any, are extremely small, at least from a conventional perspective on academic disciplinary work. It's not clear, either to me or to my students, what the use might be of the knowledge of education/éducation they have now (re)produced or what it will or should lead to, if anything. But from the perspective of discipline as practice, this is normal. There will be more writing, more (disciplinary) work, more knowledge (re)production, and the knowledge, as contingent and always emergent, will always be in need of renewal, like the disciplinary knowledge that is, in fact, the always-emergent outcome of disciplinary practice.

This counter notion of discipline is suggested in the characterization of the history of the field of composition that Bartholomae offered in his 1989 address as chair of CCCC. According to Bartholomae, it is a history of repeated, but largely failed, attempts "to reconstruct a unified field, to discipline this unruly discourse, to translate anxiety into security" ("Freshman" 44). From the perspective of dominant academic professional disciplinarity, this would constitute if not a condemnation of, then a requiem for, composition. But Bartholomae argues instead that this result is "fortunate" (44). While Bartholomae is loath to refuse the term *discipline* itself, he avers that "we may be a discipline, but we are surely not disciplined in any usual sense of the term" (48). For if composition is a discipline, it is one, for Bartholomae, whose

> central purpose has been to make room for . . . many voices, . . . a multivocal, dialogical discipline that reflects in its actions its theoretical opposition to a unifying, dominant discourse. . . . a willed and courageous resistance to the luxury of order and tradition. . . . to resist the temptations of rank and status. (49)

I read Bartholomae's address as wrestling with the limitations of the dominant definition, model, and ideology of academic professional disciplinarity. "I am suspicious," he says, "of calls for coherence. I suspect that most of the problems of academic life—problems of teaching, problems of thinking—come from disciplinary boundaries and disciplinary habits" (49). And so, he seems at times to be calling for a lack of discipline—at least as ordinarily defined. For example, in place of disciplinary courses in, say, the "American Novel," Bartholomae notes, there is no way of telling what might be going on in the course in freshman English that, at the time of his address, as well as before and since, continues to be the focus of much of the field's instruction. That is a problem, he admits, but, he says, it has also been "its greatest attraction, since it put its members in a position to make up English [as the subject, as the language, and the language as subject] as they went along" (42).[29]

Bartholomae's solution to his suspicions about identifying the discipline of composition with a stable body of knowledge with set boundaries and methods is to identify it in space and time as a materially, institutionally situated activity. For example, he describes composition as providing a "site where English was open for negotiation (or renegotiation)" or as "enabl[ing] the expression of a fundamental anxiety about 'required English'" that "produced new ways of talking about language, writing, and pedagogy," remaining something "we can never simply study" (44, 45). Composition, he suggests, is not only or merely "an abstract subject" but also "something materially present, a course and its students" (47).

In a sense, then, Bartholomae in his address can be seen as attempting to rewrite academic professional disciplinarity, at least so far as composition is concerned. His difficulties in doing so arise partly from a limitation of strategy, of defining composition primarily in terms of what it is not, which leaves unchallenged those terms themselves as the proper identifications of disciplinarity. Alternatively, we might say that composition's failure to achieve such disciplinarity marks it not so much as distinct from other disciplines, or as failing to achieve what they have, but, instead, as a sign of its steady reluctance—its refusal, even—to accept the false terms in exchange for which the dominant offers disciplinary status. For example, as Bartholomae notes, a proposal in the 1950s to amend CCCC's constitution to focus its efforts "upon a discipline rather than a course or a particular group of teachers" was defeated (Bartholomae 47).

I take such moves to reject not disciplinarity *per se* but the sense of order, coherence, and tradition Bartholomae identifies with disciplinarity, a false representation of what disciplinarity in practice, as practice, entails, a representation like and linked to the representation of languages as discrete and stable entities—such as "English"—to be studied. Composition is well positioned to call into question such representations. For composition not only has repeatedly failed to achieve such a sense of order, coherence, and tradition (not surprising from this perspective but, instead, inevitable)—it has also repeatedly insisted on pursuing a model of disciplinarity understood as material social practice, with all the contingencies that term entails.

While often enough that model of disciplinarity would appear to be one that the field is forced to recognize through the imposition of conditions restricting its practice—such as the conditions of linguistic heterogeneity it has (lately) been forced to recognize—it also appears to be a model that the field has, if sometimes fitfully, embraced as more true to the experience of those working in composition, in their teaching and scholarship, just as its history is marked by the recurring turn to a more fluid understanding of language(s) in contest with dominant English monolingualism. And just as studies of writing have revealed writing to be anything but coherent, ordered, and respectful of boundaries, linguistic or disciplinary, at least in the ordinary senses of these terms, so our experience of disciplinary work shows it to be, at its best, willing and even eager to cross disciplinary boundaries, remake tradition, and develop in seemingly incoherent and unordered ways, following a pace often frustratingly slow and rarely predictable.[30] The "gains" often appear to be, and are, small, seemingly inconsequential, and, if circulated, often misunderstood and misused—or, rather, the notion of "gain" is not applicable to the disciplinary work of rewriting language and knowledge. But this, composition has learned, is normal practice in actual disciplinary work.

Pursuing such work, understood in such terms, takes above all a sense of humility, of the ordinariness of the work we as well as our students do and its contingent, contestable character as engagement in the paradox of reproduction, making the old—again, and thereby—new. Humility is often taken to mean an acknowledgment of one's subordinate status to others. But *humility* traces to the Latin *humus*, or earth. To embrace humility is, then, to embrace one's groundedness in a particular time and space. Composition's deserved humility, the kind it sometimes does and, I argue, should embrace, is a sign of its grounded location and perspective, its recognition and grounding of its work in the ordinary, the day-to-day, not as something beneath contempt or study as a known entity but, rather, as the base and basis of all its labor and its fruit. Discipline in composition is what keeps us so grounded. Far from embracing a mechanical understanding of the ordinary as "merely" ordinary, "just" composition (and its teaching), it insists on the necessity to learn and relearn, to work and rework, that ground on which we stand and where we live and work, as both the same and yet different, to find in the ordinary and its iteration the extraordinary, meriting and requiring continual (re)translation.

Admittedly, the glamour of this work is not readily apparent. *Glamour*, of course, derives from "grammar," with which composition is commonly associated, sometimes to its chagrin. But "grammar" in its etymology refers not to syntax but, rather, to learning, and especially the art of letters and writing, as well as to magic, incantation, spells (*OED*). It is discipline that enables us to reclaim that inheritance, the briar patch now called simply *composition*. Discipline is the practice of discovering once again new meanings in such old, familiar, denigrated, ordinary terms—to rewrite composition.

* * *

I have argued that knowledge, like language, is the ongoing, always-emergent outcome of practices, practices that we can best understand as disciplinary. Against dominant notions of professional academic disciplinarity resting on a denial of the dependence of knowledge on the labor of such practices, we can understand discipline as a return to such labor, embraced not as alternative but, rather, the ground of our knowing. Language, broadly defined, is both the material of that labor and its always-emerging outcome, the end and means toward and through which we work in pursuit of such knowing. That labor enables us to rework whatever terms have been given for and to our work. It is through that labor that our discipline rewrites composition.

Epilogue

I have argued in this book that in terms like *Composition*, *Language*, *Labor*, *Value*, and *Discipline* we need to learn to recognize the presence of composition, language, labor, value, and discipline. (Iterations, recall, are never, can never be the same.) Rather than imagining the latter as mere manifestations of the former, we need to understand the former as instead no more than the ever-emergent outcomes of the practices signified by the "latter": that Composition is the always-emergent outcome of the practices still identified with the lowly term composition; that in place of understanding Language, Labor, Value, and Discipline as entities imbued with discrete agency, we recall that these upper-case designations represent mere abstractions of, and give a misleading sense of stability, internal uniformity, and discrete character to, the practices of language, labor, value, and discipline inhering in acts of composition. Such designations are, of course, themselves practices contributing to trajectories of language, labor, value, and discipline and (thereby) to composition and to the ongoing historical project called Composition. To fail to recognize these designations as practices themselves is to reinforce and participate in their rendering of the practices they abstract from their full social historical materiality.

Recognizing practices of language, labor, value, and discipline as they inhere in acts of composition and contribute to the project of Composition runs counter to dominant ideologies of these practices as something other than practices: ideologies by which practitioners appear subordinate to some larger entity acting on them, and on history, from some point outside history. It also runs counter to spurious notions, equally powerful and perhaps more attractive, of practitioners as "free" agents masters of their work—notions that understand agency as set against the material social realm, divorced from history. Against both of these I have argued for a view of composition as involving neither enslavement to nor free mastery over that realm but, instead, an engagement with it. We rewrite composition, ourselves, our history and our conditions, and thereby Composition, in response to and to shape composition, ourselves, our history and conditions, and Composition.

Understood thus, composition is "practice" not in the sense of being preparatory to some other, future activity, but in the sense of being work itself, "an activity which adapts material for some purpose or other" (Marx, *Contribution* 36). To rewrite composition is to engage in the labor of adapting the material of past representations of composition—and language, labor, value, and discipline—to some purpose or other. In this book, I have tried to adapt such material to a purpose different than what I see dominant ideologies of labor, value, disciplinarity, language, and composition propose for us by reworking the meanings we ascribe to these terms and our practice of them. In so doing, I cannot claim to be offering anything new, at least in the sense in which the "new" is ordinarily understood—for example, as deviation from the conventional and ordinary. Instead, I have argued for rediscovering what is deemed extraordinary in what we have learned to (mis)recognize as merely ordinary by rethinking, and thereby reclaiming, the terms themselves, and our work, from their dominant designations.

The laboriousness of such reworking of terms will have been painfully evident to even the most sympathetic of my readers. Indeed, given the seemingly self-evident meaning of such terms, my labor over their (possible) meanings may well seem not merely laborious but an exercise in belaboring—an unnecessary, unproductive, unmeaningful exercise in rendering difficult what is, in fact, easy and in no need of labor at all. To which I can reply only that denials of such labor offer in fact neither a retreat nor escape from labor but, rather, participation, however unwitting, in the labor of reiterating—and giving renewed life to—meanings to those terms as "self-evident," with all the consequences such labor brings. We labor to effect even, and perhaps especially, when we do not recognize our labor as labor—as "an activity which adapts material for some purpose or other. . . . a natural condition of human existence."

Another book on composition. The phrase itself seems tedious, bespeaking a belaboring of a subject that cannot possibly merit book-length discussion, certainly not another one. That sense of tedium is, I have argued, a consequence of how we have come to think of composition: as in itself inadequate, in need, lacking any disciplinary subject matter of value—the mere copy, well or poorly done, of language. Rewriting composition thus requires not giving new terms in exchange for *composition*, which would leave unchallenged the valuations assigned by the dominant to *composition*. Instead, we need to refuse the legitimacy and stability of such valuations, to insist on the discipline of taking up, and the necessity of taking up, continually, the labor of rewriting composition as a term whose meaning and value are the always-emerging outcome and product of that labor.

Composition is an ongoing historical project: the name given to work done in colleges and universities, mostly in the United States, by students and teachers as they engage and mediate differences in written language. That is the definition I am willing to offer, knowing that it is at best only a beginning, and necessarily incomplete.

NOTES WORKS CITED INDEX

Notes

1. Composition

1. On definitional anxiety as a defining characteristic of composition as a field, see Dobrin, *Postcomposition* 17–18; Hesse, foreword; Bartholomae, "What"; Horner and Lu, "Working." I discuss ideologies of disciplinarity in chapter 5.

2. I am of course poaching and twisting the notion of a "discourse of need" from Sharon Crowley ("Composition's Ethic"), who has critiqued the field of composition for its reliance on a discourse of *student* need to justify the universal first-year composition requirement. I differ from Crowley in identifying a discourse about composition itself as in need, and in challenging traditional academic disciplinarity as a goal for composition to aspire to.

3. See Bourdieu's caution:

> The practical privilege in which all scientific activity arises never more subtly governs that activity (insofar as science presupposes not only an epistemological break but also a social separation) than when, unrecognized as privilege, it leads to an implicit theory of practice which is the corollary of neglect of the social conditions in which science is possible. (Outline 1)

Alternatively, as Lynn Worsham reminds us, theory should be engaged as "a rhetorical (and political) *event* that emerges out of and responds to the world, to social and political situations that are available to understanding through interpretation" ("Coming" 103, emphasis added).

4. For a different analysis of illogicalities in Smit, see Herberg.

5. For recent discussions of the transferability of writing knowledge, see Nowacek, Wardle, and Yancey et al. I discuss issues of transfer in chapter 2.

6. Gidden, *Central Problems*. In *Terms of Work* (126–31), I critique the normative functionalist approach taken by several writers whose arguments align with Smit's and on whose work he draws.

7. Smit is explicitly reiterating a position articulated by Jeff Smith. For critiques of Smith's position invoked by Smit, see Horner, "Students, Authorship" 510; Horner, *Terms of Work* 129; Lu and Horner, "Problematic" 265.

8. I'm thinking here, for example, of works by Blommaert, Brandt, Cintron, Cushman (*Struggle*), Duffy, Gere, Gilyard (*Voices*), Graff, Barton and Hamilton, Hawisher and Selfe, Heath, Ivanič (*Writing*), Kress, Lillis (*Student*), Moss, Prior (*Writing/Disciplinarity*), Rose, Royster, Scribner and Cole, Street, and B. Williams (among countless others).

9. See, for example, Dobrin's complaint against composition studies' "historical foundations as an educational initiative—one more closely akin to the work of schools of education than other humanities disciplines, generally, and English, specifically" (28).

10. Lefebvre's critique is apposite here:

> Consider questions about space, for example: taken out of the context of practice, projected onto the place of a knowledge that considers itself to be "pure" and imagines itself to be "productive" (as indeed it is—but only of verbiage), such questions assume a philosophizing and degenerate character. What they degenerate into are mere general considerations on intellectual space—on "writing" as the intellectual space of a people, as the mental space of a period, and so on. (Production 415)

11. On "globalism" as distinct from globalization and "globality," see Beck 9–11. For a recent critique of the immateriality of this discourse, see Sutherland.

12. Dobrin is disputing Nedra Reynolds's statement that "the whole world is *not* in the Web" (*Geographies of Writing* 35, emphasis in original; qtd. in Dobrin 144).

13. "J. K. Gibson-Graham" is the name and identity taken by co-authors Katherine Gibson and (the late) Julie Graham. In their coauthored writing they have alternated between self-identifying in the singular ("I," "my," "mine") and the plural ("we," "our," "ours"). I have adopted the latter except where quotations from their work make it less confusing to use the singular, but some ambiguity is inevitable.

14. On the distinction between hegemony and the hegemonic, see R. Williams, *Marxism* 111, and discussion below.

15. In saying this, I echo Davila's review.

16. For a quite different but compelling analysis of Dobrin in these terms, see Gunner, "Disciplinary Purification."

17. We can see this invocation of an undifferentiated, stable, all-powerful monolith in the following statements: "In the local place of the wpa, hegemony becomes the very mechanism of control manifest in managerial presence: curriculum, policy, orientation, practicum" (96); "In no way can the local wpa operate outside of the context of the WPA. The wpa and the WPA are inseparable parts

of the larger complex administrative system" (97); "There can be no composition studies without the WPA in the same way that there can be no WPA or wpa without composition studies" (100); "No local wpa can exist outside of the formation of the WPA Empire, that all wpas feed the WPA Empire. Any local work toward emancipation is always work in support of the Empire's homogenization" (110); "The wpa is the occupied body used—not empowered—by the WPA. The WPA, then, is constituted by multiple wpa bodies giving subjectivity and authority over to the WPA" (219); "Theory attached to classroom practice is necessarily, always already co-opted and cannot, by definition, be emancipatory since classroom practice is sanctioned by the institution" (13).

18. According to Google Scholar, as of the time this chapter is being written, Slevin's book, published in 2001, has been cited in twenty-seven sources; Smit's book, published in 2004, has been cited in seventy-three sources, almost three times as many. Dobrin's book, published in 2011 (ten years after Slevin's) has already been cited in twelve sources, almost half the number accrued by Slevin but in one-sixth the time Slevin's book has been available.

19. From a quite different perspective, Fulkerson likewise identifies critical theory as the source infiltrating composition ("Composition at the Turn" 657).

20. For a useful and more elaborated analysis of theory/practice relations than I present here, see Zebroski, "Toward" 37ff.

21. See, for example, among many others, Goleman; Jung; Lu, "Professing"; R. Miller, "Fault"; Zebroski, *Thinking*.

22. I rehearse here suggestions Min-Zhan Lu and I make in "Working" (483). As we argue there, many of these are inevitably taken up under the rubric of courses or course titles advertising a more commodified notion of rhetoric and "its" history.

23. However, Bazerman identifies the source of his own study of writing in his experience teaching (and writing).

24. Downs and Wardle, in their separate responses to Miles et al., reject the interpretation that they see their proposed course as intending to represent the entire discipline (Downs, Wardle).

25. For a counterview, see J. Williams and Colomb.

26. For an exemplary articulation of this position, see the statement "To the Student" in William E. Coles Jr.'s *The Plural* I.

27. Trimbur alludes to this, noting that "after all, asking students to study writing is something writing teachers do and have always done" ("Changing" 18).

28. Trimbur suggests something like this in challenging the common distinction between the FYC "workshop" and the "seminar." We might also model FYC (and other) composition courses after graduate seminars, in the root sense of these. For one example of this, see the course for students designated as basic readers and writers described in David Bartholomae and Anthony Petrosky's *Facts, Artifacts, Counterfacts*.

29. See, for example, Horner, *Terms*; Thaiss and Zawacki.

30. We can see the pressures of this imperative leading Kathleen Blake Yancey, for example, to admit, in her Conference on College Composition and Communication (CCCC) Chair's Address, to wondering "if in some pretty important ways and within the relatively short space of not quite ten years, we [in composition] may already have become anachronistic" ("Made" 302). For similar arguments, see Daley, and Rowsell 2–3, 76–77, 148, 152.

31. See Calvet, 7 and passim; Gal and Irvine; Milroy 540–41; Mühlhäusler 328, qtd. in Milroy 540–41.

32. For a more developed discussion of these issues on which I draw here, see Horner, Lockridge, and Selfe.

33. Cf. Brian Street's observation that

> for many researchers and practitioners, especially those in the field of education, it is often assumed that what is "new" [in New Literacy Studies] is the "literacy" that is being described [such as "new" literacy technologies]. . . . But, in the "New Literacy Studies" the term "new" refers not so much to these [new] forms [of literacy] but rather to the studies themselves; that is, it is the ways in which literacy is conceptualised and researched that is "new" in the "New Literacy Studies." ("New" 27–28)

For similar arguments, see Wysocki's redefinition of what constitutes the "new" of "new media" ("Opening" 15), and Shipka 9.

34. For examples of calls for such additive curricular models, see Miles et al.; Rowsell. I discuss the limitations of an additive model of multilingualism in chapter 2.

35. See, for example, Yancey, "Made" 315. Selfe argues for a different model whereby the first-year composition course might simply initiate students' attention to a broad range of semiotic resources, attention that would be developed by particular students in advanced courses offered by different disciplines, such as art, digital audio design, etc. ("Response" 606–7).

36. It is telling, in this respect, that Kress and Van Leeuwen, in *Multimodal Discourse*, invoke a term advanced by much-studied nineteenth-century German composer Richard Wagner, ordinarily identified as a musician, to name the "multimodal" character of "the avant-gardes of 'high culture' arts" that, they assert, have "[only just] begun to use an increasing variety of materials and to cross the boundaries between the various art, design, and performance disciplines" (Kress and Van Leeuwen, *Multimodal Discourse* 1). Kress and Van Leeuwen suggest that "in the age of digitization" the "different modes have technically become the same at some level of representation," obviating the need for the hierarchically organized teams of specialists, each in charge of a specific mode, whose work was then brought together during editing (for example, bringing together sound and image in the production of film). But

there is a slippage here between production of specific media—sound and images—and the multimodal character of engagements with these—for example, the work with images that film music composition requires; the assumptions of music and film shots (and acting, and scenery, etc.) invoked in the writing of film scripts.

37. See for example Bartholomae, "Inventing"; Canagarajah, *Geopolitics*; Herrington and Curtis; Prior; Rose; Sternglass; Sullivan et al.; Thaiss and Zawacki. Work in "academic literacies" and *litteracies universitaires* has of course also made significant contributions to this understanding (see Defays et al.; Ivanič; Ivanič et al.; Lea and Street; Lillis, *Student*; Lillis and Curry).

2. *Language*

1. For a useful overview of conceptualizations of language as the outcome of practices, see Cooper, "Being."

2. The exception might be standard courses in the history of the English language, though even there, English is typically understood not in relation to other existing languages (now and in the past) but as a distinct entity, however much emerging from its "roots" in other languages (cf. Saraceni).

3. As Raymond Williams explains, "The living speech of human beings in their specific social relationships in the world was theoretically reduced to instances and examples of a system which lay beyond them" (*Marxism* 27). For a useful overview of the monolingualism and monolingualist effects of structural linguistics, see Canagarajah, *Translingual* 20–24.

4. For a more general account of the relegation of "language-in-use" to a subordinate position vis-à-vis language as system, see R. Williams, *Marxism* 25–28. For a different account of the changing status of "language" in composition, see MacDonald.

5. For useful overviews of this division, see Paul Kei Matsuda's "Composition Studies" and "Second Language Writing."

6. A view exemplified in Leonard Bloomfield's dismissive statement, "Writing is not language but merely a way of recording language by means of visible marks" (21).

7. For an overview, see Roberts and Street.

8. I have developed this argument in "Ideologies of Literacy."

9. A highly partial/selective list of work in basic writing addressing language difference includes Bartholomae, "Study," "Writing on the Margins," "Tidy House"; Brodkey, "On the Subjects"; Epes, "Tracing"; Farrell, "Developing"; Fox, "Basic"; Hull et al., "Remediation"; Kroll and Schafer; Lu, "Professing"; Rodby, *Appropriating*; Schwalm; Shaughnessy, *Errors*; J. Williams, "Phenomenology." The professional organizational statements on language difference include, in addition to SRTOL, the "CCCC Statement on Second Language Writing and Writers," the "CCCC Guideline on the National Language Policy"

position statement, the NCTE "Resolution on English as a Second Language and Bilingual Education," "Resolution on English as the 'Official Language,'" and "Position Statement . . . on Issues in ESL and Bilingual Education." The literature on language differences of students appearing in composition courses and arguments supporting a rapprochement between composition studies and ESL scholarship includes Bean et al.; Canagarajah, *Literacy*, "Place"; Fraiberg; Hall; Harklau et al., *Generation*; Hesford et al.; Horner and Kopelson; Horner, Lu, and Matsuda; Horner and Trimbur; Horner, Lu, Royster, and Trimbur; Jordan; Kells, Balester, and Villanueva; Kirklighter, Cárdenas, and Murphy; Lu, "Essay"; Lunsford and Ouzgane; Martinez and Young; Matsuda, "Basic"; Matsuda, Fruit, and Lamm; Nero, *Dialects*, *Englishes*; Scott, Straker, and Katz; Severino, Guerra, and Butler; Smitherman and Villanueva; Tardy; Trimbur, "Dartmouth"; Valdès.

10. I rehearse here the argument presented in my "Mapping." Bartholomae's "The Study of Error" is an exemplary illustration of the application of theories of second language learning to the errors in basic writing students' texts.

11. On this conceptualization of representation (in Calvet and others), see Moore and Gajo; Kramsch, "Contrepont"; and Moore and Py.

12. On that controversy, see Smitherman, "CCCC's Role in the Struggle"; Gilyard, "African American." The statement in largely unchanged form was "reaffirmed" in 2003. This is not to say that SRTOL had no effects or does not serve as a touchstone for pedagogical projects (see, for example, Gilyard and Richardson; Horner et al., "Language"; Kinloch; Wible, "Pedagogies"). But those projects have been hampered by the assumptions about language driving SROTL (see, again, Wible, "Pedagogies"). That said, Gilyard and Richardson's caution is apposite here:

> We should bear in mind that collaboration on a document like SRTOL does not necessarily mean that its composers were of identical theoretical persuasion, nor does the existence of SRTOL imply that strict uniformity exists among the practitioners supportive of the manifesto. (38)

They subsequently observe that "[t]here was never a shortage of ideas about how SRTOL could be implemented beyond a liberal pluralist paradigm, just a shortage of empirical models" (39), leading to their presentation of one such model.

13. Cf. Keith Gilyard's wry observation, "Social relations are a far more vital factor for Black students in school than differences of language variety" (*Voices* 74).

14. For an eloquently useful analysis of this effect, see Vershawn Ashanti Young's "'Nah." Tellingly, this is a peril that only those groups associated with subordinated social identities face: those enjoying more privileged status can afford to mix it up. Indeed, doing so advertises their privileged status—like

those who don clothing styles of the homeless to advertise their possession of sufficient status to not worry about being mistaken for being homeless.

15. Lu, drawing on Baldwin, gives an alternate inflection to the notion of language users aligned with the argument presented here ("Essay").

16. For similar models, see Pennycook, *Language*; Canagarajah, *Translingual* chapter 1. Min-Zhan Lu and I elaborate on this model in "Translingual Literacy."

17. See Canagarajah, *Translingual*, *Literacy*; Horner et al., "Language"; Horner, Donahue, and NeCamp, "Toward"; Pennycook, *Language*.

18. The same would of course be true for other equivalent theoretical monsters, for example, "Chinese," "French," and so on (see Qu).

19. Cf. R. Williams on the selectivity of what is "the tradition" (*Marxism* 115–16).

20. Other terms, not used in identical ways but with significant overlap, include *diversalité*, *plurilingual*, and *post-monolingual* (see Confiant; Khubchandani; Yildiz).

21. This is in addition to the failure to address writing's mediation of abstracted speech varieties—the fact that, as Gilyard observes, there are "no reputable studies demonstrating that speech varieties translate neatly into writing varieties" (*True* 129).

22. Cf. Kramsch:

> Peu d'apprenants ont conscience du rôle qu'ils jouent en tant que locateurs/acteurs non-natifs sur la vie ou la mort d'une langue, son développement, son usage, son potentiel sémiotique. . . . L'apprentissage d'une langue étrangère, avec tout ce qu'elle apporte de décentration, de conflit et de découvertes, est une des matières scolaires les plus propices à . . . redonner aux apprenants la puissance d'agir discursive dont ils pensent manquer [Few learners are aware of the role they play as non-native speakers/actors in the life or death of a language, its development, its use, its semiotic potential. . . . Learning a foreign language, with all the decentering, conflict, and discoveries this brings, is one of the school subjects most likely to restore to learners the discursive agency that they think they lack]. ("Contrepont" 322)

23. For example, my own family situation has made the use of particular phrases in Shanghainese ("dong shin," "ver shaw der") seem the most apposite and "natural" for me (and specific family members), at least some of the time, but I don't anticipate these will gain broader traction in U.S. culture. But if they do, they will be relocalized and therefore carry a different significance than the significance of their use by me and my family in specific moments in my family's history.

24. For a more extended analysis of ELF as model for composition on which I draw here, see Horner and Lu, "(Re)Writing English."

25. The study was first presented in Canagarajah, "Multlingual Strategies."

26. For a similar point, see Canagarajah, "Multilingual" 28–29.

27. Cf. Constant Leung's conclusion from his review of challenges to sociolinguistic certainties, that "communicative competence is not a set of knowledge and skills that one can prescribe in advance; it is an outcome of how people use their knowledge and skills" ("The Social" 307).

28. For a similar argument, see DePalma and Ringer's reconceptualization of transfer as "adaptive" transfer, understood as "the conscious or intuitive process of applying or *reshaping* learned writing knowledge in new and potentially unfamiliar writing situations" (141, emphasis added).

29. See DePalma and Ringer on the neglect of agency in dominant models of transfer.

30. As Driscoll and Wells observe, "Perkins et al. argue that dispositions are not static; learners develop particular dispositions as they move through activity systems. Research has shown that some dispositions may be context-specific (e.g., valuing learning in one context but not another) or broadly generalized (underlying value systems, such that 'learning is good')."

3. Labor

1. There is of course a burgeoning literature addressing labor in composition, and in the academy more broadly, in just such terms. I discuss some of this literature below and in chapter 4. For a sampling, see Bousquet, *How*; Bousquet et al.; Harris, "Meet"; Herman; Hendricks, "Teaching"; Horner, "Class"; Schell; Schell and Stock; Strickland; Tuell.

2. As Maurizio Lazzarato puts it, "labor produces commodities, but first and foremost it produces the capital relation" ("General").

3. On the feminization of composition work, see Holbrook; S. Miller, "Feminization"; Tuell; Schell. For more general accounts of the low status and poor working conditions of composition teaching, see Bousquet et al. Those compositionists who enjoy better working conditions often do so as compensation for taking on the responsibility of managing these others, a responsibility for social relations that likewise is not recognized as "productive" in the economy of academic institutional value (see Strickland). I discuss these matters in greater detail in chapter 4. In chapter 1 of *Terms of Work* I discuss composition's difficulties in defining and laying claim to work.

4. Hence efforts to reduce unemployment by increasing the amount of time spent on production of material goods are misdirected insofar as such efforts deny "the productive power of living labor" (55). There is no lack of work to be done. What is needed, then, is not more work, Marazzi argues, but rather "*freeing up blocks of living time* . . . because reducing work time is above all an objective tied to the *quality of life*, and not to the need to create new jobs" (55, emphasis in original).

5. We have here an instance of what Gibson-Graham describe as "subjects 'made' and as 'making themselves' in and through discourse and practices of governmentality" (*Post-Capitalist* 23). Chapter 2 of their book *Post-Capitalist* describes "devices of 'meaning production'" sustaining "belief in the naturalness of [what the (Latrobe, Australia) valley] economy was" that "obstructed movement and sustained [residents'] continued subjection" (25).

6. A recent ill-advised suggestion at my home institution that the school year be made twelve month instead of ten month in order to make use of faculty's continued local presence forced articulation of this fact. The suggestion was quickly retracted.

7. There is of course an argument that students in the United States be paid for their work as students, as students are elsewhere, rather than being required to pay others for the privilege of being students. While I am in favor of such a policy, it does not in itself necessarily constitute recognition of the labor students perform on and with language. More often, it is understood as an investment by the state to prepare students with skills necessary for their work in the future, after graduation. And thus it is conceivable that were such a policy to be adopted, the terms of the policy might inscribe more conventional notions of merit in exchange for pay, measured by, say, test scores for admission and continued tenure as students, with those students admitted under continual threat of being sacked, rather than their income being unconditional.

8. As Gibson-Graham and David Ruccio observe in arguing for a reconceptualization of class as process, traditionally,

> In that class is . . . primarily bestowed by location in an economic structure, and this structure is in turn dominated by capitalism . . . , it is not surprising that, as a conceptual tool, the categorical notion of class has not been able to break away from capitalocentric visions. (170)

9. I identify these assumptions with "monolingual-ist" ideology insofar as they not only underlie, for example, English Only (and equivalent) political movements but, as ideological, also pervade ordinary cultural practices even among those individuals who are indifferent or hostile to such movements, and insofar as the ideology is not tied to the number of languages an individual might claim to know. Monolinguals, for example, might not follow monolingualist ideology, and multilinguals might.

10. Recall, for example, advertisements during the 2008 U.S. Republican presidential primary campaign sponsored by opponents of Mitt Romney that attacked him for his ability to speak French as well as English.

11. For a more extended analysis of "friction" and language pedagogy on which I draw here, see Horner and Lu, "Toward a Labor Economy."

12. See chapter 2 for a discussion of Calvet and this model of the relations between languages and practices.

13. This transmission is attempted, of course, through a variety of strategies intended to enable students to learn or acquire the language, including, for example, not only "drill" but also "immersion."

14. As Calvet observes,

> communication cannot be reduced to a code or a model for sentence production. The codes, which are necessary but not sufficient to communication, are the constantly evolving product of a need to communicate, a quest for communication and an awareness of this communication. Furthermore, individuals may understand each other perfectly well by using codes which on analysis can be considered to be different. (5–6)

15. On the necessity of "friction" to such transactions, see Anna Lowenhaupt Tsing, discussed above.

16. We can see this use of language as such a proxy in the revision to a job posting for ESL instructors: the request for "NATIVE SPEAKING, EXPATRIATE ENGLISH TEACHERS FOR FOREIGN STUDENTS [*sic*]" apparently drew the wrong kind of native-English-speaking applicants, so the posting was revised to read as follows: "NATIVE SPEAKING, CAUCASIAN ENGLISH TEACHERS FOR FOREIGN STUDENTS" (Kandiah, "Epiphanies" 79).

17. Declining to authorize any one explanation, within their narrative, Miller and Cripps offer four competing "versions" of the changes made to the Rutgers University writing program.

18. See chapter 2 for a fuller discussion of this approach to difference in language.

19. For a discussion of the pedagogical necessity of approaching language politics in terms of dispositions, see Horner and Lu, "Rewriting."

20. On translingual writing, see Horner et al., "Language."

21. This would alleviate the common pressure on WPAs to offer all incoming students enrollment in the course their first semester, which typically results in both the lowering of hiring criteria, and the need to fire course instructors the next semester for lack of available course assignments, a boom-bust cycle that itself exacerbates the difficulty of finding qualified instructors to teach during the predictable fall semester "boom" demand.

22. For accounts of such efforts at local institutions, and the strategies undertaken, see Hesford et al., Sullivan et al., and Tardy.

23. There is significant work on translingual approaches to reading and writing in modern languages (see for example, Kramsch, "Privilege"; Yildiz). The Modern Language Association is in some ways ahead of CCCC and the National Council of Teachers of English (NCTE) in considering such approaches (see, for example, Modern Language Association Ad Hoc).

24. On this possibility, see Cameron, "Globalization," and Dor.

4. *Value/Evaluation*

1. The distinction here between a discourse of "unionism," on the one hand, and discourse on unions, on the other, parallels that between "globalism" and discourse on globalization (see Beck 9–11).

2. I discuss the way in which social relations constitute a real if unrecognized "productive force" in chapter 3.

3. I present an extended argument on this point in *Terms of Work*, chapter 1.

4. This is the perspective articulated in one version of Miller and Cripps's argument, discussed in chapter 3, that virtually anyone can teach first-year writing, rendering the pool of available labor enormous and growing.

5. This friction is also a necessary component to the "transfer" of writing skills, discussed in chapter 2.

6. For an example of breathless advocacy of such for-profit, "distance ed." providers, see Taylor, chapter 8. For more sober analyses of distance education, see Cornford and Pollock, and Crook.

7. For discussions of the effects of fast-capitalist, neoliberal market economies on workers, see Bauman, Beck, Sennett.

8. This is not to give credence to the popular belief that teaching (or learning) "the basics" of writing is simple. There is now a significant body of scholarship demonstrating the complexity of producing as well as interpreting those aspects of writing commonly categorized and denigrated as "basic skills" (see, for example, Bartholomae, "Study"; Horner, "Rethinking"; Hull; Lees; Lu, "Professing"; Shaughnessy; Tricomi; J. Williams). In short, treating writing in terms of "basic skills" is of a piece with the commodification of writing and reading, which, as I have been arguing, contributes to the denigration of the work of composition in which teachers and students engage. Conversely one might focus precisely on such "basics" but in ways that bring out their unrecognized complexity, in the same way that physics courses explore complexity in such "basics" as energy and matter.

5. *Discipline*

1. Cf. Orlikowski, "Material Knowing and Scaffolding."

2. As Halliday puts it, "Language is not a *domain* of human knowledge. . . . Language is the essential condition of knowing" (94, original emphasis).

3. There is of course a large corpus of scholarship on academic disciplinarity, the professions, and academic professions (see, for example, Bledstein; Larson; Messer-Davidow et al.; Ohmann, *Politics*). Likewise, the professionalization of composition, its status as an academic discipline, and the consequences of these have been the subject of ongoing debate for some time now (see, for example, Connors; Ferry; France et al.; Horner, *Terms*; Spellmeyer, "Marginal," "Travels"; Trimbur, "Writing Instruction"). Chris Gallagher provides an intriguing

overview, discussed below, of that debate (along with an argument about the relationship of disciplinarity to professionalism) in "We Compositionists." Readers anticipating that a chapter on discipline and its relation to knowledge will necessarily engage directly with the writings of Michel Foucault will have to settle for the following quotation from Foucault, whose import I ignore regarding Marx but follow regarding Foucault: "I quote Marx without saying so. . . . When a physicist writes a work of physics, does he feel it necessary to quote Newton and Einstein?" (Foucault, *Power/Knowledge* 52).

4. As Wilfred Carr and Stephen Kemmis note, the clientele (as well as work and conditions treated by the work) of teachers, unlike that of, say, medical doctors, is diffuse (8–9).

5. Gallagher (chapter 5, *Radical*) argues similarly for making composition a "pedagogy-centered" (vs. "student-centered") discipline.

6. Of course, attention to the arguments of Haswell and Fulkerson is also merited by Haswell's status as a scholar and as the sponsor and director (with Glenn Blalock) of *CompPile*, the best online bibliographical resource for compositionists, and Fulkerson's status as periodic assessor of trends in approaches to composition teaching, a status endorsed by the publication of his assessments ("Four," "Composition in the 1980s," "Composition at") in *College Composition and Communication*, the field's flagship journal.

7. The statement is attributed to Wilfred Carr and Stephen Kemmis's *Becoming Critical* (8). However, it misquotes from, and misrepresents, Carr and Kemmis's argument. Haswell's epitaph, attributed to Carr and Kemmis, reads, "No profession can exist without a body of systematically produced knowledge" (Haswell 198). The passage on page 8 of Carr and Kemmis closest to this is as follows:

> Briefly, these [criteria normally employed in distinguishing professional from non-professional occupations] are, first, that the methods and procedures employed by members of a profession are based on a body of theoretical knowledge and research. Part of the reason why medicine, law and engineering are regarded as professional occupations is because they involve techniques and skills supported by a body of systematically produced knowledge. (7–8)

Carr and Kemmis argue that teachers are not regarded as professionals for a variety of reasons, including not only the limited role theory and research play in teaching but also the lack of a clearly defined clientele for teachers or of a relationship of teachers to that clientele, and, most seriously, lack of teacher autonomy to make decisions (8–9ff.). Contrary to the implied alignment of their argument with Haswell's suggested by his invocation of them in his epigraph, Carr and Kemmis reject "*positivist notions of rationality, objectivity, and truth*," calling instead for a "critical approach" to theory and practice (129, emphasis in original).

8. For a recent review of replication in educational research practices, as well as in a broad range of other disciplines, countering this normative view of replication research (while supporting its importance), see Makel and Plucker.

9. Comparable support is also, of course, necessary for other kinds of research (see Lindquist).

10. For example, Bartholomae advocated and modeled precisely the application of such training to reading student writing in his early study of error ("Study").

11. See Goodman et al., *Whose Knowledge Counts in Government Literacy Policies*; Lubienski, Scott, and DeBray; Daly et al.; Trujillo; Scott and Jabbar; Ness and Gandára; Goldie et al.; McDonald.

12. The history of compositionists' use of William Perry's research, presented in his *Forms of Intellectual and Ethical Development in the College Years*, is instructive. Haswell cites this research as evidence that RAD-based research contributes to the "growth" of scholarship. But the history of compositionists' engagements with Perry's ideas has been decidedly mixed (cf. Hays, "Models"; Kogen; and Bizzell, "William Perry").

13. For an aligned and amplified argument, see Trimbur, "Writing Instruction."

14. This is not to say that Fulkerson is uninterested in research or scholarship, or that he sees no value in using research as a way to test, support, or invalidate particular teaching practices, only that trends in scholarship are not the primary focus of his article.

15. This sense is reiterated in the sentences immediately following:

> Compositionists have developed more academically challenging courses than had been expected in a traditional curriculum, despite the general impression (most often by those not directly attached to the course) that these intro courses merely teach new teachers of writing how to grade assignments, teach mechanics, oversee classrooms, and the like. (2, emphasis added)

It's worth emphasizing that Dobrin is here (and passim) describing common positions taken regarding such practica rather than describing a position he himself would advocate.

16. Coles puts it this way: "The only substantive knowledge connected with the teaching of writing which is worthy of the name is knowledge that has been made more than knowledge by the teacher himself" ("New Presbyters" 9).

17. For a review of comparable conclusions drawn about the effects of the politicization of sociology on the professional academic disciplinary status of sociology, see Burawoy 17–18.

18. I draw here from my afterword to Martins's collection.

19. For a review of the various kinds of replication in research and their value, see Schmidt.

20. Just as "music" and "literature" (and even "English") can serve simultaneously as descriptors and honorifics.

21. Cf. Gallagher's discussion of concerns that work in composition should somehow "matter" to the students and the larger public, as in the 2004 CCCC theme "Making Composition Matter" and calls for a "public" turn, service-learning, and attention to "everyday literacies."

22. See for example Slaughter and Rhodes, and Lillis and Curry.

23. For a more elaborated version of this argument, see Lu and Horner, "Composing."

24. There is a long tradition of complaint against such writing. For a representative sampling, see Coles, "Freshman"; France, "Assigning Places"; S. Miller, *Textual*; Petraglia; Trimbur, "Circulation." I elaborate this point in "Re-valuing Student Writing."

25. Writing in the disciplines programs that eliminate FYC altogether exemplify this in moving both the students and their writing out of the course.

26. Recall here Freire's observation, "Within the word we find two dimensions, reflection and action, in such radical interaction that if one is sacrificed—even in part—the other immediately suffers" (87).

27. On the inevitability of and need to embrace opacity as a feature of all communicative efforts, see Bernabé, Chamoiseau, and Confiant 52.

28. Cf. accounts by Crane et al. of the "moments of friction and hesitancy" arising from the translations in which translingual research engages them ("More Than Just Translation" 40).

29. By "English" Bartholomae appears to mean the subject, the language, and the language as subject. He subsequently traces ongoing debates in the field's scholarship between language as abstraction and as practice, as an ideal and as common property (44).

30. For an especially useful discussion of this, see Lindquist, "Time."

Works Cited

Anson, Chris, and Christiane Donahue. "Curricular Topographia: Deconstructing 'Writing Program Administration' in an International Context." Martins 21–47.

Apple, Michael W., Jane Kenway, and Michael Singh, eds. *Globalizing Education: Policies, Pedagogies, and Politics.* New York: Lang, 2005. Print.

Auer, Peter. "Monolingual Bias in Bilingualism Research, or: Why Bilingual Talk Is (Still) a Challenge for Linguistics." Heller 319–39.

Baca, Damián. "Rethinking Composition, Five Hundred Years Later." *JAC* 29.1–2 (2009): 229–42. Print.

Banocy-Payne, Marge. "Program in Course Redesign, Tallahassee Community College." Web. 1 June 2005. <http://www.center.rpi.edu/PewGrant/RD3%20Award/TCCplan.html>.

Barbour, Stephen. "Language, Nationalism, and Globalism: Educational Consequences of Changing Patterns of Language Use." *Beyond Boundaries: Language and Identity in Contemporary Europe.* Ed. Paul Gubbins and Mike Holt. Clevedon, UK: Multilingual Matters, 2002. 11–18. Print.

Barnard, Ian. "The Ruse of Clarity." *College Composition and Communication* 61.3 (2010): 434–51. Print.

Barthes, Roland. "Writers, Teachers, Intellectuals." *Image-Music-Text.* Trans. Stephen Heath. London: HarperCollins, 1977. 190–216. Print.

Bartholomae, David. "Basic Writing: An Alternative to Basic Skills." *Journal of Basic Writing* 2.2 (1979): 85–109. Print.

———. "Freshman English, Composition, and CCCC." *College Composition and Communication* 40.1 (1989): 38–50. Print.

———. "Inventing the University." *When a Writer Can't Write: Studies in Writer's Block and Other Composing Problems.* Ed. Mike Rose. New York: Guildford, 1985. 134–65. Print.

———. "The Study of Error." *College Composition and Communication* 31 (1980): 253–69. Print.

———. "The Tidy House: Basic Writing in the American Curriculum." *Journal of Basic Writing* 12.1 (Spring 1993): 4–21. Print.

———. "What Is Composition and (If You Know What That Is) Why Do We Teach It?" Bloom et al. 11–28.

———. "Writing Assignments: Where Writing Begins." *Writing on the Margins: Essays on Composition and Teaching.* Boston: Bedford/St. Martins, 2005. 171–91. Print.

Bartholomae, David, and Anthony Petrosky. *Facts, Artifacts, Counterfacts: Theory and Method for a Course in Basic Reading and Writing.* Portsmouth, NH: Boynton Cook/Heinmann, 1986. Print.

Barton, David, and Mary Hamilton. *Local Literacies: Reading and Writing in One Community.* London: Routledge, 1998. Print.

Barton, David, Mary Hamilton, and Roz Ivanič, eds. *Situated Literacies: Reading and Writing in Context.* New York: Routledge, 2000. Print.

Bauman, Marcy. "hours per week." WPA-L listserv posting. <http://lists.asu.edu/archives/wpa-l.html>. 25 June 2005.

Bauman, Zygmunt. *Globalization: The Human Consequences.* New York: Columbia UP, 1998. Print.

Bawarshi, Anis, and Mary Jo Reiff. *Genre: An Introduction to History, Theory, Research, and Pedagogy.* West Lafayette, IN: Parlor, 2010. Print.

Baynham, Mike, and Mastin Prinsloo, eds. *The Future of Literacy Studies.* Basingstoke, UK: Palgrave Macmillan, 2009. Print.

Bazerman, Charles. "The Case for Writing Studies as a Major Discipline." Olson and Worsham 32–38.

———. "From Cultural Criticism to Disciplinary Participation: Living with Powerful Words." *Writing, Teaching, and Learning in the Disciplines.* Ed. Anne Herrington and Charles Moran. New York: Modern Language Association, 1992. 61–68. Print.

———. "Response: Curricular Responsibilities and Professional Definition." Petraglia 249–59.

Beach, King. "Consequential Transitions: A Sociocultural Expedition beyond Transfer in Education." *Review of Research in Education* 24.1 (1999): 101–39. Print.

Bean, Janet, Maryann Cucchiara, Robert Eddy, Peter Elbow, Rhonda Grego, Rich Haswell, Patricia Irvine, Eileen Kennedy, Ellie Kutz, Al Lehner, and Paul Kei Matsuda. "Should We Invite Students to Write in Home Languages? Complicating the Yes/No Debate." *Composition Studies* 31.1 (Spring 2003): 25–42. Print.

Beck, Ulrich. *What Is Globalization*? Trans. Patrick Camiller. Cambridge: Polity, 2000. Print.

Bernabé, Jean, Patrick Chamoiseau, and Raphaël Confiant. *Éloge de la créolité.* Paris: Gallimard, 1989. Rpt. as *Éloge de la créolité/In Praise of*

Creoleness. Trans. M. B. Taleb-Khyar. Baltimore: Johns Hopkins UP, 1990. Print.

Bernhardt, Steve. "Seeing the Text." *College Composition and Communication* 37.1 (1986): 66–78. Print.

Bizzell, Patricia. "William Perry and Liberal Education." *College English* 46 (September 1984): 447–54. Print.

———. "Marxist Ideas in Composition Studies." *Contending with Words*. Ed. Patricia Harkin and John Schilb. New York: Modern Language Association, 1991. 52–68. Print.

Björk, Lennart, Gerd Bräuer, Lottie Rienecker, and Peter Stray Jörgensen, eds. *Teaching Academic Writing in European Higher Education*. New York: Springer, 2003. Print.

Blanchet, Philippe. "Quels fondements et quels objectifs pour une sociodidactique de la pluralité linguistique et culturelle? Enjeux épistémologiques, théoriques et interventionnistes [Foundations and Goals for a Socio-didactic/Didacticism of Linguistic and Cultural Plurality: Epistemological, Theoretical, and Interventionist Stakes]." *(Mé)Tisser les langues à l'école?* Dir. Stéphanie Clerc. *Cahiers de Linguistique* 37.2 (2011): 183–92. Print.

Bledstein, Burton. *The Culture of Professionalism: The Middle Class and the Development of Higher Education in America*. New York: Norton, 1978. Print.

Blommaert, Jan. *Grassroots Literacy: Writing, Identity and Voice in Central Africa*. New York: Routledge, 2008. Print.

Bloom, Lynn Z., Donald A. Daiker, and Edward M. White, eds. *Composition in the Twenty-first Century: Crisis and Change*. Carbondale: Southern Illinois UP, 1996. Print.

Bloomfield, Leonard. *Language*. New York: Holt, 1933. Print.

Bolter, Jay David, and Richard Grusin. *Remediation: Understanding New Media*. Cambridge: MIT P, 2000. Print.

Bourdieu, Pierre. *Language and Symbolic Power*. Ed. John B. Thompson. Trans. Gino Raymond and Matthew Adamson. Cambridge, MA: Harvard UP, 1991. Print.

———. *Outline of a Theory of Practice*. Trans. Richard Nice. Cambridge: Cambridge UP, 1977. Print.

Bousquet, Marc. "Composition as Management Science: Toward a University without a WPA." *JAC* 22 (2002): 493–526. Rpt. Bousquet et al. 11–35.

———. *How the University Works: Higher Education and the Low Wage Nation*. New York: New York UP, 2008. Print.

Bousquet, Marc, Tony Scott, and Leo Parascondola, eds. *Tenured Bosses and Disposable Teachers: Writing Instruction in the Managed University*. Carbondale: Southern Illinois UP, 2004. Print.

Boutang, Yann Moulier. *Le Capitalisme cognitif.* Éditions Amsterdam, 2008. *Cognitive Capitalism.* Trans. Ed Emery. New York: Polity, 2011. Print.

Boyer, Ernest L. *Scholarship Reconsidered: Priorities for the Professoriate.* Princeton: Carnegie Foundation for the Advancement of Teaching, 1990. Print.

Brandt, Deborah. *Literacy in American Lives.* Cambridge: Cambridge UP, 2001. Print.

Braun, M. J. "The Prospects for Rhetoric in a First-Year Composition Program: Deliberative Discourse as a Vehicle for Change?" *Writing Program Administration* 31.3 (2008): 89–109. Print.

Brodkey, Linda. "On the Subjects of Class and Gender in 'The Literacy Letters.'" *College English* 51.2 (1989): 125–41. Print.

Brutt-Griffler, Janina. *World English: A Study of Its Development.* Clevedon, UK: Multilingual Matters, 2002. Print.

Burawoy, Michael. "For Public Sociology." *American Sociological Review* 70.1 (2005): 4–28. Print.

Byram, Michael. *Teaching and Assessing Intercultural Communicative Competence.* Clevedon, UK: Multilingual Matters, 1997. Print.

Calhoon-Dillahunt, Carolyn. "Important Focus, Limited Perspective." *College Composition and Communication* 63.3 (2012): 495–99. Print.

Calvet, Louis-Jean. *Pour une écologie des langues du monde.* Plon, 1999. Trans. Andrew Brown, *Towards an Ecology of World Languages.* London: Polity, 2006. Print.

Cameron, Deborah. "Globalization and the Teaching of 'Communication Skills.'" *Globalization and Language Teaching.* Ed. David Block and Deborah Cameron. London: Routledge, 2002. 67–82. Print.

———. *Verbal Hygiene.* Rev. ed. London: Routledge, 2012. Print.

Canagarajah, A. Suresh. "The Ecology of Global English." *International Multilingual Research Journal* 1.2 (2007): 89–100. Print.

———. *A Geopolitics of Academic Writing.* Pittsburgh: U of Pittsburgh P, 2002. Print.

———. "Lingua Franca English, Multilingual Communities, and Language Acquisition." *Modern Language Journal* 91 (2007): 923–39. Print.

———, ed. *Literacy as Translingual Practice: Between Communities and Classrooms.* New York: Routledge, 2013. Print.

———. "Multilingual Strategies of Negotiating English: From Conversation to Writing." *JAC* 29.1–2 (2009): 17–48. Print.

———. "Negotiating the Local in English as a Lingua Franca." *Annual Review of Applied Linguistics* 26 (2006): 197–218. Print.

———. "'Nondiscursive' Requirements in Academic Publishing, Material Resources of Periphery Scholars, and the Politics of Knowledge Production." *Written Communication* 13 (1996): 435–72. Print.

———. "The Place of World Englishes in Composition: Pluralization Continued." *College Composition and Communication* 57 (2006): 586–619. Print.

———. *Translingual Practice: Global Englishes and Cosmopolitan Relations.* London: Routledge, 2013. Print.

Carr, Wilfred, and Stephen Kemmis. *Becoming Critical: Education Knowledge and Action Research.* Deakin UP, 1986. Rpt. Milton Park, UK: Falmer, 1988.

Carter, Christopher. "Bureaucratic Essentialism and the Corporatization of Composition." Bousquet et al. 186–92.

Chase, Geoffrey. "Redefining Composition, Managing Change, and the Role of the WPA." *Writing Program Administration* 21 (Fall 1997): 46–54. Rpt. Ward and Carpenter 243–51.

Chiang, Yuet-Sim D., and Mary Schmida. "Language Identity and Language Ownership: Linguistic Conflicts of First-Year University Writing Students." Harklau et al. 81–96.

Chaput, Catherine. "Fear, Affective Energy, and the Political Economy of Global Capitalism." *Entertaining Fear: Rhetoric and the Political Economy of Social Control.* Ed. Catherine Chaput, M. J. Braun, and Danika M. Brown. New York: Lang, 2010. 1–28. Print.

Cintron, Ralph. *Angels Town: Chero Ways, Gang Life, and the Rhetoric of Everyday.* Boston: Beacon, 1998. Print.

Clanchy, M. T. *From Memory to Written Record: England 1066–1307.* Cambridge, MA: Harvard UP, 1979. Print.

Code Switch. Radio news program. National Public Radio. http://www.npr.org/blogs/codeswitch/.

Coleman, Lisa Hill, and Lorien Goodman, eds. "Rhetoric/Composition: Intersections/Impasses/Differends." *Enculturation* 5.1 (2003), 5.2 (2004). Web. 30 Nov. 2006.

Coles, William E., Jr. "Freshman Composition: The Circle of Unbelief." *College English* 31 (1969): 134–42. Print.

———. "New Presbyters as Old Priests: A Forewarning." *CEA Critic* 41.1 (1978): 3–9. Print.

———. *The Plural I: The Teaching of Writing.* New York: Holt, 1978. Print.

Conference on College Composition and Communication. CCCC Guideline on the National Language Policy. National Council of Teachers of English. NCTE, 1988; updated 1992. Web. 19 Aug. 2008.

———. CCCC Statement on Second Language Writing and Writers. National Council of Teachers of English. NCTE, 2001; revised Nov. 2009. Web. 9 Dec. 2009.

———. Students' Right to Their Own Language. National Council of Teachers of English. NCTE, 1974. Web. 31 Aug. 2009.

Confiant, Raphaël. "Créolité et francophonie: Un éloge de la diversalité." *Potomitan*, n.d. Web. 26 Oct. 2010.

Connors, Robert. "Rhetoric in the Modern University: The Creation of an Underclass." Trimbur and Bullock 55–84.

Cook, Vivian. *Linguistics and Second Language Acquisition.* New York: St. Martin's, 1993. Print.

Cooper, Marilyn M. "The Being of Language." Horner and Kopelson 13–30.

Cornford, James, and Neil Pollock. "The University Campus as a 'Resourceful Constraint': Process and Practice in the Construction of the Virtual University." Lea and Nicoll 170–81.

Council of Writing Program Administrators. "Evaluating the Intellectual Work of Writing Administration." [1998]. 24 January 2007. Web. <http://wpacouncil.org/positions/intellectualwork.html>.

Coupland, Nikolas. "Review: Sociolinguistic Prevarication about 'Standard English.'" *Journal of Sociolinguistics* 4.4 (2000): 622–34. Print.

Crane, L. G., M. B. Lombard, and E. M. Tenz. "More Than Just Translation: Challenges and Opportunities in Translingual Research." *Social Geography* 4 (2009): 39–46. Print.

Cronin, Michael. *Translation and Globalization.* London: Routledge, 2003. Print.

Crook, Charles. "Learning as Cultural Practice." Lea and Nicoll 152–69.

Crowley, Sharon. "Composition Is Not Rhetoric." *Enculturation* 5.1 (2003): n. pag. Web. 2 Sept. 2009.

———. "Composition's Ethic of Service, the Universal Requirement, and the Discourse of Student Need." *JAC* 15.2 (1995): 227–40. Print.

———. "Linguistics and Composition Instruction: 1950–1980." *Written Communication* 6.4 (1989): 480–505. Print.

Crystal, David. *English as a Global Language*, 2nd ed. Cambridge: Cambridge UP, 2003. Print.

Cushman, Ellen. *The Cherokee Syllabary: Writing the People's Perseverance.* Norman: U of Oklahoma P, 2011. Print.

———. *The Struggle and the Tools: Oral and Literate Strategies in an Inner City Community.* Albany: State U of New York P, 1998. Print.

Daly, Alan J., Kara S. Finnigan, Stuart Jordan, Nienke M. Moolenaar, and Jing Che. "Misalignment and Perverse Incentives: Examining the Politics of District Leaders as Brokers in the Use of Research Evidence." *Educational Policy* 28 (2014): 145–74.

Daley, Elizabeth. "Expanding the Concept of Literacy." *Educause Review* 38.2 (2003): 33–40. Print.

Darrah, Charles. "Complicating the Concept of Skill Requirements: Scenes from a Workplace." *Changing Work, Changing Workers: Critical Perspectives on Language, Literacy, and Skills.* Ed. Glynda Hull. Albany: State U of New York P, 1997. 249–72. Print.

Dauney, Bertrand. "The Evolution of the French Field of *La Didactique de l'écrit* (Didactics of Language Practices): Theorizing the Teaching Practices of Writing in the Disciplines." *L1—Educational Studies in Language and Literature* 8.2 (2007): 13–34. Print.

Declining by Degrees: Higher Education at Risk. Documentary. PBS, 2005.

Defays, Jean-Marc, Annick Englebert, Marie-Christine Pollet, Francine Thyrion, et Laurence Rosier, dir. *Actes du colloque international les discours universitaires: formes, pratiques, mutations*. Paris: L'Harmattan, 2009. Print.

Davila, Bethany. Review of *The End of Composition Studies*, by David W. Smit. *Composition Studies* 34.2 (2006). Web.

D'Eloia, Sarah G. "Teaching Standard Written English." *Journal of Basic Writing* 1.1 (Spring 1975): 5–13. Print.

DePalma, Michael-John, and Jeffrey M. Ringer. "Toward a Theory of Adaptive Transfer: Expanding Disciplinary Discussions of 'Transfer' in Second-Language Writing and Composition Studies." *Journal of Second Language Writing* 20 (2011): 134–47. Print.

Dingo, Rebecca, Rachel Reidner, and Jennifer Wingard. "Disposable Drudgery: Outsourcing Goes to College." Martins 265–88.

Dobrin, Sidney I. "Introduction: Finding Space for the Composition Practicum." *Don't Call It That: The Composition Practicum*. Ed. Sidney I. Dobrin. Urbana, IL: National Council of Teachers of English, 2005. 1–34. Print.

———. *Postcomposition*. Carbondale: Southern Illinois UP, 2011. Print.

Donahue, Christiane. "'Internationalization' and Composition Studies: Reorienting the Discourse." *College Composition and Communication* 61.2 (2009): 212–43. Print.

———. "Writing and Teaching the Disciplines in France: Current Conversations and Connections." *Arts and Humanities in Higher Education* 3 (2004): 59–79. Print.

Donovan, Timothy R., and Ben W. McClelland, eds. *Eight Approaches to Teaching Composition*. Urbana, IL: National Council of Teachers of English, 1980. Print.

Dor, Daniel. "From Englishization to Imposed Multilingualism: Globalization, the Internet, and the Political Economy of the Linguistic Code." *Public Culture* 16.1 (2004): 97–118. Print.

Downing, David B., Claude Mark Hurlbert, and Paula Mathieu, eds. *Beyond English Inc.: Curricular Reform in a Global Economy*. Portsmouth, NH: Boynton/Cook, 2002. Print.

Downs, Douglas. Response to Miles et al. *College Composition and Communication* 60.1 (2008): 171–75. Print.

Downs, Douglas, and Elizabeth Wardle. "Teaching about Writing, Righting Misconceptions: (Re)envisioning 'First-Year Composition' as 'Introduction to Writing Studies.'" *College Composition and Communication* 58.4 (2007): 552–84. Print.

Driscoll, Dana Lynn, and Jennifer Wells. "Beyond Knowledge and Skills: Writing Transfer and the Role of Student Dispositions." *Composition Forum* 26 (Fall 2012). Web.

Dubin, Fraida. "Situating Literacy within Traditions of Communicative Competence." *Applied Linguistics* 10.2 (1989): 171–81. Print.

Duffy, John. *Writing from These Roots: The Historical Development of Literacy in a Hmong American Community*. Honolulu: U of Hawaii P, 2007. Print.

Durst, Russel. *Collision Course: Conflict, Negotiation, and Learning in College Composition*. Urbana, IL: National Council of Teachers of English, 1999. Print.

Edwards, Anne. "User Engagement and the Processes of Educational Research." Fenwick and Farrell 44–57.

Elbow, Peter. "Response." *College Composition and Communication* 46 (1995): 87–92. Print.

———. *Vernacular Eloquence: What Speech Can Bring to Writing*. New York: Oxford UP, 2011. Print.

Epes, Mary. "Tracing Errors to Their Sources: A Study of the Encoding Processes of Adult Basic Writers." *Journal of Basic Writing* 4 (1985): 4–33. Print.

Faigley, Lester. *Fragments of Rationality: Postmodernity and the Subject of Composition*. Pittsburgh: U of Pittsburgh P, 1992. Print.

———. "The Study of Writing and the Study of Language." *Rhetoric Review* 7.2 (1989): 240–56. Print.

Fairclough, Norman. "The Appropriacy of Appropriateness." *Critical Language Awareness*. Ed. Norman Fairclough. London: Longman, 1992. 31–56. Print.

Farrell, Thomas J. "Developing Literacy: Walter J. Ong and Basic Writing." *Journal of Basic Writing* 2.1 (Fall/Winter 1978): 30–51. Print.

Farris, Christine, and Chris M. Anson, eds. *Under Construction: Working at the Intersections of Composition Theory, Research, and Practice*. Logan: Utah State UP, 1998. Print.

Fenwick, Tara, and Lesley Farrell, eds. *Knowledge Mobilization and Educational Research: Politics, Languages and Responsibilities*. London: Routledge, 2012. Print.

Ferry, Christopher. "Theory, Research, Practice, Work." Farris and Anson 11–18.

Firth, Alan, and Johannes Wagner. "On Discourse, Communication, and (Some) Fundamental Concepts in SLA Research." *Modern Language Journal* 81.3 (1997): 285–300. Print.

Fontaine, Sheryl, and Susan Hunter, eds. *Writing Ourselves into the Story: Unheard Voices from Composition Studies*. Carbondale: Southern Illinois UP, 1992. Print.

Foucault, Michel, and Colin Gordon. *Power/Knowledge: Selected Interviews and Other Writings, 1972–1977.* New York: Pantheon, 1980. Print.

Fox, Tom. "Basic Writing as Cultural Conflict." *Journal of Education* 171.1 (1990): 65–83. Print.

———. *The Social Uses of Writing: Politics and Pedagogy.* Norwood, NJ: Ablex, 1990. Print.

Fraiberg, Steven. "Composition 2.0: Toward a Multilingual and Multimodal Framework." *College Composition and Communication* 62.1 (2010): 100–26. Print.

France, Alan W. "Assigning Places: The Function of Introductory Composition as a Cultural Discourse." *College English* 55 (1993): 593–609. Print.

France, Alan W., William B. Lalicker, and Chris Teutsch. "Perpetrating Fraud upon the Laity?" *College Composition and Communication* 52.2 (2000): 278–81. Print.

Freire, Paulo. *Pedagogy of the Oppressed.* Trans. Myra Bergman Ramos. New York: Continuum, 1970. Print.

Friedrich, Patricia, and Aya Matsuda. "When Five Words Are Not Enough: A Conceptual and Terminological Discussion of English as a Lingua Franca." *International Multilingual Research Journal* 4 (2010): 20–30. Print.

Fulkerson, Richard. "Composition Theory in the Eighties: Axiological Consensus and Paradigmatic Diversity." *College Composition and Communication* 41.4 (1990): 409–29. Print.

———. "Composition at the Turn of the Twenty-First Century." *College Composition and Communication* 56.4 (2005): 654–87. Print.

———. "Four Philosophies of Composition." *College Composition and Communication* 30.4 (1979): 343–48. Print.

Gage, John T. "On 'Rhetoric' and 'Composition.'" *An Introduction to Composition Studies.* Ed. Erika Lindemann and Gary Tate. New York: Oxford UP, 1991. 15–32. Print.

Gal, Susan, and Judith T. Irvine. "The Boundaries of Languages and Disciplines: How Ideologies Construct Difference." *Social Research* 62 (1995): 967–1001. Print.

Gallagher, Chris W. *Radical Departures: Composition and Progressive Pedagogy.* Urbana, IL: National Council of Teachers of English, 2002. Print.

———. "We Compositionists: Toward Engaged Professionalism." *JAC* 25.1 (2005): 75–99. Print.

Ganobcsik-Williams, Lisa. *Teaching Academic Writing in UK Higher Education: Theories, Practices, and Models.* Houndmill, England: Palgrave Macmillan, 2006. Print.

Gee, James Paul. "New Literacy Studies: From 'Socially Situated' to the Work of the Social." Barton, Hamilton, and Ivanič 180–96. Print.

———. "New People in New Worlds: Networks, the New Capitalism and Schools." *Multiliteracies: Literacy Learning and the Design of Social Futures*. Ed. Bill Cope and Mary Kalantzis. London: Routledge, 1999. 43–68. Print.

Gee, James Paul, Glynda Hull, and Colin Lankshear. *The New Work Order: Behind the Language of the New Capitalism*. Boulder, CO: Westview, 1998. Print.

George, Diana, ed. *Kitchen Cooks, Plate Twirlers, and Troubadours: Writing Program Administrators Tell Their Stories*. Portsmouth, NH: Boynton/Cook, 1999. Print.

Gere, Anne Ruggles. *Writing Groups: History, Theory, and Applications*. Carbondale: Southern Illinois UP, 1987. Print.

Gibson-Graham, J. K. *The End of Capitalism (as We Knew It): A Feminist Critique of Political Economy*. Blackwell, 1996. New Edition Minneapolis: U of Minnesota P, 2006. Print.

———. *A Postcapitalist Politics*. Minneapolis and London: U of Minnesota P, 2006. Print.

Gibson-Graham, J. K., and David Ruccio. "'After' Development: Re-imagining Economy and Class." Gibson-Graham, Resnick, and Wolff 158–81.

Gibson-Graham, J. K., Stephen Resnick, and Richard D. Wolff, eds. *Re/presenting Class: Essays in Postmodern Marxism*. Durham, NC, and London: Duke UP, 2001. Print.

Gibson-Graham, J. K., Stephen Resnick, and Richard Wolff. "Toward a Poststructuralist Political Economy." Gibson-Graham, Resnick, and Wolff 1–22.

Giddens, Anthony. *Central Problems in Social Theory: Action, Structure and Contradiction in Social Analysis*. Berkeley: U of California P, 1979. Print.

Gilyard, Keith. "African American Contributions to Composition Studies." *College Composition and Communication* 50.4 (1999): 626–44. Print.

———. *True to the Language Game: African American Discourse, Cultural Politics, and Pedagogy*. New York: Routledge, 2011. Print.

———. *Voices of the Self: A Study of Language Competence*. Detroit: Wayne State UP, 1991. Print.

Gilyard, Keith, and Elaine Richardson. "Students' Right to Possibility: Basic Writing and African American Rhetoric." *Insurrections: Approaches to Resistance in Composition Studies*. Ed. Andrea Greenbaum. Albany: State U of New York P, 2001. 37–51. Print.

Gladstein, Jill M., and Dara Rossman Regaignon. *Writing Program Administration at Small Liberal Arts Colleges*. Anderson, SC: Parlor Press, 2012. Print.

Godley, Amanda, and Jennifer Seibel Trainor. "Embracing the Logic of the Marketplace: New Rhetorics for the Old Problem of Labor in Composition." Bousquet et al. 11–85.

Goldie, David, Matthew Linick, Huriya Jabbar, and Christopher Lubienski. "Using Bibliometric and Social Media Analyses to Explore the 'Echo Chamber' Hypothesis." *Educational Policy* 28 (2014): 281–305. Print.

Goleman, Judith. *Working Theory: Critical Composition Studies for Students and Teachers.* Westport, CT: Bergin, 1995. Print.

Goodman, Kenneth S., Robert C. Calfee, and Yetta M. Goodman, eds. *Whose Knowledge Counts in Government Literacy Policies? Why Expertise Matters.* New York: Taylor and Francis, 2014. Print.

Grabill, Jeffrey T., James E. Porter, Stuart Blythe, and Libby Miles. "Institutional Critique Revisited." *Works and Days* 21 (2003): 219–37. Print.

Graff, Harvey J. *The Labyrinths of Literacy: Reflections on Literacy Past and Present.* Rev. ed. Pittsburgh: U of Pittsburgh P, 1995. Print.

Grosjean, François. "The Bilingual as a Competent but Specific Speaker-hearer." *Journal of Multilingual and Multicultural Development* 6 (1985): 467–77. Print.

Gunner, Jeanne. "Disciplinary Purification: The Writing Program as Institutional Brand." *JAC* 32.3–4 (2012): 615–43. Print.

———. "Everything That Rises. . . ." *College Composition and Communication* 63.3 (2012): 491–95. Print.

Hall, Jonathan. "Multilinguality Is the Mainstream." Horner and Kopelson 31–48.

Halliday, M. A. K. "Towards a Language-based Theory of Learning." *Linguistics and Education* 5 (1993): 93–116. Print.

Hardt, Michael. Introduction: Language at Work. Marazzi 7–11.

Harklau, Linda, Kay M. Losey, and Meryl Siegal, eds. *Generation 1.5 Meets College Composition: Issues in the Teaching of Writing to U.S.-Educated Learners of ESL.* Mahwah, NJ: Erlbaum, 1999. Print.

Harklau, Linda, Meryl Siegal, and Kay M. Losey. "Linguistically Diverse Students and College Writing: What Is Equitable and Appropriate?" Harklau et al. 1–14.

Harris, Joseph. "Behind Blue Eyes: A Response to Marc Bousquet." *JAC* 22 (2002): 891–98. Print.

———. "Meet the New Boss, Same as the Old Boss: Class Consciousness in Composition." *College Composition and Communication* 52 (2000): 43–68. Print.

———. *A Teaching Subject: Composition since 1966.* New Edition. Logan: Utah State UP, 2012. Print.

Hartwell, Patrick. "Grammar, Grammars, and the Teaching of Grammar." *College English* 47.2 (1985): 105–27. Print.

Harvey, David. *The Limits to Capital.* London: Verso, 2006. Print.

Haswell, Richard H. "Methodologically Adrift." *College Composition and Communication* 63.3 (2012): 487–91. Print.

———. "Minimal Marking." *College English* 45.6 (1983): 600–604. Print.

———. "NCTE/CCCC's Recent War on Scholarship." *Written Communication* 22.2 (2005): 198–223. Print.

Haswell, Richard H., and Glenn Blalock, eds. *CompPile: A Research Bibliography*. Web.

Hawisher, Gail, and Cynthia L. Selfe. *Literate Lives in the Information Age: Narratives of Literacy from the United States*. New York: Routledge, 2004. Print.

Hays, Janice N. "Models of Intellectual Development and Writing: A Response to Myra Kogen et al." *Journal of Basic Writing* 6.1 (1987): 11–27. Print.

———. "Socio-cognitive Development and Argumentative Writing: Issues and Implications from One Research Project." *Journal of Basic Writing* 7.2 (1988): 42–67. Print.

Heath, Shirley Brice. *Ways with Words: Language, Life, and Work in Communities and Classrooms*. Cambridge: Cambridge UP, 1984. Print.

Heller, Monica, ed. *Bilingualism: A Social Approach*. Basingstoke: Macmillan, 2007. Print.

Hendricks, Bill. "Making a Place for Labor: Composition and Unions." Bousquet et al. 83–99.

———. "Teaching Work: Academic Labor and Social Class." *JAC* 25 (2005): 587–615. Print.

Herberg, Erin. Review of *The End of Composition Studies*, by David W. Smit. *Rhetoric Society Quarterly* 36 (2006): 129–33. Print.

Herman, Peter C., ed. *Day Late, Dollar Short: The Next Generation and the New Academy*. Albany: State U of New York P, 2000. Print.

Herrington, Anne J., and Marcia Curtis. *Persons in Process: Four Stories of Writing and Personal Development in College*. Urbana, IL: National Council of Teachers of English, 2000. Print.

Hesford, Wendy, Eddie Singleton, and Ivonne M. García. "Laboring to Globalize a First-Year Writing Program." *The Writing Program Interrupted: Making Space for Critical Discourse*. Ed. Donna Strickland and Jeanne Gunner. Portsmouth, NH: Boynton/Cook, 2009. 113–25. Print.

Hesse, Doug D. Foreword. Smit ix–xiii.

———. "Understanding Larger Discourses in Higher Education: Practical Advice for WPAs." Ward and Carpenter 299–314.

Holbrook, Sue Ellen. "Women's Work: The Feminizing of Composition." *Rhetoric Review* 9 (1991): 201–29. Print.

Horner, Bruce. Afterword. Martins 332–42.

———. "Class, Class Consciousness, and 'Good Teaching Jobs.'" *JAC* 26 (2006): 139–55. Print.

———. "Ideologies of Literacy, 'Academic Literacies,' and Composition Studies." *Literacy in Composition Studies* 1.1 (2013): 1–9. Print.

———. "Mapping Errors and Expectations for Basic Writing: From the 'Frontier Field' to 'Border Country.'" *Representing the "Other": Basic Writers and the Teaching of Basic Writing*. Bruce Horner and Min-Zhan Lu. Urbana, IL: National Council of Teachers of English, 1999. 117–36. Print.

———. "Rethinking the 'Sociality' of Error: Teaching Editing as Negotiation." *Rhetoric Review* 11 (1992): 172–99. Print.

———. "Re-Valuing Student Writing." *Teaching with Student Texts: Essays toward an Informed Practice*. Ed. Joseph Harris, John Miles, and Charles Paine. Logan: Utah State UP, 2010. 9–23. Print.

———. Review of *Tenured Bosses and Disposable Teachers: Writing Instruction in the Managed University*, ed. Marc Bousquet, Tony Scott, and Leo Parascondola. *College Composition and Communication* 56 (2004): 351–55. Print.

———. "Students, Authorship, and the Work of Composition." *College English* 59.5 (1997): 505–29. Print.

———. *Terms of Work for Composition: A Materialist Critique*. Albany: State U of New York P, 2000. Print.

Horner, Bruce, Christiane Donahue, and Samantha NeCamp. "Toward a Multilingual Composition Scholarship: From English Only to a Translingual Norm." *College Composition and Communication* 63 (2011): 269–300. Print.

Horner, Bruce, Brice Nordquist, and Susan Ryan, eds. *Economies of Writing: Revaluations in Rhetoric and Composition*. Logan: Utah State UP, forthcoming.

Horner, Bruce, and John Trimbur. "English Only and U.S. College Composition." *College Composition and Communication* 53 (2002): 594–630. Print.

Horner, Bruce, and Karen Kopelson, eds. *Reworking English in Rhetoric and Composition: Global Interrogations, Local Interventions*. Carbondale: Southern Illinois UP, 2014. Print.

Horner, Bruce, and Min-Zhan Lu. "Resisting Monolingualism in 'English': Reading and Writing the Politics of Language." *Rethinking English in Schools: A New and Constructive Stage*. Ed. Viv Ellis, Carol Fox, and Brian Street. London: Continuum, 2007. 141–57. Print.

———. "Rewriting English: Putting English in Translation." *English—A Changing Medium for Education*. Ed. Constant Leung and Brian Street. Bristol, UK: Multilingual Matters, 2012. 59–78. Print.

———. "Rhetoric and (?) Composition." *The Sage Handbook of Rhetorical Studies*. Ed. Andrea A. Lunsford, Kirt H. Wilson, and Rosa E. Eberly. Los Angeles: Sage, 2009. 293–315. Print.

———. "Toward a Labor Economy of Academic Literacy: Exploring Academic Frictions." *Literacy, Economy and Power: Writing and Research after* Literacy in American Lives. Ed. John Duffy, Julie Nelson Christoph, Eli Goldblatt, Nelson Graff, Rebecca Nowacek, and Bryan Trabold. Carbondale: Southern Illinois UP, 2014. 111–26. Print.

———. "Working Rhetoric and Composition." *College English* 72 (2010): 470–94. Print.

Horner, Bruce, Min-Zhan Lu, and Paul Kei Matsuda, eds. *Cross-Language Relations in Composition.* Carbondale: Southern Illinois UP, 2010. Print.

Horner, Bruce, Min-Zhan Lu, Jacqueline Jones Royster, and John Trimbur. "Language Difference in Writing: Toward a Translingual Approach." *College English* 73.3 (2011): 303–21. Print.

Horner, Bruce, Tim Lockridge, and Cynthia L. Selfe. "Translinguality, Transmodality, and Difference: Exploring Dispositions and Change in Language and Learning." Digital monograph. *Enculturation Intermezzo.* Web.

"hours per week." WPA-L listserv thread. Web. <http://lists.asu.edu/archives/wpa-l.html>. June 2005.

House, Juliane. "English as a Lingua Franca: A Threat to Multilingualism?" *Journal of Sociolinguistics* 7.4 (2003): 556–78. Print.

Hull, Glynda. "Acts of Wonderment: Fixing Mistakes and Correcting Errors." Bartholomae and Petrosky 199–226.

———. "Research on Error and Correction." *Perspectives on Research and Scholarship in Composition.* Ed. Ben W. McClelland and Timothy R. Donovan. New York: Modern Language Association, 1985. 162–84. Print.

Hull, Glynda, Mike Rose, Kay Losey Fraser, and Marisa Castellano. "Remediation as Social Construct: Perspectives from an Analysis of Classroom Discourse." *College Composition and Communication* 42 (1991): 299–329. Print.

Ivanič, Roz. "Bringing Literacy Studies into Research on Learning across the Curriculum." Baynham and Prinsloo 100–22.

———. *Writing and Identity: The Discoursal Construction of Identity in Academic Writing.* Amsterdam/Philadelphia: Benjamins, 1998. Print.

Ivanič, Roz, Richard Edwards, David Barton, Marilyn Martin-Jones, Zoe Fowler, Buddug Hughes, Greg Mannion, Kate Miller, Candice Satchwell, and June Smith. *Improving Learning in College: Rethinking Literacies across the Curriculum.* Milton Park: Routledge, 2009. Print.

Jacobsohn, Walter. "The Real Scandal in Higher Education." Schell and Stock 159–84.

Janković-Paus, Svjetlana. "Theory, Practice, and Research on Academic Writing in Europe and Outside Europe." *Monitor ISH Journal for the Humanities and Social Sciences* (2009): 147–63. Print.

Jaschik, Scott. "Outsourced Grading." *Inside Higher Ed* 22 September 2005. Web. <http://insidehighered.com/news/2005/09/22/outsource.html.>.

Jenkins, Jennifer. "Current Perspectives on Teaching World Englishes and English as a Lingua Franca." *TESOL Quarterly* 40 (2006): 157–81. Print.

Johnson-Eilola, Johndan. *Nostalgic Angels: Rearticulating Hypertext Writing.* Norwood, NJ: Ablex, 1997. Print.

Jordan, Jay. *Redesigning Composition for Multilingual Realities.* Urbana, IL: Conference on College Composition and Communication/National Council of Teachers of English, 2012. Print.

Jung, Julie. *Revisionary Rhetoric, Feminist Pedagogy, and Multigenre Texts.* Carbondale: Southern Illinois UP, 2005. Print.

Kachru, Braj. *The Alchemy of English: The Spread, Functions, and Models of Non-native Englishes.* Urbana: U of Illinois P, 1990. Print.

Kandiah, Thiru. "Epiphanies of the Deathless Native User's Manifold Avatars: A Post-colonial Perspective on the Native Speaker." Singh 79–110.

Keller, Evelyn Fox. *Refiguring Life: Metaphors of Twentieth-Century Biology.* New York: Columbia UP, 1995. Print.

Kells, Michelle Hall, Valerie Balester, and Victor Villanueva, eds. *Latino/a Discourses: On Language, Identity and Literacy Education.* Portsmouth, NH: Boynton/Cook Heinemann, 2004. Print.

Khubchandani, Lachman M. "A Plurilingual Ethos: A Peep into the Sociology of Language." *Indian Journal of Applied Linguistics* 24 (1998): 5–37. Print.

Kiefson, Ruth. "The Politics and Economics of the Super-Exploitation of Adjuncts." Bousquet et al. 143–52.

Kinkead, Joyce, and Jeanne Simpson. "The Administrative Audience: A Rhetorical Problem." Ward and Carpenter 68–77.

Kinloch, Valery Felita. "Revisiting the Promise of Students' Right to Their Own Language: Pedagogical Strategies." *College Composition and Communication* 57 (2005): 83–113. Print.

Kirklighter, Cristina, Diana Cárdenas, and Susan Wolff Murphy, eds. *Teaching Writing with Latino/a Students: Lessons Learned at Hispanic-Serving Institutions.* Albany: State U of New York P, 2007. Print.

Kogen, Myra. "The Conventions of Expository Writing." *Journal of Basic Writing* 5.1 (1986): 24–37. Print.

Kopelson, Karen. "Sp(l)itting Images: Or, Back to the Future of (Rhetoric and?) Composition." *College Composition and Communication* 59.4 (2008): 750–80. Print.

Kramsch, Claire. "Contrepont." Zarate, Lévy, et Kramsch 319–23.

———. "The Privilege of the Intercultural Speaker." *Language Learning in Intercultural Perspective: Approaches through Drama and Ethnography.* Ed. Michael Byram and Michael Fleming. Cambridge: Cambridge UP, 1998. 16–31. Print.

———. "The Traffic in Meaning." *Asia Pacific Journal of Education* 26.1 (2006): 99–104. Print.

Kress, Gunther. *Literacy in the New Media Age.* London: Routledge, 2003. Print.

Kress, Gunther, and Theo Van Leeuwen. *Multimodal Discourse: The Modes and Media of Contemporary Communication.* London: Arnold, 2001. Print.

Kroll, Barry M., and John C. Schafer. "Error Analysis and the Teaching of Composition." *College Composition and Communication* 29 (1978): 242–48. Print.

Kuhn, Thomas. *The Structure of Scientific Revolutions*, 2nd ed. U of Chicago P, 1970. Print.

Kusterer, Ken C. *Know-how on the Job: The Important Working Knowledge of "Unskilled" Workers*. Boulder, CO: Westview, 1978. Print.

Larson, Magali Sarfatti. *The Rise of Professionalism: A Sociological Analysis*. Berkeley: U of California P, 1979. Print.

Laurence, Patricia. "Error's Endless Train: Why Students Don't Perceive Errors." *Journal of Basic Writing* 1.1 (Spring 1975): 23–42. Print.

Lazzarato, Maurizio. "General Intellect: Towards an Inquiry into Immaterial Labour." Trans. Ed Emery. *Generation-online.org*. Web. 15 Apr. 2014. <http://www.geocities.ws/immateriallabour/lazzarato-immaterial-labour.html>.

———. "Immaterial Labor." *Generation-online.org*. Web. http://www.generation-online.org/c/fcimmateriallabour3.htm. 14 Apr. 2014.

Lauter, Paul. "From Adelphi to Enron—And Back." Bousquet et al. 72–82.

Lea, Mary R., and Brian V. Street. "The 'Academic Literacies' Model: Theory and Applications." *Theory into Practice* 45.4 (2006): 368–77. Print.

———. "Student Writing in Higher Education: An Academic Literacies Approach." *Studies in Higher Education* 23 (1998): 157–72. Print.

Lea, Mary R., and Kathy Nicoll, eds. *Distributed Learning: Social and Cultural Approaches to Practice*. London: Routledge, 2002. Print.

Lees, Elaine O. "Proofreading as Reading, Errors as Embarrassments." *A Sourcebook for Basic Writing Teachers*. Ed. Theresa Enos. New York: Random, 1987. 216–30. Print.

———. "'The Exceptable Way of the Society': Stanley Fish's Theory of Reading and the Task of the Teacher of Editing." *Reclaiming Pedagogy: The Rhetoric of the Classroom*. Ed. Patricia Donahue and Ellen Quandahl. Carbondale: Southern Illinois UP, 1989. 144–63. Print.

LeFebvre, Henri. *The Production of Space*. Trans. D. Nicholson-Smith. Oxford: Blackwell, 1991. Print.

Leung, Constant. "Convivial Communication: Recontextualizing Communicative Competence." *International Journal of Applied Linguistics* 15.2 (2005): 120–44. Print.

———. "The 'Social' in English Language Teaching: Abstracted Norms versus Situated Enactments." *Journal of English as a Lingua Franca* 2.2 (2013): 283–313.

Leung, Constant, Roxy Harris, and Ben Rampton. "The Idealised Native Speaker, Reified Ethnicities, and Classroom Realities." *TESOL Quarterly* 31 (1997): 543–75. Print.

Levin, Ben, and Amanda Cooper. "Theory, Research and Practice in Mobilizing Research Knowledge in Education." Fenwick and Farrell 17–29.

Lillis, Theresa. *The Sociolinguistics of Writing.* Edinburgh: Edinburgh UP, 2013. Print.

———. *Student Writing: Access, Regulation, Desire.* London: Routledge, 2001. Print.

Lillis, Theresa, and Mary Jane Curry. "Professional Academic Writing by Multilingual Scholars: Interactions with Literacy Brokers in the Production of English-Medium Texts." *Written Communication* 23 (2006): 3–35. Print.

Lindquist, Julie. "Time to Grow Them: Practicing Slow Research in a Fast Field." *JAC* 32.3–4 (2012): 645–66. Print.

Lingard, Bob, Ian Hardy, and Stephen Heimans. "Deparochializing Educational Research: Three Critical, Illustrative Narratives." Fenwick and Farrell 211–36.

Lippi-Green, Rosina. *English with an Accent: Language, Ideology and Discrimination in the United States.* London: Routledge, 1997. Print.

Lipson, Carol, and Molly Voorheis. "The Material and the Cultural as Interconnected Texts: Revising Material Conditions for Part-Time Faculty at Syracuse University." Schell and Stock 107–31.

Lu, Min-Zhan. "An Essay on the Work of Composition: Composing English against the Order of Fast Capitalism." *College Composition and Communication* 56 (2004): 16–50. Print.

———. "Living English Work." *College English* 68 (2006): 605–18. Print.

———. "Metaphors Matter: Transcultural Literacy." *JAC* 29.1–2 (2009): 285–93. Print.

———. "Professing Multiculturalism: The Politics of Style in the Contact Zone." *College Composition and Communication* 54 (1994): 442–58. Print.

Lu, Min-Zhan, and Bruce Horner. "Composing in a Global-local Context: Careers, Mobility, Skill." *College English* 72.2 (2009): 109–29. Print.

———. "The Problematic of Experience: Redefining Critical Work in Ethnography and Pedagogy." *College English* 60 (1998): 257–77. Print.

———. "Translingual Literacy, Language Difference, and Matters of Agency." *College English* 75 (2013): 586–611. Print.

Lubienski, Christopher, Janelle Scott, and Elizabeth DeBray, eds. Politics of Education Association Special Issue Theme: The Politics of Research Utilization. *Educational Policy* 28 (2014). Print.

———. "The Politics of Research Production, Promotion, and Utilization in Educational Policy." *Educational Policy* 28 (2014): 131–44. Print.

Luke, Allan. "Getting Over Method: Literacy Teaching as Work in 'New Times.'" *Language Arts* April 1998: 305–13. Print.

Lunsford, Andrea A. "Cognitive Development and the Basic Writer." *College English* 41 (1979): 38–46. Print.

Lunsford, Andrea A., and Lahoucine Ouzgane, eds. *Crossing Borderlands: Composition and Postcolonial Studies.* Pittsburgh: U of Pittsburgh P, 2004. Print.

MacDonald, Susan. "The Erasure of Language." *College Composition and Communication* 58.4 (2007): 585–625. Print.

Makel, Matthew C., and Jonathan A. Plucker. "Facts Are More Important than Novelty: Replication in the Education Sciences." *Educational Researcher* 43 (2014): 304–16. Print.

"Making Faculty Work Visible: Reinterpreting Professional Service, Teaching, and Research in the Fields of Language and Literature." Report of the MLA Commission on Professional Service. New York: Modern Language Association, 1996. Print.

Makoni, Sinfree. "African Languages as European Scripts: The Shaping of Communal Memory." *Negotiating the Past: The Making of Memory in South Africa.* Ed. S. Nuttall and C. Coetzee. Oxford: Oxford UP, 1998. 242–48. Print.

Malcolm, Katherine. "(Re)writing Economies in a Community College: Funding, Labor, and Basic Writing." Horner, Nordquist, and Ryan, n.p.

Mao, LuMing. "Studying the Chinese Rhetorical Tradition in the Present: Re-presenting the Native's Point of View." *College English* 69.3 (2007): 216–37. Print.

———. "'Why Don't We Speak with an Accent?': Practicing Interdependence-in-Difference." Horner, Lu, and Matsuda 189–95.

Marazzi, Christian. *Capital and Language: From the New Economy to the War Economy.* Trans. Gregory Conti. Los Angeles, CA; Semiotext(e), 2008 [DeriveApprodi 2002]. Print.

Marshall, Eric. "Teaching Writing in a Managed Environment." Bousquet et al. 111–21.

Martin-Jones, Marilyn. "Bilingualism, Education and the Regulation of Access to Language Resources." Heller 161–82.

Martins, David S., ed. *Transnational Writing Program Administration.* Logan: Utah State UP, 2015. Print.

Marx, Karl. *Capital, I: A Critique of Political Economy.* Trans. Ben Fowkes. New York: Vintage, 1976. Print.

———. *A Contribution to the Critique of Political Economy.* Ed. Maurice Dobb. Trans. S. W. Ryazanskaya. London and New York: International Publishers, 1970. Print.

Matsuda, Paul Kei. "Alternative Discourses: A Synthesis." *ALT/DIS: Alternative Discourses and the Academy.* Ed. Christopher Schroeder, Helen Fox, and Patricia Bizzell. Portsmouth, NH: Boynton/Cook, 2002. 191–96. Print.

———. "Basic Writing and Second Language Writers: Toward an Inclusive Definition." *Journal of Basic Writing* 22.2 (2003): 67–89. Print.

———. "Composition Studies and ESL Writing: A Disciplinary Division of Labor." *College Composition and Communication* 50 (1999): 699–721. Print.

———. "The Myth of Linguistic Homogeneity in U.S. College Composition." *College English* 68 (2006): 637–51. Print.

———. "Second Language Writing in the Twentieth Century: A Situated Historical Perspective." *Exploring the Dynamics of Second Language Writing*. Ed. Barbara Kroll. New York: Cambridge UP, 2003. 15–34. Print.

Matsuda, Paul Kei, Maria Fruit, and Tamara Lee Burton Lamm, eds. "Bridging the Disciplinary Divide: Integrating a Second-Language Perspective into Writing Programs." Special issue of *WPA: Writing Program Administration* 30.1–2 (2006). Print.

McConnel, Frances Ruhlen. "Freeway Flyers: The Migrant Workers of the Academy." Fontaine and Hunter 40–58.

McDonald, Lauren. "Think Tanks and the Media: How the Conservative Movement Gained Entry into the Education Policy Arena." *Educational Policy* 28 (2014): 845–80. Print.

McKay, Sandra Lee. "EIL Curriculum Development." Rubdy and Saraceni 114–29.

———. "Toward an Appropriate EIL Pedagogy: Re-Examining Common ELT Assumptions." *International Journal of Applied Linguistics* 13.1 (2003): 1–22. Print.

Meierkord, Cristina. "Syntactic Variation in Interactions across International Englishes." *English World-Wide* 25.1 (2004): 109–32. Print.

Messer-Davidow, Ellen, David R. Shumway, and David J. Sylvan, eds. *Knowledges: Historical and Critical Studies in Disciplinarity*. Charlottesville: U of Virginia P, 1993. Print.

Micciche, Laura. "More Than a Feeling: Disappointment and WPA Work." *College English* 64 (2002): 432–58. Print.

Miles, Libby, Michael Pennell, Kim Hensley Owens, Jeremiah Dyehouse, Helen O'Grady, Nedra Reynolds, Robert Schwegler, and Linda Shamoon. "Commenting on Douglas Downs and Elizabeth Wardle's 'Teaching about Writing, Righting Misconceptions.'" *College Composition and Communication* 59.3 (2008): 503–11. Print.

Miller, Carolyn. "Genre as Social Action." *Quarterly Journal of Speech* 70 (1984): 151–67. Print.

Miller, Richard. "Fault Lines in the Contact Zone." *College English* 56 (1994): 389–48. Print.

Miller, Richard E., and Michael J. Cripps. "Minimum Qualifications: Who Should Teach First-Year Writing?" *Discord and Direction: The Postmodern Writing Program Administrator*. Ed. Sharon James McGee and Carolyn Handa. Logan: Utah State UP, 2005. 123–39. Print.

Miller, Susan. "The Feminization of Composition." Trimbur and Bullock 39–53.

———. *Textual Carnivals: The Politics of Composition*. Carbondale: Southern Illinois UP, 1991. Print.

———. "Writing Studies as a Mode of Inquiry." Olson and Worsham 41–54.

Milroy, James. "Language Ideologies and the Consequences of Standardization." *Journal of Sociolinguistics* 5.4 (2001): 530–55. Print.

Modern Language Association Ad Hoc Committee on Foreign Languages. "Foreign Languages and Higher Education: New Structures for a Changed World." Modern Language Association, 2007. Web. 28 Aug. 2009.

Moore, Danièle, et Bernard Py. "Introduction: Discours sur les langues et représentations sociales." Zarate, Lévy, et Kramsch 271–79.

Moore, Danièle, and Laurent Gajo. "Introduction: French Voices on Plurilingualism and Pluriculturalism: Theory, Significance and Perspectives." *International Journal of Multilingualism* 6.2 (2009): 137–53. Print.

Morton, Deb Balzhiser. "Re: hours per week." WPA-L listserv posting 25 June 2005. Web.

Moss, Beverly. *A Community Text Arises: A Literate Text and a Literacy Tradition in African American Churches*. Cresskill, NJ: Hampton, 2003. Print.

Mühlhäusler, Peter. *Linguistic Ecology*. Oxford: Blackwell 1996. Print.

Mulderig, Gerald. "Is There Still a Place for Rhetorical History in Composition Studies?" *History, Reflection, and Narrative: The Professionalization of Composition, 1963–1983*. Ed. Mary Rosner, Beth Boehm, and Debra Journet. Stamford, CT: Ablex, 1999. 163–76. Print.

Murphy, James. "Rhetorical History as a Guide to the Salvation of American Reading and Writing: A Plea for Curricular Courage." *The Rhetorical Tradition and Modern Writing*. Ed. James Murphy. New York: Modern Language Association, 1982. 3–12. Print.

National Council of Teachers of English. Position Statement Prepared by the NCTE Committee on Issues in ESL and Bilingual Education. National Council of Teachers of English. NCTE, 1981; updated 2008. Web. 14 Aug. 2008.

———. Resolution on English as a Second Language and Bilingual Education. National Council of Teachers of English. NCTE, 1982; updated 2008. Web. 8 Aug. 2008.

———. Resolution on English as the "Official Language." National Council of Teachers of English. NCTE, 1986; updated 2008. Web. 8 Aug. 2008.

Nero, Shondel J, ed. *Dialects, Englishes, Creoles, and Education*. Mahwah, NJ: Erlbaum, 2006. Print.

———. *Englishes in Contact: Anglophone Caribbean Students in an Urban College*. Cresskill: Hampton P, 2001. Print.

Ness, Erik C., and Denisa Gándara. "Ideological Think Tanks in the States: An Inventory of Their Prevalence, Networks, and Higher Education Policy Activity." *Educational Policy* 28 (2014): 258–80. Print.

"New Brand Composition." WPA-L listserv Thread, #227–231. 25–30 July 2008. Web.

Nowacek, Rebecca S. *Agents of Integration: Understanding Transfer as a Rhetorical Act.* Carbondale: Southern Illinois UP, 2011. Print.

Ohmann, Richard. Introduction to the 1995 Edition. *English in America: A Radical View of the Profession.* Hanover, NH: Wesleyan UP, 1996. xiii–lii. Print.

———. *The Politics of Knowledge: The Commercialization of the University, the Professions, and Print Culture.* Middletown, CT: Wesleyan UP, 2003. Print.

Olson, Gary, and Lynn Worsham, eds. *Rhetoric and Composition as Intellectual Work.* Carbondale: Southern Illinois UP, 2002. Print.

O'Neill, Peggy. "Unpacking Assumptions, Providing Context: A Response to Marc Bousquet." *JAC* 22 (2002): 906–16. Print.

Orlikowski, Wanda J. "Material Knowing: the Scaffolding of Human Knowledgeability." *European Journal of Information Systems* 15 (2006): 460–66. Print.

Ozga, Jenny. "Knowledge Stocks and Flows: Data and Education Governance." Fenwick and Farrell 73–85.

Paikeday, Thomas M. *The Native Speaker Is Dead!* Toronto and New York: Lexicography, 2003. Print.

Palmeri, Jason. *Remixing Composition: A History of Multimodal Writing Pedagogy.* Carbondale: Southern Illinois UP, 2012. Print.

Parakrama, Arjuna. *De-Hegemonizing Language Standards: Learning from (Post)Colonial Englishes about "English."* London: MacMillan, 1995.

Pearson. Pearson Knowledge Technologies' industry-leading automated essay assessment. <http://www.knowledge-technologies.com/>. Web.

Pennycook, Alastair. "English as a Language Always in Translation." *European Journal of English Studies* 12 (2008): 33–47. Print.

———. *Language as a Local Practice.* London: Routledge, 2010. Print.

Perry, William G., Jr. *Forms of Intellectual and Ethical Development in the College Years.* New York: Holt, 1970. Print.

Petraglia, Joseph, ed. *Reconceiving Writing, Rethinking Writing Instruction.* Mahwah, NJ: Erlbaum, 1995. Print.

Prior, Paul A. "Moving Multimodality beyond the Binaries: A Response to Gunther Kress' 'Gains and Losses.'" *Computers and Composition* 22 (2005): 23–30. Print.

———. *Writing/Disciplinarity: A Sociohistoric Account of Literate Activity in the Academy.* New York: Routledge, 1998. Print.

Probyn, Elspeth. *Sexing the Self: Gendered Positions in Cultural Studies.* New York: Routledge, 1993. Print.

Qu, Weiguo. "Critical Literacy and Writing in English: Teaching English in a Cross-Cultural Context." Horner and Kopelson 64–74.

Raduntz, Helen. "The Marketization of Education." Apple et al. 231–45.

Rai, Saritha. "A Tutor Half a World Away, But as Close as a Keyboard." *New York Times* 7 September 2005. Web.

Ramonet, Ignacio. "La pensée unique." *Le monde diplomatique* January 1995. Web.

Ratcliffe, Krista. "The Current State of Composition Scholar/Teachers: Is Rhetoric Gone or Just Hiding Out?" *Enculturation* 5.1 (Fall 2003): http://enculturation.net/5_1/index51.html. Web.

Redd, Teresa. "An HBCU Perspective on *Academically Adrift*." *College Composition and Communication* 63.3 (2012): 499–506. Print.

Resnick, Stephen A., and Richard D. Wolff. *Knowledge and Class: A Marxian Critique of Political Economy*. Chicago: U of Chicago P, 1989. Print.

"Responsibilities of Teaching Assistants and Academic Staff." University of Wisconsin-Milwaukee English Department Composition Advisory Committee, 2004. Brochure.

Reynolds, Nedra. *Geographies of Writing: Inhabiting Places and Encountering Difference*. Carbondale: Southern Illinois UP, 2004. Print.

Rhoades, Gary. "Afterword: Educating for Literacy, Working for Dignity." Bousquet et al. 256–72.

———. *Managed Professionals: Unionized Faculty and Restructuring Academic Labor*. Albany: State U of New York P, 1998. Print.

Rhodes, Keith. "Marketing Composition for the 21st Century." *WPA: Writing Program Administration* 23.3 (2000): 51–69. Print.

———. "You Are What You Sell: Branding the Way to Composition's Better Future." *WPA: Writing Program Administration* 33.3 (2010): 58–77. Print.

Richardson, Elaine. *African American Literacies*. London: Routledge, 2003. Print.

Roberts, Celia, and Brian Street. "Spoken and Written Language." *The Handbook of Sociolinguistics*. Ed. F. Coulmas. Oxford and Cambridge, MA: Blackwell, 1997. 168–86. Print.

Rodby, Judith. *Appropriating Literacy: Writing and Reading in English as a Second Language*. Portsmouth, NH: Boynton/Cook, 1992. Print.

Rose, Mike. *The Mind at Work: Valuing the Intelligence of the American Worker*. New York: Penguin, 2005. Print.

———. "Narrowing the Mind and Page: Remedial Writers and Cognitive Reductionism." *College Composition and Communication* 39 (1988): 267–302. Print.

Roskelly, Hephzibah, ed. "Survival of the Fittest: Ten Years in a Basic Writing Program." *Journal of Basic Writing* 7.1 (1988): 13–29. Print.

Royster, Jacqueline Jones. *Traces of a Stream: Literacy and Social Change among African American Women*. Pittsburgh: U of Pittsburgh P, 2000. Print.

Rowsell, Jennifer. *Working with Multimodality: Rethinking Literacy in a Digital Age*. New York: Routledge, 2013. Print.

Rubdy, Rani, and Mario Saraceni, eds. *English in the World: Global Rules, Global Roles*. London: Continuum, 2006. Print.

Russell, David R. "Looking Beyond the Interface: Activity Theory and Distributed Learning." Lea and Nicoll 64–82.

Saraceni, Mario. "Reflections on the Rhetorics on the (Re-)Location of English." *Changing English* 8.3 (2011): 271–79. Print.

Schell, Eileen E. *Gypsy Academics and Mother-Teachers: Gender, Contingent Labor, and Writing Instruction*. Portsmouth, NH: Boynton/Cook, 1998. Print.

Schell, Eileen E., and Patricia Lambert Stock, eds. *Moving a Mountain: Transforming the Role of Contingent Faculty in Composition Studies and Higher Education*. Urbana, IL: National Council of Teachers of English, 2001. Print.

Schmied, Josef, ed. *Academic Writing in Europe: Empirical Perspectives*. Research in English and Applied Linguistics. REAL Studies 5. Göttingen, Germany: Cuvillier, 2011. Print.

Schmidt, Stefan. "Shall We Really Do It Again? The Powerful Concept of Replication Is Neglected in the Social Sciences." *Review of General Psychology* 13 (2009): 90–100. Print.

Schwalm, David. "Re: New Brand Composition." WPA-L listserv posting, 26 July 2008.

———. "The Writing Program (Administrator) in Context: Where Am I, and Can I Still Behave Like a Faculty Member?" Ward and Carpenter 9–22.

Scott, James C. *Domination and the Arts of Resistance: Hidden Transcripts*. New Haven, CT: Yale UP, 1990. Print.

Scott, Janelle, and Huriya Jabbar. "The Hub and the Spokes: Foundations, Intermediary Organizations, Incentivist Reforms, and the Politics of Research Evidence." *Educational Policy* 28 (2014): 233–57. Print.

Scott, Jerrie Cobb, Dolores Y. Straker, and Laurie Katz, eds. *Affirming Students' Right to Their Own Language: Bridging Language Policies and Pedagogical Practices*. New York: Routledge/Urbana, IL: National Council of Teachers of English, 2009. Print.

Scott, Tony. *Dangerous Writing: Understanding the Political Economy of Composition*. Logan: Utah State UP, 2009. Print.

———. "The Politics of Valuation in Writing Assessment." Horner, Nordquist, and Ryan, n.p.

Scribner, Sylvia. "Literacy in Three Metaphors." *American Journal of Education* 93 (1984): 6–21. Print.

Scribner, Sylvia, and Michael Cole. *The Psychology of Literacy*. Cambridge, MA: Harvard UP, 1981. Print.

Seidlhofer, Barbara. "Research Perspectives on Teaching English as a Lingua Franca." *Annual Review of Applied Linguistics* 24 (2004): 209–39. Print.

Selfe, Cynthia L. "The Movement of Air, the Breath of Meaning: Aurality and Multimodal Composing." *College Composition and Communication* 60.4 (2009): 616–63. Print.

———. "Response to Doug Hesse." *College Composition and Communication* 61.3 (2010): 606–10. Print.

———. *Technology and Literacy in the Twenty-First Century: The Importance of Paying Attention.* Carbondale: Southern Illinois UP, 1999. Print.

Sennett, Richard. *The Corrosion of Character: The Personal Consequences of Work in the New Capitalism.* New York: Norton, 1998. Print.

Severino, Carol, Juan C. Guerra, and Johnnella E. Butler, eds. *Writing in Multicultural Settings.* New York: Modern Language Association, 1997. Print.

Shaughnessy, Mina P. *Errors and Expectations: A Guide for the Teacher of Basic Writing.* New York: Oxford UP, 1977. Print.

———. "The Miserable Truth." *Journal of Basic Writing* 3.1 (Fall/Winter 1980): 109–14. Print.

Shipka, Jody. *Toward a Composition Made Whole.* Pittsburgh: U of Pittsburgh P, 2011. Print.

Sifakis, Nikos. "Teaching EIL—Teaching International or Intercultural English? What Teachers Should Know." Rubdy and Saraceni 151–68.

Singh, Rajendra, ed. *The Native Speaker: Multilingual Perspectives.* New Delhi: Sage, 1998. Print.

Slaughter, Sheila, and Gary Rhoades. *Academic Capitalism and the New Economy: Markets, State, and Higher Education.* Baltimore: Johns Hopkins UP, 2004. Print.

Sledd, James. "A Comment on "Freshman Composition as a Middle-Class Enterprise." *College English* 59 (1997): 712–14. Print.

———. "Why the Wyoming Resolution Had to Be Emasculated: A History and a Quixoticism." *JAC* 11 (1991): 269–81. Print.

Slevin, James. "Depoliticizing and Politicizing Composition Studies." Trimbur and Bullock 1–21.

———. "Disciplining Students: Whom Should Composition Teach and What Should They Know?" Bloom et al. 153–65.

———. *Introducing English: Essays in the Intellectual Work of Composition.* Pittsburgh: U of Pittsburgh P, 2001. Print.

Smarthinking. 24 January 2007. <http://www.smarthinking.com/static/colleges/>.

Smit, David W. *The End of Composition Studies.* Carbondale: Southern Illinois UP, 2004. Print.

Smith, Jeff. "Students' Goals, Gatekeeping, and Some Questions of Ethics." *College English* 59 (1997): 299–320. Print.

Smitherman, Geneva. "CCCC's Role in the Struggle for Language Rights." *College Composition and Communication* 50.3 (1999): 349–76. Print.

Smitherman, Geneva, and Victor Villanueva, eds. *Language Diversity in the Classroom: From Intention to Practice.* Carbondale: Southern Illinois UP, 2003. Print.

Spellmeyer, Kurt. "Marginal Prospects." *WPA* 21.2–3 (1998): 162–82. Print.

———. "Travels to the Heart of the Forest: Dilettantes, Professionals, and Knowledge." *College English* 56.7 (1994): 788–809. Print.

Stanforth, Sherry Cook. "The Dangerous Intersection of Home and School." Durst 159–69.

Sternglass, Marilyn. *Time to Know Them: A Longitudinal Study of Writing and Learning at the College Level.* Mahwah, NJ: Erlbaum, 1997. Print.

Street, Brian. *Literacy in Theory and Practice.* Cambridge: Cambridge UP, 1984. Print.

———. "The Future of 'Social Literacies.'" Baynham and Prinsloo 21–37.

———. "New Literacy Studies." *Language, Ethnography, and Education: Bridging New Literacy Studies and Bourdieu.* Ed. Michael Grenfell, David Bloome, Cheryl Hardy, Kate Pahl, Jennifer Rowsell, and Brian Street. London: Routledge, 2012. 27–49. Print.

Strickland, Donna. "Taking Dictation: The Emergence of Writing Programs and the Cultural Contradictions of the Composition Teacher." *College English* 63 (2001): 457–79. Print.

Sullivan, Francis J., Arabella Lyon, Dennis Lebofsky, Susan Wells, and Eli Goldblatt. "Student Needs and Strong Composition: The Dialectics of Writing Program Reform." *College Composition and Communication* 48 (1997): 372–91. Print.

Sutherland, Thomas. "Liquid Networks and the Metaphysics of Flux: Ontologies of Flow in an Age of Speed and Mobility." *Theory, Culture, and Society* 30.5 (2013): 3–23. Print.

Swearingen, C. J. "Rhetoric and Composition as a Coherent Intellectual Discipline: A Meditation." Olson and Worsham 12–22. Print.

Syverson, Margaret A. *The Wealth of Reality: An Ecology of Composition.* Carbondale: Southern Illinois UP, 1999. Print.

Tardy, Christine. "Enacting and Transforming Local Language Policies." *College Composition and Communication* 62.4 (2011): 634–61. Print.

Tate, Gary, Amy Rupiper, and Kurt Schick, eds. *A Guide to Composition Pedagogies.* New York: Oxford, 2001. Print.

Taylor, Mark C. *The Moment of Complexity: Emerging Network Culture.* Chicago: U of Chicago P, 2001. Print.

Thaiss, Chris, and Terry Zawacki. *Engaged Writers, Dynamic Disciplines: Research on the Academic Writing Life.* Portsmouth, NH: Boynton/Cook Heinemann, 2006. Print.

Thaiss, Chris, Gerd Bräuer, Paula Carlino, Lisa Ganobcsik-Williams, and Aparna Sinha, eds. *Writing Programs Worldwide: Profiles of Academic*

Writing in Many Places. Fort Collins, CO: WAC Clearinghouse; Anderson, SC: Parlor Press, 2012. Web.

Tingle, Nicholas, and Judy Kirscht. "A Place to Stand: The Role of Unions in the Development of Writing Programs." Schell and Stock 218–32.

Tricomi, Elizabeth Taylor. "Krashen's Second-Language Acquisition Theory and the Teaching of Edited American English." *Journal of Basic Writing* 5.2 (Fall 1986): 59–69. Print.

Trimbur, John. "Changing the Question: Should Writing Be Studied?" *Composition Studies* 31.1 (2003): 15–24. Print.

———. "Composition and the Circulation of Writing." *College Composition and Communication* 52.2 (2000): 188–219. Print.

———. "The Dartmouth Conference and the Geohistory of the Native Speaker." *College English* 71.2 (2008): 142–69. Print.

———. "Delivering the Message: Typography and the Materiality of Writing." Olson and Worsham 188–202.

———. "Literacy and the Discourse of Crisis." Trimbur and Bullock 277–95.

———. "Writing Instruction and the Politics of Professionalization." Bloom et al. 133–45.

Trimbur, John, and Richard Bullock, eds. *The Politics of Writing Instruction: Postsecondary*. Portsmouth, NH: Boynton/Cook, 1991. Print.

Trimbur, John, and Karen Press. "When Was Multimodality? Modality and the Rhetoric of Transparency." *Multimodality in Writing: The State of the Art in Theory, Methodology, and Pedagogy*. Ed. Arlene Archer and Esther Breuer. Leiden, Holland: Brill, forthcoming.

Trujillo, Tina. "The Modern Cult of Efficiency: Intermediary Organizations and the New Scientific Management." *Educational Policy* 28 (2014): 207–32.

Tsing, Anna Lowenhaupt. *Friction: An Ethnography of Global Connection*. Princeton: Princeton UP, 2005. Print.

Tuell, Cynthia. "Composition Teaching as 'Women's Work': Daughters, Handmaids, Whores, and Mothers." Fontaine and Hunter 123–39.

Tusting, Karin. "New Literacy Studies and Time: An Exploration." Barton, Hamilton, and Ivanič 35–51.

Ungerleider, Charles. "Affairs of the Smart: Will Education Researchers and Decision-Makers 'Hook Up'?" Fenwick and Farrell 61–72.

Valdés, Guadalupe. "Bilingual Minorities and Language Issues in Writing." *Written Communication* 9 (1992): 85–136. Print.

Vance, John. "Code-Meshing Meshed Codes: Some Complications and Possibilities." *JAC* 29.1–2 (2009): 281–84. Print.

Vaughn, William. "I Was an Adjunct Administrator." Bousquet et al. 165–70.

Virno, Paolo. "Notes on the 'General Intellect.'" *Marxism beyond Marxism*. Ed. Saree Makdisi, Cesare Casarino, and Rebecca E. Karl. New York: Routledge, 1996. 265–72. Print.

Ward, Irene, and William J. Carpenter, eds. *The Allyn and Bacon Sourcebook for Writing Program Administrators.* New York: Longman, 2002. Print.

Wardle, Elizabeth. "Continuing the Dialogue: Follow-Up Comments on 'Teaching about Writing, Righting Misconceptions.'" *College Composition and Communication* 60.1 (2008): 175–81. Print.

———. "Creative Repurposing for Expansive Learning: Considering 'Problem-Exploring' and 'Answer-Getting' Dispositions in Individuals and Fields." *Composition Forum* 26 (2012). Web.

———, ed. Writing and Transfer. *Composition Forum* special issue. 2012. Web.

Watkins, Evans. "Managing Comp." *JAC* 22 (2002): 899–905. Print.

———. *Work Time: English Departments and the Circulation of Cultural Value.* Palo Alto, CA: Stanford UP, 1989. Print.

Wible, Scott. "Pedagogies of the 'Students' Right' Era: The Language Curriculum Research Group's Project for Linguistic Diversity." *College Composition and Communication* 57.3 (2006): 442–78. Print.

Widdowson, Henry G. "The Ownership of English." *TESOL Quarterly* 28 (1994): 377–89. Print.

Williams, Bronwyn. *Shimmering Literacies: Popular Culture and Reading and Writing Online.* New York: Lang, 2009. Print.

Williams, Joseph M. "The Phenomenology of Error." *College Composition and Communication* 32 (1981): 152–68. Print.

Williams, Joseph, and Gregory G. Colomb. "The Case for Explicit Teaching: Why What You Don't Know Won't Help You." *Research in the Teaching of English* 27.3 (1993): 252–64. Print.

Williams, Raymond. *Keywords: A Vocabulary of Culture and Society.* Rev. ed. New York: Oxford UP, 1983. Print.

———. *Marxism and Literature.* Oxford: Oxford UP, 1977. Print.

. *Problems in Materialism and Culture.* London: Verso, 1980. Print.

Willis, Paul. *Learning to Labor: How Working Class Kids Get Working Class Jobs.* Morningside Edition. New York: Columbia UP, 1977, 1981. Print.

Winterowd, W. Ross. *Composition/Rhetoric: A Synthesis.* Carbondale: Southern Illinois UP, 1986. Print.

"Work load, vacation time, and course release (was news alert)." WPA-L listserv thread. <http://lists.asu.edu/archives/wpa-l.html>. June 2005.

Worsham, Lynn "Coming to Terms: Theory, Writing, Politics." Olson and Worsham 101–14. Print.

Wysocki, Anne Frances. "Opening New Media to Writing: Openings and Justifications." *Writing New Media: Theory and Applications for Expanding the Teaching of Composition.* Anne Frances Wysocki, Johndan Johnson-Eilola, Cynthia L. Selfe, and Geoffrey Sirc. Logan: Utah State UP, 2004. 1–41. Print.

Yancey, Kathleen Blake. "Made Not Only in Words: Composition in a New Key." *College Composition and Communication* 56.2 (2004): 297–328. Print.

Yancey, Kathleen Blake, Liane Robertson, and Kara Taczak. *Writing across Contexts: Transfer, Composition, and Sites of Writing*. Logan: Utah State UP, 2014. Print.

Yildiz, Yasemin. *Beyond the Mother Tongue: The Postmonolingual Condition*. New York: Fordham UP, 2012. Print.

Young, Vershawn Ashanti. "'Nah, We Straight': An Argument against Code Switching." *JAC* 29.1–2 (2009): 29–46. Print.

Young, Vershawn Ashanti, and Aja Martinez, eds. *Code-Meshing as World English: Policy, Pedagogy, Performance*. Urbana, IL: National Council of Teachers of English, 2011. Print.

Zarate, Geneviève, Danielle Lévy, & Claire Kramsch, dirs. *Précis du plurilinguisme et du pluriculturalisme*. Paris: Éditions des archives contemporaines, 2008. Print.

Zebroski, James T. *Thinking through Theory: Vygotskian Perspectives on the Teaching of Writing*. Portsmouth, NH: Boynton/Cook, 1994. Print.

———. "Toward a Theory of Theory for Composition Studies." Farris and Anson 30–50.

Ziguras, Christopher. "International Trade in Education Services: Governing the Liberalization and Regulation of Private Enterprise." Apple et al. 93–112.

Index

abstraction: labor as, 145–46, 192, 195; of language from wide range of practices, 23, 48, 59–60, 62, 82–83, 161
Academically Adrift (Arum et al.), 176
academic literacies model, 16–17
academic socialization model, 16–17
activity systems, 56, 83–85, 90
activity theory (AT), 84–85
adaptive strategies, 31–32, 35, 89
additive models, 36, 50, 63–64
administrative imperative, 20
administrators, 142–43. *See also* writing program administrators (WPAs)
affordances, 49, 53, 59–60
African American Vernacular English (AAVE), 74–76
agency, 64–65, 71, 206–7; form and, 83–85; of student, 87–89; transfer theory, 86–90
alliances of writing instructors, 187–88
alternatives to composition, 9–11
ambiguities, 78–81
analysis, 73–74, 83
Anson, Chris, 189
answer-getting disposition, 88–89
apocalyptic rhetoric, 12–13, 31, 36, 186
apprenticeship models, 16–17, 19
Arum, Richard, 176
attention economy, 97
autonomous model of literacy, 80–81
autonomy, myth of, 188

Bartholomae, David, 71, 105, 176, 202–3, 224n29
basic writing, 60, 105, 221n8
Bauman, Marcy, 138–39
Bauman, Zygmunt, 151
Bawarshi, Anis, 84
Bazerman, Charles, 22, 40, 46, 171
Beach, King, 87
Bean, Janet, 192, 193
bilingualism, 106–7
border crossing, 86
bordering, 86
Bourdieu, Pierre, 12, 64, 88, 142, 211n3
Bousquet, Marc, 133–35
Boutang, Yann Moulier, 97–98, 99
Boyer, Ernest, 126
Boyer commissions, 147, 157
branding, 146–48
brokering, 6, 121, 123, 140–60; alternatives to dominant view, 156–57; English-center literacy, 144–45; sites of, 143–44. *See also* writing program administrators (WPAs)
Byram, Michael, 189–90

Calvet, Louis-Jean, 4–5, 62, 64, 67, 70, 104, 220n14
Cameron, Deborah, 44
"can able to" discussion, 69–71
Canagarajah, Suresh, 62, 68, 73, 80, 128
capitalism: exploitation of workers, 123–25; global, 28; labor and work, 92–94; language as productive force, 95–97; project against, 27–33, 156–57
capitalocentric discourse, 4, 13, 27–28
Carr, Wilfred, 222n7
Carter, Christopher, 137
change, 3, 37–40; already part of traditional work, 36, 46; apocalyptic terms, 12–13, 31, 36; consensus, lack of, 14–15; fast pace of, 25–26
Chase, Geoffrey, 142–43, 151, 154–56
class identities, 101
class relations, 118
classroom conditions, 195–96, 198–99
classroom ethnography, 173–74
code meshing, 72–73
code switching, 72–73
codification: autonomous model of literacy, 80–81; English as a Lingua Franca, 78–80; monolingualism and, 102–3
cognitive development, 61, 105
Coles, William, 182
collective bargaining, 134, 135, 136
Collision Course (Durst), 178
colonization, 33, 69
commodification, 94, 136, 145–49; attempts to export, 188–89; courses as exchangeable, 150; disciplinary accession to, 163–68, 170, 183; of English-center literacy, 144–45; of knowledge, 163–66, 180–81, 186; of labor as abstract skills, 145–46, 192; of language, 101–2, 104, 119; of work of composition, 5–6, 12
competence, 82, 112
complexity theory, 26
composition: calls for changes to, 9–11; change already part of traditional work, 36, 46; de-disciplinizing effect, 184–85; definitions, 8, 196–97, 208; denigration of, 4, 9–11, 21, 36; denigration of instructors, 92, 122–23, 149–52; end of, 4, 11–12; as failed delivery of marketable writing skills, 14–20; feminization of, 95, 218n3; as foil to rhetoric, writing studies, and the multimodal, 35–53; as hegemony in student training and management, 20–27, 34–35; as intellectual work, 4, 13, 33–35, 125–31; labor issue, 95, 98; lack of professional recognition, 172–73; material social conditions, 8–9, 33–34, 46, 52; moving beyond, 24, 25, 27, 34; multimodal, 36, 47–53, 91, 214–15n36; official charge assigned to, 10–11, 14, 26, 194–95; as ongoing historical project, 8, 208; problematics of, 3–4, 167–90; professionalization of, 164–67; relation to dominant conceptualizations, 2–3, 9–11; as service work, 43, 45, 52, 124, 130–31; as set of activities and practices, 34, 40; as term, 1, 8, 206–8; value of as skills production, 131–33; as writing studies, 40–47
"Composition as Management Science" (Bousquet), 133–35

"Composition at the Turn of the Twenty-First Century" (Fulkerson), 168, 177–82
CompPile bibliography, 176, 222n6
conduit model, 103
Conference on College Composition and Communication (CCCC), 168–76, 183, 202–3; Statement on "Students' Right to Their Own Language", 61, 64, 65–66, 216n12
consensus, lack of, 14–15
consistency, 151–52
consumer model, 18–19, 113, 140
content, 41–42, 45–46, 195, 199–200
context: autonomous model of literacy, 80–82; recontextualization, 28, 68, 87–90; transfer theory, 86–90; vernacular expression, 75
contingent faculty, 95, 98–100, 118; scholarship on, 153; terms for, 150
contract period, 99
Cook, Vivian, 106–7
Cooper, Amanda, 174–75, 176–77
Council of Writing Program Administrators (CWPA), 122, 125, 146
course descriptions, 18–19
Cripps, Michael, 110–14, 116, 151–52, 154–55
critical/cultural studies (CCS) pedagogy, 178, 181, 192–93
Cronin, Michael, 103–4
Crowley, Sharon, 58, 60, 211n2
cultural capital, 24–25, 37, 185
curriculum, 45; multimodality and, 50–51; redesigning, 135–36, 181–82; vertical, 41, 51; (re)writing and, 77–78
Curry, Mary, 144–45
cycle of crises/pleas/complaints, 132–33
Dar Al-Hekma (DAH) College (Saudi Arabia), 189
DePalma, Michael-John, 89
dialogic pedagogy, 80
difference, 3, 13; denigration for, 61–62; as deviation from sameness, 20; as inevitable, 35; language and, 4, 56, 60–66, 180; linguistic, 71–72; monolingualism and, 102–3; as norm, 67; problematics of composition, 3–4; temporal, 67–70, 73–74; touristic stance, 189–90
digital communication technologies, 22, 52
discipline, 1, 6, 163–205; academic socialization model, 16–17; accession to commodification, 163–68, 170, 183; composition teaching and professional academic disciplinarity, 177–82; contingent character, 200–201; counter notion of, 202–4; de-disciplinizing effect, 184–85; definitions, 165; elision of labor, 166–67; as material social practice, 204; policy choices, 174–75; problematics of composition as professional, 167–90; professionalization of composition, 164–67; rethinking terms of discourse, 27–33; rewriting, in composition, 190–96; of rewriting composition, 196–205; status and regime of flexible accumulation, 183–90; teaching as central to, 166–67
distance learning schools, 149–50
Dobrin, Sidney, 4, 11–12, 20–27, 30–32, 40, 142, 186, 223n15; intellectual work, view of, 33–35; phenomena of writing, 22–23, 25, 45; on practicum, 180

dominant views, 2; acceptance of, 26–27, 161; ambiguities not acceptable, 81; brokering alternatives to, 156–57; capitalocentric discourse, 27–28; challenges to, 9–11; fast capitalism, 2, 4, 12, 25, 31; limited conceptions of composition, 9–13, 20–21, 23–25, 31–32, 36, 39, 45, 47, 49, 52–53; of multimodality, 50–52; not concerned with course content, 195, 199–200; not monolithic, 32–33; opposition to change, 117–18; titles for graduate programs, 9–10; unionism supports, 136–37. *See also* monolingualism; terms
Donahue, Christiane, 189
Downs, Doug, 40–41, 43, 46, 166
Durst, Russel, 178, 179–82

economics, 27–33, 35; capitalocentric discourse, 27–28; linguistic-cognitive character, 95–97
education, 25, 202, 212n9
Elbow, Peter, 199
End of Capitalism (as We Knew It), The: A Feminist Critique of Political Economy (Gibson-Graham), 27–29
end of composition, 4, 11–12
End of Composition Studies, The (Smit), 11–12, 14–20
English, 4, 215n2; as always in translation, 67–68, 119; assumed threats to, 102–3; borrowings from "other" languages, 76–78; as collaborative project, 76–77, 81–82; as commodity, 5; fetishization of, 104–5; idealized notion of, 63; language equated with, 55, 56–60; as language *tout court*, 56–57; "Native-Speaker English" as norm, 108–9; re(learning), 76–82; reworking, 62, 76–78, 107; stability attributed to, 58, 74, 76, 103, 109–10; as term, 37; vernacular expression, 74–76; world Englishes, 106, 109. *See also* language; language practices; Standard Written English (SWE)
English as a Lingua Franca (ELF), 5, 78–82, 107–8, 116, 123, 141
English as a Second Language (ESL), 58
English-only ideology, 55–56, 58, 102–4
eradicationist view, 69
ethics, 133–40
"Evaluating the Intellectual Work of Writing Administration" (Council of Writing Program Administrators), 122, 125–31
evaluation, 43–44. *See also* value/evaluation
exchange value, 95, 121, 123–24, 132–33, 140, 195; knowledge and, 164–65
expert-novice model, 17–18
external relevance, 142–43, 152

Faigley, Lester, 58, 59, 60
fast capitalism, 2, 4, 12, 25, 31, 123, 141; technological imperative, 52–53
feminist critiques, 131
fetishism, 63, 104, 137, 145
"fighting back," 187–88
first-year composition (FYC), 15, 40–43, 213n28; calls to abolish, 153; restrictions on student writing, 194–95, 198–99; Rutgers University program, 110–16, 151–52; skills production, 150–53; universal requirement, 157–58

Fish, Stanley, 185
"flexibility," 52, 150–51, 153, 179
flexible accumulation, regime of, 183–90
form, 83–85, 185
for-profit schools, 149–50
Foucault, Michel, 222n3
Freire, Paulo, 24, 39, 224n26
Fulkerson, Richard, 39, 168, 177–82, 186–87, 192–93, 222n6
functional normativity, 17, 83–84, 171–72

Gal, Susan, 102
Gallagher, Chris, 190–92, 224n21
Gee, James, 75, 81, 93–94, 96
general intellect, 96, 163
general writing skills, focus on, 19, 132, 150, 158–59
genre, 83–84
"Genre as Social Action" (Miller), 84
Gibson-Graham, J. K., 4, 13, 27–33, 35, 186, 212n13, 219nn5, 8
Giddens, Anthony, 16
Gilman, Holly, 135
Gilyard, Keith, 69, 75, 216nn12, 13, 217n21
glamour, 205
global lingua franca, 119
globalism, 25, 31–32, 119, 142; composition instructors as "flexible" labor, 150; literacy brokering, 144–45; There Is No Alternative, 26, 99, 155; WPA response to challenges, 156–57. *See also* market
graduate programs and students, 40, 110; practicum, 180–82; titles, 9–10
graduation requirements, 117
grammar, 205
"Grammar, Grammars, and the Teaching of Grammar" (Hartwell), 171–72, 174
"great man" theory, 71
Grosjean, François, 106
guaranteed social income, 97–98, 99, 101
Gunner, Jeanne, 184

habitus, 82, 88
Hardt, Michael, 96–97
Harris, Joseph, 11, 168
Hartwell, Patrick, 171–72, 174
Harvey, David, 156
Haswell, Richard, 168–76, 186, 192, 222n6
hegemonic, 2, 12, 31, 82, 195
hegemony, 2, 31, 195; of capitalism, 27–29; student, 20–27
Hendricks, Bill, 136–37
Hesse, Doug, 143
Horner, Bruce, 50
House, Juliane, 79, 107
human capital, 153
humility, 204–5

import/export model, 189
Improving Learning in College: Rethinking Literacies across the Curriculum (Ivanič), 86
indoctrination, 179–80
intellectual work, 4, 13, 33–35, 81–82, 201; boundaries for, 129–30; in hierarchy of work, 95, 98; of students, 100–101, 196–97, 219n7; value of composition work, 125–31, 139
interlanguage, 61, 105
internationalization, 6, 119, 189, 201
"Inventing the University" (Bartholomae), 71

Irvine, Judith T., 102
Ivanič, Roz, 86, 88

JAC, 133
Johnson, Billy "White Shoes," 71
Johnson-Eilola, Johndan, 52
journals, 168–76
justice, 133–40

Kemmis, Stephen, 222n7
Kiefson, Ruth, 137
Kinkead, Joyce, 143
knowledge: as always emergent, 164, 200, 205; commodification of, 163–66, 170, 175, 180–82, 186; esoteric, 165–66; as material social historical project, 177; as object, 163, 168, 170; use value, 163
knowledge mobilization, 6, 168, 177, 180–82, 198
knowledge/information economy, 123, 141
Kress, Gunther, 48–49, 94, 96, 214n36

labor, 1, 5, 92–120; as abstract skills, 145–46, 192, 195; alternative notions, 99–100; commodification of, 123–25; concrete practices, 123–24; contradiction in understanding of workforce, 97–98; definitions, 92–93; "flexibility" of, 52, 150–51, 153, 179; friction as productive, 103, 107–8, 119, 123, 148, 180, 189–90; job searches, 97, 99–100; language as productive force, 95–97; as material interchange, 92–93; monolingualism and composition, 98–108; as natural condition of human existence, 92–93; occluded, 102, 104, 123–24, 132, 139, 145–46, 161, 166–67, 181, 192–93; recognition and, 93–94; skills as commodities, 110–11; staffing, 13, 41, 109–11; of students, 100–101, 113–14, 117–19; translingual approach to composition, 108–20; value and, 123–25; well-resourced laborers, 113, 160. *See also* work
labor relations, 95, 136
language, 1, 55–91; abstracted from wide range of practices, 23, 48, 59–60, 62, 82–83, 161; agency and, 64–65; as always emergent, 56, 66–68, 74, 107, 200, 205; beyond the sentence, 82–90; as commodity, 101–2, 104, 119; denigration for differences, 61–62; difference, 4, 56, 60–66, 180; discipline of rewriting composition, 196–205; English equated with, 55, 56–60; global practice of, 57; as local practice, 4–5, 55–56, 67, 84; as noncount noun, 59; as ongoing outcome of practices, 55, 64, 75, 200; as outside material social realm, 59–60; parole vs. langue, 4, 58, 65, 73–74, 76, 83; (re)production, 2, 56, 65–66, 71, 102; as productive force in capitalism, 95–97; representations of, 55, 62, 64–66; social acceptability and, 64–65; as system, 57; terms for, 62–63. *See also* English; writing
language learning, 76–82
language practices, 66–76; always in translation, 67–68, 119; changing forms, 71–72; code meshing, 72–73; countermodels, 66–67, 156; difference and, 180; discrimination against people, 63–65,

103; as form of labor, 95–97; gaps, 72–73; linguistic heterogeneity, 114–15, 118–19, 201, 204; meso-political activity, 75; negotiation, 69–71; role of, 56; sedimentation practices, 68–70, 76–77, 84; self-doubt about, 64–65; social identities of users, 57–58; speech privileged, 59–60; as temporal, 67–70, 73–74; value contingent on, 121–22, 200. *See also* English
language rights, 61, 63–66
Lauter, Paul, 137
Lea, Mary R., 16–17
Lees, Elaine, 176
Lefebvre, Henri, 212n10
Leung, Constant, 218n27
Levin, Ben, 174–75, 176–77
Lillis, Theresa, 4, 13, 27, 29–33, 35, 44, 46; English-center literacy, 144–45; on modality, 48
linear developmental model, 105–6
Lingard, Bob, 175
linguistic heterogeneity, 114–15, 118–19, 201, 204
linguistics, 58
literacy, as term, 37
literacy brokering, 144–45
literacy work, 185–86
local character, 147–48, 153–54
Lockridge, Tim, 50
lone scholar, 174, 200
Lu, Min-Zhan, 37, 69–71
Lunsford, Andrea, 38

"Making Faculty Work Visible" report, 126
Malcolm, Katie, 135
managerial discourse, 134, 185
Marazzi, Christian, 96–97
market: composition as failed delivery of marketable writing skills, 14–20; expert-novice model, 17–18; language as productive force, 95–96; made possible by "friction," 103, 107–8, 119, 123, 148, 180, 189–90. *See also* globalism
"Marketing Composition for the 21st Century" (Rhodes), 146
"marketization" of education, 145
Marshall, Eric, 135
Marx, Karl, 92, 96, 104, 137, 145, 163, 207
Marxian theory, 1, 38, 92–93
mastery, 78
material social realm, 1–2, 140–41; composition and, 8–9, 33–34, 46, 52; composition positioned in, 167–68; curriculum redesign, 135–36; discipline as, 204; labor as material interchange, 92–93; language as outside, 59–60; necessity of locating knowledge in, 176–77; occluded by commodification, 123–24, 126–27, 166–67; scholarship on composition and, 172–74; theory works within, 11–13, 32, 35, 140–41
Matsuda, Paul Kei, 119
meaning, 94
meso-political activity, 75
Miles, Libby, 41–42, 43, 46
Miller, Carolyn, 84
Miller, Richard, 110–14, 116, 151–52, 154–55
Miller, Susan, 40, 44, 148–49
misrecognition, 5, 12, 32, 49, 53–54, 89
MLA Commission on Professional Service, 126

models, limitations of, 83–85
monolingualism, 5, 55–58, 73, 219n10; denigration for difference, 61–62; disciplinary accession to, 164; dominant appropriation of, 65–66; hiring limitations, 115–16; labor in composition, 98–108; pluralization of, 64, 65, 112, 114; single language user, 67; sustains exploitative working conditions, 102
monomodality, 47–48
Morton, Deb, 138
multicompetence, 106–7
multimodality, 36, 47–53, 91, 214–15n36; dominant view, 50–52; transmodal approach, 50–51

National Council of Teachers of English (NCTE), 168–76
"NCTE/CCCC's Recent War on Scholarship" (Haswell), 168–76
need, discourse of, 3–4, 9, 11, 21, 26–27, 35–36, 53, 208, 211n2; challenges not addressed, 13; failed delivery of marketable writing skills, 14–20
neoliberal ideology, 99, 104, 147
"new," "alternative," "better," "different," 3–4, 10–11, 30, 49–50; language and, 55, 66
New Literacy Studies, 93–94, 214n33
nonacademic sites, 44
noncapitalist activities, 28
normative functionalist view, 17, 83–84
notations, 48
Nowacek, Rebecca, 87

Ohmann, Richard, 168, 183–88, 191, 195, 199–200
Ozga, Jenny, 174

parole, 4, 58, 65, 73–74, 76, 83
paternalism, 134
pedagogical imperative, 11, 20, 43–45
pedagogy: content knowledge, 42, 45–46; intellectual work within, 33–34; linguistically based, 58; rethinking and reworking, 24; as training and management, 20–27, 34–35; transmission model, 14, 15, 19–20, 67, 101, 179
Pennycook, Alastair, 4, 56, 67, 75, 84, 103
periphery scholars, 128
Perry, William, 223n12
policy choices, 174–75
political economy, 93, 119
politicization, 38–39, 183–84
Post-Capitalism (Lillis), 27–33
Post-Capitalist Politics (Gibson-Graham), 27, 29
postcomposition, 20–27
Postcomposition (Dobrin), 11–12, 20–27, 30–32, 142
post-fordist economy, 97, 147
postpedagogy, 21
power relations, 12, 16, 112, 144
practical consciousness, 71–72
practical criticism, 199
practice, 207
practicum, 180–82
pre-professional training, 51–52
Press, Karen, 47
"problem-exploring" disposition, 88–89
Probyn, Elspeth, 38–39
production: activity of, 8; commodification of, 123; of social relations, 94–95
productivity, 100
professional development, 99–100, 113, 151, 153, 159–60

professionalization, 164–67
program coherence, 151–52, 157
public school education, 136, 140

racism, 75
"RAD"—"replicable, aggregable, and data-supported" studies, 169–72, 186, 192, 193, 201, 223n12
Raduntz, Helen, 145
realistic, as term, 155
recognition, 5, 56, 84, 89, 93–94
re-cognization, 32
recontextualization, 28, 68, 87–90
Reiff, Mary Jo, 84
repetitions, 69
representation, 23, 34; bias toward timeless structure, 83; of disciplines, 200–201; of language, 55, 62, 64–66
(re)production, 2, 56, 65–66, 75, 81, 202; labor and, 102, 166–67
repurposing, 88, 90
Resnick, Stephen, 1
resources, lack of, 113, 134–35, 177, 195
rethinking: language differences, 67; rather than abandoning, 30–31; terms for language, 62–63
reworking, 24, 30–31, 46, 200, 206–7; curriculum design, 181–82; English, 62, 76–78, 107; teaching composition, 181; transnational writing programs, 188–89
rewriting, 30–31, 53–54, 71, 76–78, 101–2; disciplinarity in composition, 190–96; hiring practices, 114–16; language and discipline of, 196–205
rhetoric, 36–37, 39–40
rhetorical approach, 179
rhetorical axiology, 39
Rhoades, Gary, 136
Rhodes, Keith, 146–48, 150, 158
Richardson, Elaine, 74–76
Ringer, Jeffrey M., 89
Rowsell, Jennifer, 53
Ruccio, David, 219n8
Russell, David, 84–85
Rutgers University composition program, 110–16, 151–52

sameness, 3–4, 13, 20, 84
scholarship, 42–43, 60, 168, 221–22n3; bibliographies of research, 169, 171–72, 176, 222n6; classroom ethnography, 173–74; ideology, role of, 174–76; not interchangeable with teaching, 191–92; "RAD"—"replicable, aggregable, and data-supported" studies, 169–72; on teaching practices, 177–82
Scholarship Reconsidered: Priorities of the Professoriate (Boyer), 126
schooling, as private good, 149
Schwalm, David, 143–44, 149–50, 159
second language writing, 58, 80, 105
sedimented practices, 68–70, 76–77, 84
Selfe, Cynthia, 48, 50, 214n35
seminars, 213n28
semiodiversity, 107, 115
sensory engagements, 48–49
service category, 24–25, 96
Shaughnessy, Mina, 39
Sifakis, Nicos, 79
Simpson, Jeanne, 143
situation, 83–84
skills production, 131–33
Slevin, James, 4, 33–35, 45, 100–101, 164–65, 167, 197
Smit, David, 4, 11–12, 14–20, 26–27, 186; alternatives envisioned, 30–31; intellectual work, view of, 33–35

social relations, 5
social security, 97–98
sociolinguistics of writing, 4, 13, 27–33, 35; marginalization of writing, 29–30
speech, 29–30, 58–60, 215n3; English as a Lingua Franca, 78–80; writing as transcription of, 58–59
stability, 212–13n17; assumption of, 12–13; attributed to English, 58, 74, 76, 103, 109–10; challenged by ELF, 78–80; of language, 63, 66; monolingualism assumes, 102–3; of rhetoric, 39–40
staff development, 128–29
staffing, 13, 41, 109–11
Standard English, 73
Standard Written English (SWE), 63, 65, 109–10, 119
Statement on "Students' Right to Their Own Language" (SRTOL), 61, 64, 65–66, 216n12
Street, Brian, 16–17, 49, 80, 214n33
structures of feeling, 72
students, 211n2; agency, 87–89; as consumers, 18–19, 113, 140; discipline, centrality to, 167; indoctrination of, 179–80; as intellectuals, 34, 41–42, 45, 197, 219n7; labor of, 100–101, 113–14, 117–19; practical criticism and, 199; representation of language practices to, 70; restrictions on writing, 194–95, 198–99; reworking curriculum design, 181–82; rhetoric reworked by, 39–40; subjectivities, 20–21; training and management, 20–27, 34–35; writing movement, 33–34
study skills model, 16
subjectivity, 20–21
substitutability, 156–59
survival culture, 74, 75
Syverson, Margaret, 25–26

"target" language, 106, 109–10
Taylor, Mark C., 25
teacherscholars, 201
teaching, 5, 12; as central to discipline, 166–67; not interchangeable with scholarship, 191–92; professional academic disciplinarity and, 177–82
teaching assistants, 110–11
Teaching of English to Speakers of Other Languages (TESOL), 61
teaching subjects, 11, 31, 163, 168
"Teaching Writing in a Managed Environment" (Marshall), 135
technicians, 198
technological imperative, 52–53
temporal location, 67–70, 73–74, 83–85, 91
Tenured Bosses and Disposable Teachers: Writing Instruction in the Managed University (Bousquet et al.), 133–34, 136, 137
terms, 1–2; alternative, 161–62; apocalyptic, 12–13, 31, 36; for capitalism, 27–28; composition as, 1, 8, 9–10, 206–8; for contingent faculty, 150; countering dominant, 4–7, 28, 206–7; English as, 37; familiarity with, 35; labor and, 5; for language, 62–63; redefinition needed, 12; rethinking, 3, 27–33. *See also* dominant views
theory: activity theory (AT), 84–85; challenges to dominant view, 1, 10–11; as escape from limitations, 13, 23–24; Marxian, 1, 38, 92–93; as material social practice, 11–13, 32, 35, 140–41; postcomposition, 21–22; rethinking terms

of disciplinary discourse, 27–33; transfer theory, 86–90, 186–87
Total Quality Management (TQM), 147, 150
touristic stance, 189–90
"Toward a Theory of Theory in Composition" (Zebroski), 24
transfer theory, 86–90, 186–87
translation, 103–4, 149; disciplinary work and, 201–2; hiring practices and, 114–16
translingual approach, 5, 56, 62, 67–71, 198, 220n23; code meshing, 72–73; English as a Lingua Franca, 78–82; labor in composition, 108–20
translinguals, 73
transmission model of pedagogy, 14, 15, 19, 101, 113–14, 179
transmodal approach, 50–51
transnational writing program administration, 188–89
trappings, payoff of, 190–91
Trimbur, John, 42–43, 45, 46–47, 131
Tsing, Anna Lowenhaupt, 103, 148, 180
tuition, 124
Tusting, Karin, 68

uniformity, 110–11
unionism, discourse of, 122, 133–37, 221n1
units of analysis, 56, 83–85, 90–91
use value, 123–24, 132–33, 140, 163, 193–95; rewriting courses, 198–99

value/evaluation, 1, 5–6, 121–62; alternative terms, 161–62; brokering value of composition, 140–60; composition work as "intellectual," 125–31; composition work as skills production, 131–33; contingent on language, 121–22, 200; ethics, 133–40; exchange and use values, 95, 121, 123–24, 132–33, 140; knowledge, forms of, 128–29; substitutability, 156–59
Van Leeuwen, Theo, 214n36
vernacular expression, 74–76
vertical curriculum, 41, 51
violence, language of, 26
visual, the, 48

"war" on scholarship rhetoric, 169, 170, 174
Wardle, Elizabeth, 40–41, 43, 46, 87–88, 166
Watkins, Evan, 195
"Who Should Teach First-Year Writing?" (Miller and Cripps), 110–14
"Why Johnny Can't Write," 131
Williams, Raymond, 2, 32, 48, 71–74, 155, 215n3; on work and labor, 92, 94
Wolff, Richard, 1
work, 92, 121; gender discrimination, 94–95, 149; "hard," 138–39; "real work," 94–95, 102, 117, 125–26; recognition and, 93–94; value and, 123–25. *See also* labor
working conditions, 6–8, 13, 93; exchange and use value, 132–33; lack of resources, 134–35, 177, 195; monolingualist ideology sustains, 102; professionalization and, 165–66; regime of flexible accumulation, 185; substitutability, 156–59; valuing other than skills instruction, 158–60; well-resourced laborers, 113
Worsham, Lynn, 24, 211n3

WPA-L listserv, 133, 138
writing: as abstract, 23, 59–60; contradictory understandings of, 15–16; hyper-circulatory nature of, 23, 25, 26; marginalization of, 29–30; as noun, 42–43; as participial, 42–43; phenomena of, 22–23, 25, 45; as second-language acquisition, 61; as socialization, 16; as stable entity, 12, 20; as task, 197–98; as term, 37; as topic, 196–98; as transcription of speech, 58–59. *See also* language; rewriting
"Writing about Writing" ("WAW"), 40–41, 166
writing in the disciplines (WID), 16, 31, 112, 114
writing movement, 33–34
writing program administrators (WPAs), 5, 6, 212–13n17, 220n21; brokering of value, 123, 140–60; collective proposal, 134–35; commodification and, 124–25; discourse of, 122, 124; ethics and the value of composition work, 133–40; five categories of characteristic work, 127; hours worked, focus on, 135–36, 138–39; inexperienced, 135; "intellectual" work of, 124; justification of expenses, 153; larger forces not addressed, 154–55; local conditions and solutions, 153–56; paternalism of, 135; professional development, 99, 113, 151, 153, 159–60; program coherence, 151–52; at research universities, 141; as retailers of commodities, 145; scholarship, 127–29; sourcebook for, 142–43; staff development, 128–29; transnational administration, 188–89; unionism, discourse of, 122, 133–37; value of composition work as skills production, 131–33; work seen as service, 125–26, 130
writing studies, 21–23, 35; attempts to change composition to, 36; composition as, 40–47; evaluative role, 43–44; major, 40–41; student participation in designing, 46
Wysocki, Anne, 51

Young, Vershawn Ashanti, 216–17n14

Zebroski, James T., 24

Bruce Horner is the Endowed Chair in Rhetoric and Composition at the University of Louisville, where he teaches courses in composition, composition theory and pedagogy, and literacy studies. His previous books include *Reworking English in Rhetoric and Composition: Global Interrogations, Local Interventions*, coedited with Karen Kopelson; *Terms of Work for Composition: A Materialist Critique*, winner of the 2001 W. Ross Winterowd Award for Most Outstanding Book in Composition Theory; and *Cross-Language Relations in Composition*, coedited with Min-Zhan Lu and Paul Kei Matsuda and winner of the 2012 Conference on College Composition and Communication Outstanding Book Award.